Project Evaluation
and Development

CONSTRUCTION TECHNOLOGY AND MANAGEMENT

A series published in association with the Chartered Institute of Building.

The series will, when complete, cover every important aspect of construction. It will be of particular relevance to the needs of students taking the CIOB Member Examinations, Parts 1 and 2, but will also be suitable for degree courses, other professional examinations, and practitioners in building, architecture, surveying and related fields.

Published

Project Evaluation and Development
Alexander Rougvie

Practical Building Law
Margaret Wilkie with Richard Howells

Building Technology 1:
Site Organisation and Method
Ian Chandler

Building Technology 2: Performance
Ian Chandler

Building Technology 3:
Design, Production and Maintenance
Ian Chandler

The Economics of the Construction Industry
Geoffrey Briscoe

Project Evaluation and Development

ALEXANDER ROUGVIE

MITCHELL · *LONDON*

in association with the Chartered Institute of Building

To Janet, Hannah, Duncan and Kate,
for putting up with it.

© Alexander Rougvie 1987

First published 1987

Reprinted 1988

Filmset by Deltatype, Ellesmere Port
and printed in Great Britain by
Billing & Son Ltd, Worcester

Published by The Mitchell Publishing Company Limited
4 Fitzhardinge Street, London W1H 0AH
A subsidiary of B. T. Batsford Limited

British Library Cataloguing in Publication Data

Rougvie, Alexander
    Project evaluation and development.——
    (Construction management)
    1. Construction industry——Management
    2. Industrial project management
    I. Title   II. Chartered Institute of
    Building   III. Series
    690'.068'4   TH438

ISBN 0–7134–5075–4

Contents

Acknowledgements

The author and publishers wish to gratefully acknowledge the permission given to reproduce material from the following sources.

Reproduction of the RIBA plan of work (figs. 8 and 15) and the recommended fee scales (figs. 11, 12 and 13) is made with the kind permission of RIBA Publications Ltd, the copyright holder.

Reproduction of parts of the ACE Conditions of Engagement (figs. 14, 15 and 16) is made with the kind permission of the Association of Consulting Engineers.

Reproduction of the project management check list, from 'Project Management in Building' (p. 211) is made with the kind permission of the Chartered Institute of Building.

Reproduction of the fee scales from 'Professional Charges for Quantity Surveying Services' (figs. 17 and 18) is made with the kind permission of Surveyors Publications, a subsidiary of Surveyors Holdings Ltd, a Royal Institution of Chartered Surveyors company.

1. Introduction to Factors in Development

As with most types of economic undertaking, the development of property demands the presence of land, labour and capital. However, these factors on their own cannot produce developments. To these must be added a further, vital factor – a motive for the production of buildings. The motives may be as simple as a concern for profit or a concern for the provision of social amenity, or may be a complex mixture of both. Before embarking upon a detailed examination of the factors it is useful to review some of their main features so that they may be placed in the overall context of developments in general.

Land

The term 'land' means the top soil and the air space above, as well as the strata below; although it is normal to talk about 'land and buildings', the latter once constructed become annexed to the land itself. The term 'real property' or 'realty' is also used to describe land (with or without buildings). Land and its ownership possess certain characteristics which do not apply to other forms of property, in that a piece of land may have ownership rights called 'legal estates' which are capable of being created and traded. Since the introduction of the Law of Property Act 1925, the only two legal estates in land are the 'freehold' and the 'leasehold' (more accurately, the 'fee simply absolute in possession' and the 'term of years absolute in possession' respectively). The freehold title is the superior interest, and is the largest estate which can be held by anyone (as in theory, all land is actually *owned* by the Crown). The freehold is perpetual, i.e. does not come to an end after a period of time. Subject of course to any other limitations, the freehold owner may occupy, enjoy and dispose of his property as he wishes. The leaseholder, often referred to as the lessee or tenant, has only the right to occupy and enjoy his property for a fixed period of time. The leaseholder will also normally pay rent to the landlord for this privilege. At the end of the lease the landlord (usually the freeholder) has the right to the return of the property, with the lessee's interest having been extinguished by the ending of the fixed period. This right owned by the landlord is termed the 'reversionary interest' in the property. In some types of lease the lessee may have a right to obtain an extension of the lease, providing that certain requirements are satisfied.

Where a tenant wishes to 'sublet' or 'assign' his interest in a property, it is normal for the tenant to have to gain the landlord's consent for such subletting or assignment. On subletting, the tenant may only grant a sublease for a period less than his own lease. The tenant then becomes the 'sublessor' and the new occupier is termed the 'sublessee' or 'underlessee'. In such transactions, the original lessee is still responsible to the landlord for performance of the conditions of the original lease, and the sublessee is in turn responsible to the sublessor. On assignment, however, the lessee, with the permission of the Landlord, transfers all his rights to the assignee for whatever term of the lease may be remaining. In assignments, the assignee than becomes directly responsible to the Landlord for the performance of the obligations contained in the original lease agreement.

In most transactions undertaken as part of the property development process, the transfer of freeholds or the granting or assignment of leases will be in writing, probably under seal. It is obviously essential that any document providing a lease contains the details of the obligations of the parties involved, in particular the terms of the lease, the amount of rent and when it is to be paid, when it is to be reviewed (if at all), and who is to be responsible for insurance and repairs. The commonest formats are the 'fully repairing and insuring' lease, where the tenant is responsible for insuring and carrying out all repairs, and the 'internal repairing' lease, where the landlord is responsible for external repairs and insurance, and the lessee carries out all internal repairs. Where a lease for a long period (e.g. 99 years) is granted, this is usually assumed to be for the use of the ground only, and may be called a ground lease. A ground rent will be paid for the use of the land, and the lessee may erect buildings for occupation or for rent. At the expiry of the lease the land and buildings revert to the landlord (except where there is a right to extension or to the purchase of the freehold).

It is usual for an 'occupation lease' to be granted where the object is to grant the use of existing buildings. A 'rack rent' is paid when the rent is the full rental value of the property, but where the rent paid is less than the full value, it is termed a 'head rent'; the difference enjoyed by the tenant is termed a 'profit rent' (i.e. the difference between the 'head rent' paid to the landlord, and the rent receivable by the tenant from his sub-tenant).

The 'fixed' quantity of land available for development has always provided a substantial motivation for people or organisations to become involved with development in order to provide investment opportunities. The economic purist will argue that land is not fixed in quantity in any absolute sense, as there have for many years been land reclamation schemes which have increased the amount of developable land. It is also true that as land values increase through scarcity, further tracts of land, previously thought to be not worth developing, will at the margin become more viable. However, the cost of providing land by reclamation is still high, and in many if not most cases the additional cost will rule out this type of development. A further avenue for the increase in land quantity may also arise through decisions by local and central government to remove restrictions on the use of certain areas of land, e.g. green belt land, and thus increase the quantity of usable land. So although there may be increases available in the pool of developable land, the areas in question are small in comparison with the total normally available, and are therefore unlikely to influence the total picture of development opportunity. What *will* be affected by such changes will be the comparative values of development land in the local economic environment, where markets are likely to be more volatile in their response to changes in land availability.

Motivation

The finite nature of land as a resource has led to increased competition for the right to develop in order to satisfy particular needs. These needs may be seen as a function of the motives of the different agencies who wish either to develop themselves, or to use the products of development. The motives themselves may be either simple or complex, but in either case it is important to be able to establish the real reason for development. In some cases the answer may be straightforward, for example an industrial company may simply need more space for production, storage or office accommodation. In others, the motive may be considerably more complex. Consider the speculative housebuilder; it may appear obvious that the housebuilder requires to buy land in order to construct houses for sale, and indeed this is the case, but further aspects must also be considered, in particular the market which the housebuilder wishes to exploit. In the past decade the proportion of housing built for owner occupation has increased enormously, but at the same time the level of discernment exercised by the customer has also increased; thanks in some measure to direct and indirect government intervention, aspirations to home ownership have increased. Housebuilders therefore can no longer purchase green field sites, cover them with 'developers' boxes' and assume that a captive market will quietly respond. Two events which are at present occurring almost in parallel exemplify the difficulty which may exist in establishing the motivation for a particular development. The first is the initiatives being pursued in the attempts to regenerate run-down inner city areas. These usually involve the re-use of derelict areas of industrial land, e.g. docklands or redundant factory sites, and these sites normally involve considerable technical difficulties in construction, with concomitant additional costs in e.g. refilling docks, providing expensive foundations, or treating contaminated soil. These problems make the sites unattractive due to the high costs and high risks involved. But at the same time the housebuilders are pleading with government that houses are in general expensive due to the high cost of (scarce) land, particularly in the south, and are attempting to persuade government that restrictions on the use of green belt land for development should be lifted. The result is a trade-off, with the housebuilders being prepared to become involved with inner city regeneration, in the hope that having been seen to be willing to respond to such initiatives, government will be prepared to make life easier in other directions. This is not to imply that the inner city work is being undertaken for altruistic reasons; the real nature of the demand for inner city housing, together with the willingness of the banks and building societies to make mortgage funds available, has meant that the inner city sites are themselves viable for developers, albeit at greater risk than might be considered normal for this type of activity. Another example of conflicts in motivation occurs in the case of urban office development. The prime movers (if not the actual developers) in this type of activity are the major financial institutions who require to find investments which will provide long-term stable income in order for the pension funds and insurance companies to be able to meet obligations which may not terminate for decades. On the face of it, the scarcity of land, coupled with the likelihood of commercial organisations' needs for office space, should validate the choice of office building as a good long-term investment. At the same time, however, the prime movers themselves are participating in the current information technology revolution, and are aware of projections that indicate a possible dramatic change in employment patterns in commerce. The most stark scenario pictures most office workers in the future working from home based computer terminals, with a corresponding reduction in the need for the corporate headquarters type of building. Although at least one major institution has heeded the analysts' advice and has started a planned reduction in office investment, this is not yet a trend. What therefore is the real motivation for the continued popularity of this type of investment solution? Do the institutions really have faith in their own (presumably more optimistic) analyses of the office market in decades to come, which substantiate their decisions (which may in time be proved right), or could it be the case that the collective body of institutional investors cannot be seen to be introducing doubts over the wisdom of such decisions, in case their doubts introduce lack of confidence in the market, followed by a real reduction in the value of the investments themselves? Are such decisions therefore based upon the institutions' perception of what the financial critics and analysts believe to be a proper and credible portfolio of investments, rather than on an objective if still speculative analysis of the future?

Further difficulties in identifying motives occur when considering developments by public bodies, in particular local authorities. Traditionally, local authorities concerned themselves only with those matters for which they had statutory responsibility, such as education, roads and sewers. Over the past decade however, there has been a considerable increase in direct property development by local government. Although the economic characteristics of the property market are the same for both private and public sector developer, there are special factors which apply to the activities of public bodies which drastically affect their freedom of action in comparison with the private sector. The first is the obvious presence of political considerations, at both national and local level, which may control the level of activity in general and on individual projects. A more difficult characteristic, which is studied in greater detail in section 3.4 in the context of procurement systems, is the matter of public accountability. This can be defined as the need to justify to those on whose behalf money is being spent that the procedures used and the decisions themselves are honest and without favour. This need is often in direct conflict with the most efficient use of resources, and public procedures at times seem to be designed to obstruct rather than promote the most efficacious employment of public funds. The notion of public accountability leads directly into the third factor, the need for the authority to take into account the effect of its development proposals on the needs of the community at large. Examples may occur in the case of an authority which wishes to expand employment opportunities in its area, and could influence this through the building of advance factories to rent. The siting of the factory estate could adversely affect the values of residential property in the area, or might affect the whole character of the area. In this example it is probable that the development would only go ahead after the widest public consultation, and at the end of the process there would be no guarantee that the authority would be able to proceed. The mixture of motives and influences described above creates problems for those involved in development projects, in deciding where the prime decision making power lies. Designers, contractors and clients themselves need to be able to recognise and relate to the *sources* of authority for decisions on legal, financial, commercial and technical matters. Where the authority for all of these types of decisions is vested in one individual or body, the process is relatively simple; unfortunately this is rarely the case in even the simplest project.

The influence of taste or fashion should not be underestimated as a motivator for development. Any investor in property will wish to ensure that his buildings correspond to present demands, and will wish to anticipate the likely future prospects for the chosen development vehicle. Recent examples of changes in taste influencing the types and form of development include the use of atria in office developments, the increased number of conversions of redundant riverside warehouses to high value residential units, and the provision of major out-of-town hypermarkets.

Finance

In the provision of finance for development, there have been interesting changes in procedures and systems over the past two decades, with the result that the financing of development, particularly prime development, can be approached in a more flexible manner than used to be the case. The two most obvious needs are for short-term finance to meet the operational costs of carrying out the acquisition of the land, the construction or adaptation of buildings, and the marketing of the completed development. Following completion, there will be a need for long-term finance to meet the cost of repaying the short-term loan, and to allow the developer to realise his profit. (This assumes that the developer wishes to retain a long-term interest in the completed project; if the completed project is sold in its entirety, there will be no need for long-term borrowing. Most developers will wish to retain an interest in the long-term profitability of the development.)

The 'traditional' pattern of provision of short- and long-term finance has been as follows:

Short-term Finance for the development process	*Long-term* Finance for the investment
Clearing banks Merchant banks	Insurance companies Pension funds Property bonds Charitable funds Unit trusts

It is now becoming more common for the boundaries between the providers of short- and long-term finance to become blurred, with some of the institutional investors being willing to provide short-term funding as well as funding the completed investment. The apportionment of the risks and yields in investment has also changed, with the institutions now being prepared to become involved in the risks attached to developing, in exchange for an increased share of the yield. It is likely that the picture will become even more flexible (if confusing) in the near future due to the changes in legislation governing the provision of financial services.

Participants

Finally, the mixture of participants in the process, their goals and aspirations, cannot safely be neglected in any discussion of the factors influencing the process of development. The position of the prime movers in development has been briefly noted above, and will be discussed in more detail in section 3.2. But other participants may play equal or even more important roles in determining the success of any development.

The members of the following cast of players will have their own goals and objectives which may coincide with or vary from the client's objectives: however, the removal, as far as is possible, of any mismatch in objectives is essential to the satisfactory completion and even survival of the project.

1.   *The planner*

The United Kingdom has consistently shown a rather schizophrenic attitude towards 'the planners' and the concept of planning itself. On the one hand the proponents of the planned economy will argue that any criticism of planning derives from the system's failures, and that one real reason for these failures lies not with the system, but with the fact that the planners have not had enough freedom or authority to deliver the initiatives and responsibilities with which they are charged. On the other hand, the free marketeer would argue that any system of planning in the economy, whether at the level of economic planning or infrastructure planning, serves only to distort the smooth operation of market forces. Between these extremes there is probably a more commonly held view that the mixed economy of the UK would undoubtedly suffer if the planning system were to disappear totally. Within the public sector, the activities of the planner have been concentrated in the establishment of a local development framework, within which the planners employed by the authority can exercise judgement on applications for permission to develop by the private sector. The role is therefore a predominantly negative one, with the emphasis on development control. The planning counterpart in the private sector is concentrated not within the development or financing organisations, but in private consultancy practices, or within private architectural or multi-disciplinary firms. This role may involve advice to either the private or public sector clients, in terms of policy formulation, or the obtaining of permissions for particular (often controversial) projects.

2.   *The valuer*

As with the planner, the valuer may find employment in either the public or the private sector, and the range of skills involved in either is likely to be similar, even if the purpose to which these skills are applied is different. In the context of the development of land, the valuer's basic function is to provide advice relating to capital and rental values, and requires an understanding of the particular market for which valuation is required. A detailed knowledge of the effects of various types of taxation is also required. Probably the most crucial role is that providing the developer with an accurate estimate of the value of the land upon which the development is to take place: from the developer's viewpoint, the value of the land is only that value which will allow him to achieve a profit after all costs have been met. This implies that the asking price, if there is one, is largely irrelevant; unless the amount which the developer can afford to pay is above the asking price, the development will not be viable unless the developer can afford to make savings elsewhere, or is prepared to reduce his required profit margin. In order for the valuer to provide the advice required, he will normally need to draw on information from other members of the development team, in particular from the architect and quantity surveyor, in order to arrive at a value which may form the basis for a bid for the site. An introduction to some of the techniques used for this purpose is given in section 2.4.

3.   *Sales and letting agency*

In many cases, this may be the same person or organisation as the valuer, but charged also with the task of finding potential buyers or occupiers for the completed project, and negotiating the sale or lease. Functions may include the assessment of the market for a proposed development, the requirements of likely occupiers, the provision of a sales or letting strategy, the assessment of price or rental levels and the review periods, as well as the actual negoti-ations. It will be clear from these functions that it would be unwise to leave deliberations on many of them until the end of the project, and it is normal therefore for the agent to be appointed early in the process: in many cases the same organisation will act as both valuers and letting agents, and will therefore be involved throughout the lifetime of the project.

4.   The architect

In spite of the range and number of participants in the development process, the long-term image of the buildings which results will almost certainly be perceived as the responsibility of the architect; in spite of the public perception of the architect as primarily an artist, something which the profession as a whole would not wish to dispel, the work of the architect impacts on a range of issues essential to the success of the development, and is by no means confined to matters aesthetic. In the traditional services provided by the architect, three main strands may be identified: obtaining planning permission for the development; designing (in conjunction with others) the building; and the overall control of the project once on site.

Although it was noted above that specialist planners may be involved in obtaining planning permission, this is usually confined to particularly difficult or controversial sites or projects; few projects have this degree of complexity, and it is more normal for permission to be sought by the architect, who will also conduct any detailed negotiations with the planning authority. The architect will also be responsible for obtaining any other approvals, e.g. building control approval. While it may be over matters relating to the aesthetics of a building that the architect receives most public scrutiny, as far as the client is concerned there will be other matters of at least equal importance, not the least of which are the functional performance and the overall financial viability of the project. The trade-off between the cost, functional performance, appearance and the final commercial desirability of the building inevitably produces a series of conflicts which must be resolved. The question of whether the education, professional training and experience of the architect are sufficient to allow him to reasonably discharge these responsibilities, together with the overall management of the project at both pre- and post- contract stages, is one which is receiving considerable public debate.

5.   The quantity surveyor

For the purposes of this section reference is made to the quantity surveying function as it is practised in the offices of the 'professional' quantity surveyor, and not his counterpart employed by a building contractor. Traditionally, the quantity surveyor's functions have been to prepare for the client estimates of cost for a proposed development, to prepare Bills of Quantities upon which contractors may tender in competition, to prepare valuations of the work done on site as a basis for the issue of certificates by the architect, and to prepare and negotiate the final account for the construction works. However, over the past decade the profession has undergone a process of self-examination, aided at least in part by the changes in the nature of construction services being offered by contractors, and by a series of criticisms by clients who, drawing on their experiences in the American market, can see no justification for the continuation of a service which is based on the use of the bill of quantities. In response, the quantity surveying profession has identified a range of services around which the QS of the future is likely to operate. These services are based on the provision of financial and management advice to clients, and will, if the initiatives are accepted by clients, provide the QS with a powerful mandate as a basis for his operations. However, such changes are likely to involve considerable adjustment to the *modus operandi* of most practices, and also to the structure of the education and training of new entrants to the profession (as well as a programme of reorientation of existing practitioners).

This list has been confined to those members of the team who can be said to have a strategic impact on the success of the development process; this is not to minimise the importance of the other possible participants: the solicitor, the structural or civil engineers, the mechanical engineers, landscape consultants, interior designers and contractors, all of whom have an input to the development. Such a review cannot be complete without a reminder of the need for some sort of overall management of the system. Many clients will wish to retain overall control of the project with their in-house staff, and most major development clients with a consistent programme of work will retain members of staff for this purpose. There has over the past ten years been an increasing and more effective recognition of the need for the whole process of development to be the subject of a single identifiable management focus, independent of any of the particular services being provided. The subject of the overall management of projects is developed in chapter 4, but it will already be apparent that given the range and complexity of services and functions required on all but the most modest of projects, there is a clear need for the identification of the needs of the particular development system, and a method of co-ordinating and implementing decisions made to satisfy those needs.

2. Project Appraisal

2.1 SOCIAL AND LEGISLATIVE CONTROL OF DEVELOPMENT

Introduction

There are probably few areas of legislation in Britain today which continually evoke as much controversy as those provisions in the statute law which seek to govern the use of land. In the development of the modern planning system, there has been a continual recognition that the owners of private land should not be allowed to be the sole judges in determining the uses and standards to be applied to land in their ownership. Irrespective of the current views of critics of modern planning legislation, it is recognised as historical fact that the laissez-faire philosophy of the ordinary law could not hope to deal with the social problems in the cities of Victorian Britain: legislation was the only way in which reform could be introduced. The public health legislation of the mid-nineteenth century has provided the impetus for over a century of evolution in land use legislation, culminating in the current situation where there is in practice little change which an owner of land can introduce without prior permission. Planning legislation may therefore be seen as a means of regulating private choice in the use of land, to the greater benefit of society as a whole. In this respect planning may be seen as an interventionist system, attempting to compensate for the inability of the free market to provide a reasonable and socially acceptable pattern of land usage.

This intervention may take one of two forms, or possibly a combination of both. First, and predominantly, is the negative form, in which the law allows planning authorities to restrict developments to those which they consider desirable for their areas. Second is the (limited) ability of the authority to promote developments itself, through the acquisition of land (via the free market or by compulsory purchase) which is then developed directly by the authority or in partnership with other bodies.

Running alongside the development of land use legislation has been the debate over how the costs and benefits of changes in land should be distributed. The law on the subject has tended to change according to the ideologies of the government of the moment, but the principle may be stated simply. Where planning permission is granted for a development, there will be a change in the value of that land and possibly the surrounding land. If, for example, permission is granted for residential development on land previously in agricultural use, and the area contains a shortage of land for housing, the land for which permission is granted will increase in value. Conversely, if permission is granted for development which is likely to emit noise or fumes, the value of surrounding property may diminish. The terms coined for such effects are 'betterment' and 'worsement' respectively. The argument runs that as society in granting such permission through its democratically elected representatives has *created* increases or decreases in land values, then society should demand a share in any increase, and should pay compensation for any decrease in value. Prior to April 1985, betterment was the subject of Development Land Tax (DLT) at the rate of 66% of the increase in value between the existing use and the new use, while compensation was payable for a limited number of actions of the authority. DLT was abolished in the 1985 Finance Act.

Due to the politically charged nature of the arguments it is unlikely that there will be any long-term stability in this area.

In addition to the legislation on land usage, there are also provisions of the common law which act to limit land usage. These provisions lie mainly in the realm of private law and exist as a result of private agreements to restrict the use of land. It is important to realise that where such restrictions run with the land, they cannot be removed merely by a grant of planning permission favourable to a particular change; the private restriction must also be removed, and this may well prove to be more difficult and expensive than obtaining public consent for the development.

Subsequent sections of this chapter will introduce the roles of the parties involved in the planning process, the methods of deciding planning policy, the machinery for dealing with planning applications, controls on amenity and conservation, and private controls on the use of land, thus providing an introduction to the overall system in use today. Land law and planning law are complex subjects, and their treatment here cannot hope to cover all of the provisions and qualifications which apply. For a more detailed treatment of some of the legal issues, the reader is advised to consult the volumes noted in the bibliography for this chapter.

Planning administration

The primary focus for the administration of the planning system in

England and Wales is the local authority within whose area the land for development lies, with other powers being possessed by certain public undertakings such as water authorities and the energy supply industries, who are also able to take decisions on planning matters directly affecting their operations. However, to assume that the planning system is totally decentralised is to understate the complexity of the relationship between local and central government. All planning authorities derive their powers from legislation created and implemented by central government, and it is therefore within the power of central government to reduce or increase the level of local control. In addition central government retains a considerable power to interfere with the activities of local planning by withholding or granting approval for particular proposals, by acting as the appeal authority should a developer object to the decision of a local authority, and by the use of its ability to influence the levels of resources available locally.

The system can therefore be described as one in which a degree of local accountability is recognised, but is circumscribed by the wide discretionary powers of supervision held centrally. The balance of power is not static, and can be expected to change according to the colour of the government of the day, and according to changes in central government's perceived need to control the allocation of land as a result of other policies – e.g. a declared policy of increasing the amount of private house ownership might be reflected in increasing pressure on local authorities to reappraise their policies to permit housing development on land which had been earmarked for public amenity use.

1. *Central government*

The first real concentration of planning power in central government's hands came as a result of the need for centralised administration and material planning to deal with the aftermath of the Second World War. Until that time the 750 different planning authorities in England and Wales had freedom to plan their areas in the way which suited them best. The trend towards central integration of planning policies began in 1951 with the establishment of the Ministry of Local Government and Planning, shortly to be reformed as the Ministry of Housing and Local Government, and reformed again in 1970 into the Department of the Environment, which survives today as one of the major Departments of State. The Department of the Environment has general responsibility in England and Wales for planning, housing and the financing and administration of local authorities, together with wide powers for the supervision of other environmental matters. The political head of the Department is the Secretary of State for the Environment, who is in addition a government minister and Cabinet member.

While the Secretary of State is accountable for all of the activities of the Department, there are relatively few matters which are referred to him for his personal adjudication. Those developers who have contact with the Department are usually those who wish to appeal against an unfavourable decision by a local authority, and normally such appeals will be dealt with by a planning inspector. The inspector is normally a member of staff of the Department (although outsiders are also used) and although there remain cases where the inspector's function is to provide a report upon which the Secretary of State's decision will be based, in practice most cases of appeal are now dealt with by the inspectors themselves without the intervention of the Secretary of State. The role of the inspectorate is in some ways an ambiguous one; conflicts of interest may be suspected where a government servant is required to act impartially in an appeal in which government policy may be at issue. Pressure for changes which would increase the inspectorate's autonomy have been resisted to date in the belief that inspectors should be well informed on government planning policy, and may be trusted to maintain an 'arms-length' relationship with the administration they serve.

2.   Local government

The 1972 Local Government Act, implemented in 1974, divided England and Wales for administrative purposes into *counties*, with these being subdivided into *districts*. The districts were further subdivided into *parishes* (in England) or *communities* (in Wales). Some counties were designated as 'metropolitan' counties, and their districts metropolitan districts.

In London, a two-tier system existed, with the Greater London Council providing some planning services for the whole area, and the London boroughs plus the Common Council of the City of London providing locally based services within their own boundaries. Part 1 of the Local Government Act 1985 abolished the metropolitan counties and the Greater London Council, and the local planning authorities for those areas are now the metropolitan districts and the London boroughs plus the Common Council of the City of London.

Since the 1980 Local Government Land and Planning Act, the balance of power in planning matters has been in favour of the district councils, and for the metropolitan districts and the London boroughs, this power has been enhanced by the 1985 Local Government Act. The county councils are limited to making broad strategic plans, with the district councils having the final decision on detailed local planning. The counties are therefore in a position to make strategic plans for their areas, but have no power to enforce their application in the districts, other than to request the Secretary of State to use his authority to 'call-in' an application for his own decision. Parish and community councils have little direct authority over planning matters, their rights being restricted to being consulted in connection with planning applications affecting land in their areas, and the right to appear at any planning inquiry in order to support any case they may wish to make.

3. *Consultation*

Although government policy is issued centrally, in the form of primary legislation, subordinate legislation and directions issued to authorities, plus advisory publications such as circulars, white papers, policy statements, etc., it would be misleading to assume that the process is unidirectional. It has become usual for government to consult widely with local authorities prior to significant changes being introduced. In many cases the final document, legislative or advisory, may be modified considerably between initial and final draft form. Thus the local authorities are often able to affect significantly the nature and content of central government instructions.

4. *European influence*

Since joining the European Economic Community in 1972, the Community legislation having a bearing on land use and environmental policy has increased considerably, and this process is likely to continue. While there have been considerable differences in enthusiasm between the member states in implementing Community directives, it is clear that there will be an increased effect on the UK planning process by European legislation on environmental matters. The philosophical difference in attitude between the EEC and the UK on planning law is based upon the fact that British planning and environmental controls are built upon a high level of local and central discretion thus allowing (in theory at least) a large amount of flexibility, while the Community's search has been for harmonisation of legislation and practice within member states, thus producing unnecessary rigidity within the system.

5. *The public sector agencies*

Those agencies charged with the provision of a wide range of public services and facilities have a major impact upon the uses of land in relation to their objectives, not the least of which is the physical size and economic importance of some of the projects undertaken; recent years have seen several major public inquiries concerning such developments, e.g. the National Coal Board's proposals for mining in the Vale of Belvoir, and the seemingly unresolvable search for a location for a third airport for London.

Most proposals for such developments involve complex inter-action between the agency concerned, the local planning authorities and central government, with the overlay of an increasing but unpredictable involvement by pressure groups lying outside the 'formal' planning machinery.

The public sector agencies may be grouped for planning purposes as follows:

(a) The Crown and government departments. These are exempt from planning controls, but submit to a voluntary process of informal consultation with local planning authorities over their proposals.

(b) The statutory undertakers. Their title implies no more than specific statutory authority for the work they carry out. Section 290(1) of the Town and Country Planning Act 1971 defines statutory undertakings as those with the authority to provide '. . . any railway, light railway, tramway, road transport, water transport, canal, inland navigation, dock, harbour, pier or light-house undertaking, or . . . the supply of electricity, gas, hydraulic power or water.' Further legislation has granted such status to the British Airports Authority, the Post Office, the Civil Aviation Authority, for at least part of their functions. In general terms, the statutory undertakers only enjoy freedom from planning legislation in relation to land required *directly* in connection with their *operations*. While most statutory undertakings are publicly owned, the privatisation and nationalisation policies of successive govern-ments have left a number of anomalies, while conversely there are also a number of major public companies which do not enjoy statutory undertaker status, e.g. the Housing Corporation and the National Coal Board.

(c) Local planning authorities. These may obtain deemed planning permission for their own developments by resolving so to do, but may also follow the procedures for ordinary applications. The fact that the authority is both developer and controller must imply some conflict of interests, together with the suspicion that the authority may be more generous in dealing with its own applications than with a comparable application from outside.

(d) Other agencies. A rich variety of other organisations exists, ranging from those within the direct control of the Crown, to those quasi-independent authorities which have a measure of delegated authority, and appear to sit, sometimes uncomfortably, in neither public nor private sectors.

Policy formulation

Any system of planning must contain a mechanism whereby

planning policy may be originated and communicated, and against which proposals may be judged. In the British planning system the vehicle used for this purpose is the development plan. Development plans exist in three forms: the *structure plan* which describes strategic policy; the *local plan*, which provides the detailed policy for an area; and the *unitary development plan*, introduced in Part I of Schedule 1 of the Local Government Act 1985, and applying only to the metropolitan districts and London boroughs. In addition, an authority may utilise informal criteria to supplement the above *statutory* plans. Further guidance to developers on the acceptability of proposals may also exist in the form of quantitative standards on matters such as density and plot ratios. Each of these types of policy statement will be examined in turn.

1. Structure plans

Responsibility for the preparation of structure plans outside London rests with the County Planning Authority. The structure plan is basically a written account of the County Planning Authority's policies for the whole or part of their area, prepared after:

(a) a survey of the area which includes physical and economic characteristics, population, communications and transport, plus any other relevant matters,

(b) formulation of strategies and alternatives,

(c) publication of the survey and public participation,

(d) draft plan,

(e) public inquiry to consider objections,

(f) publication of the Secretary of State's modifications, and consideration of objections,

(g) approval or rejection by Secretary of State,

(h) continued monitoring of the assumptions and of the plan's implementation in order to allow updating.

The plan itself need not be solely concerned with physical planning, i.e. the location and appearance of buildings; while the structure plan is primarily concerned with land usage, the authority may also take into account the social implications of their policies, and indeed it would be difficult to frame such policies without taking these matters into account.

Delay in preparing and approving structure plans has meant that it is as yet too early to assess their impact; in addition the increase in devolution to the district authorities since the 1980 Local Government Planning and Land Act has meant that the structure plan has decreased in significance in relation to the local plan.

2. Local plans

As with structure plans, local plans have statutory origins, and are intended to provide detailed information under which development control may take place, and are prepared by the district planning authority in consultation with the county.

Local plans may be divided into three types:

(a) District plans: containing a comprehensive treatment of matters relating to the development of land in a district or part of it.

(b) Action Area plans: these are comprehensive statements of planning policy in relation to areas selected for development, redevelopment or improvement.

(c) Subject plans: deal only with selected issues, not necessarily concerned with building works, e.g. recreation or green belts. These plans would often cut across district boundaries, and would be prepared as a joint effort between adjoining district or county authorities if necessary.

The preparation of local plans follows a similar pattern to that for structure plans, and although they may be prepared ahead of the approval of the structure plan, they must still conform generally to the structure plan.

3. Unitary development plans

These will apply only to the metropolitan districts and London boroughs, and will eventually replace the old development plans, structure plans and local plans for those areas. The local planning authorities will be required under the Act to prepare UDPs when the Secretary of State decides to implement paragraph 2 of Part 1 of Schedule 1 of the Local Government Act 1985. The preparation of such plans follows a roughly similar process to the structure plans and local plans. Two or more metropolitan districts of London boroughs may decide to prepare joint UDPs to allow a more comprehensive plan to be prepared. Local plans already approved may be incorporated into the UDPs. Until such time as an authority's UDP has been *fully* prepared and approved, and the old development, structure and local plans revoked, any development, structure or local plan in force on 1st April 1986 will continue. This applies also to the Greater London Development Plan, which is treated as the structure plan for Greater London.

The additional workload supplied for the London boroughs and the metropolitan districts, together with previous experience of the time scales for preparing and approving development plans, would indicate that the 'old' plans in force at 1st April 1986 are likely to form the basis for those authorities' planning strategies for some considerable time.

4. Non-statutory planning policies

It is obvious that given the need for careful surveying, detailed preparation of planning statements, several levels of public participation and scrutiny by the Department of the Environment, the preparation of structure and local plans is a slow and cumbersome process. Such plans are unlikely to be flexible enough to cope with the rapid changes which may be expected to affect even the most relaxed and rural areas.

In order to accommodate the need to avoid delays and uncertainty, many planning authorities have adopted a variety of informal statements of policy. These have no status as far as planning legislation is concerned, and may range from simple declarations of policy by the planning committee to complex and detailed statements of policy regarding an area or a planning issue. The fact that such plans do not have statutory approval does *not* mean that the authority cannot rely on their validity; authorities may validly take into account other *material* considerations not contained in the structure or local plans when adjudicating upon a proposal, and the stated policy of the authority may well provide valid criteria for judging a particular application.

5. *Other policies and standards*

Although the planning policies stated in the various types of development plans may provide substantial guidance to an authority in dealing with any individual application, it must be remembered that the authority is also granted by statute a considerable degree of discretion in the parameters used.

The Town and Country Planning Act 1971, at Section 29(1) states that '. . . the authority, in dealing with the application shall have regard to the provisions of the development plan, *so far as material to the application, and to any other material considerations*, and . . . may grant permission, either unconditionally or *subject to such conditions as they think fit*, or may refuse planning permission.'

Obviously, conditions may not be attached to a grant of permission merely at the whim of the authority, but only in pursuit of legitimate objectives. Similarly, 'other material considerations' must be applied to the judgement of the application only if they are material in respect of the application itself. Department of the Environment Circular 1/85 'The use of conditions in planning permission' (replacing 5/68 and 70/69) now provides authoritative advice on the powers which determine when and how conditions may be imposed. The circular sets out six tests for validity of conditions, i.e. they must be (a) necessary, (b) relevant to planning, (c) relevant to the development to be permitted, (d) enforceable, (e) precise, and (f) reasonable in all other respects. If the conditions fail to meet these criteria, they are liable to be rejected at a planning appeal.

Two types of policy which have been employed to 'guide' the authority's discretion are the *presumptive* policies, which have been used mainly to restrict development, by creating a presumption that a particular type of development in an area will *not* be allowed (although the reverse is also possible) and *quantitative standards*, which tend to be used to regulate developments in some detail where it may be assumed that permission will be granted.

(a) Presumptive policies

(i) A *presumption* in favour of development has been used to suggest to authorities that permission should be granted, unless the authority can justify refusal. In recent times, central government has encouraged specific types of development through the issue of circulars advising authorities that, for example, permission should be granted in favour of the release of land for housing, unless the authority could establish that a sufficient medium-term land stock was already available. However, the presumption in favour has generally been considered subservient to the presumption against permission, i.e. the policies on constraint.

(ii) *Constraint* policies: although these may appear to cause considerable frustration to developers, this form of negative control can claim considerable success in controlling urban sprawl and preserving the countryside. Around half of the total area in England and Wales is now subject to some type of constraint policy, the most commonly encountered being:

Green belts. Originally devised for restraining development around London, green belt policies are now a common policy feature in other authorities' areas in order to keep stretches of unspoilt countryside within easy reach of town-dwellers. Permission for development other than agricultural or recreational use is granted only exceptionally in these areas.

White land. Land designated 'white land' has no real legal significance, the term being used loosely to describe land in the area between the outer fringes of a town and the beginning of a green belt. In these areas, the presumption is normally in favour of development being allowed, unless there are overwhelming reasons for refusing permission.

Countryside developments. Developments in the countryside are normally restricted to those assumed to be in support of agricultural activity, and should be concentrated on existing towns and villages. While the structure or local plans may provide a useful means of regulating such development, further controls exist by the use of designations as Areas of Outstanding Natural Beauty, Sites of Special Scientific Interest, Nature Reserves, Areas of Great Landscape, Scientific or Historic Value, and Coastal Conservation Areas.

Agricultural land. This is divided into five grades with Grade 1 being of exceptionally high quality, and Grade 5 being considered of poor potential. Little development may take place on Grade 1 or 2 land, with no agricultural objections likely on Grades 4 or 5. Non-agricultural development of Grade 3 land must be the subject of consultation with the Ministry of Agriculture, Fisheries and Food, in order to ensure that an adequate supply of farmland remains available.

(b) Quantitative standards

The use of quantitative standards occurs to ensure that where permission is granted for development, the shape, bulk, location, height etc., of developments are acceptable to the authority, thus controlling the detail rather than the principle of the development. Not all planning authorities adopt predetermined standards for judging applications, and amongst those authorities which do, there is considerable variation in the way standards are adopted or publicised. Frequently non-published standards are applied as 'further guidance'.

As the subject matter of such standards may include density, layout, mix, open space, roads and parking, height and massing of buildings, daylight and sunlight, type of materials, sound insulation and landscaping, their effect will normally be felt once outline permission has been granted. These standards are capable of predetermining the form and appearance of developments, and therefore developers will wish to ascertain, in advance of application, the standards likely to be demanded by the authority. The employment of such standards allows a strong negotiating edge in favour of the authority, which need only point to its adopted standards, and force the developer to justify deviation from them. Obviously certain standards, e.g. density, will have enormous influence on the value of land on which development may take place.

(i) *Density standards*. Normally used for residential developments, the common density standards include:
 - persons per hectare
 - dwellings per hectare
 - habitable rooms per hectare (habitable rooms are living-room and bedrooms of 'normal size' but *may* also include kitchens. The term is not used with consistency.)
 - bedspaces per hectare
 - floor space in m^2 per hectare (more used for cost comparison than development control)

and may often be defined in the local plan, and in some cases in general terms in the structure plan.

(ii) *Plot ratio controls*. These serve for commercial developments the same purpose as density standards, and may be used to determine the mass of a development, normally by prescribing a ratio of permitted floorspace to site area. (A plot ratio of 6:1 could imply a six storey building covering the whole site, or a twelve storey building covering half the site.) The choice of ratio enables the authority to predetermine the density and, indirectly, the height of the building.

(iii) *Daylighting*. The common law recognises the continuing rights of existing buildings to light, normally where such light has been enjoyed for twenty years, but as such rights are private they may be 'bought out' and therefore are of no real benefit to the public at large. The use of daylighting standards by planners is to ensure that the new buildings have adequate sunlight and daylight. This is achieved by determining the spacing of parts of new buildings in relation to the existing buildings adjoining the site, and is expressed in terms of sunlight angles against the side of proposed buildings. The use of such standards in conjunction with plot ratios may have a dramatic effect on the configuration of the new building, as the sunlight angles may indicate that only part of the site may be developed, thus forcing exploitation of the plot ratio into an increase in height.

(iv) *Roads and streets*. Standards for roads normally originate from the local highway authority, but are implemented by the planning authority. The main criterion for determining the width and disposition of roads is safety, and the concentration of attention is generally on junctions, to allow adequate visibility for traffic. The highway authority may also insist on the standard of construction being acceptable where the road is to be adopted and maintained at public expense. Central government's current advice on highway standards is contained in the Department's Design Bulletin No. 32, 'Residential Roads and Footpaths', read in conjunction with DOE Circular 22/80.

(v) *Parking*. Standards for the provision of parking need to be related to the traffic policies of the area, but most authorities regard the provision of off-street parking as essential where the permission is likely to generate further traffic movement. Typical standards imposed are:

- for private residential developments: between one and three car spaces per dwelling
- for hotels: one car space per bedroom
- for other development: between one car space per 20m^2 (where space is not at a premium, and heavy use made of private transport) and 1000m^2 (in urban areas where good use is made of public transport).

In some developments where space for parking provision is severely limited, it may be possible to negotiate a relaxation or waiver of the standard, in consideration of the developer making some contribution in cash to the authority's efforts in making other parking facilities available.

(vi) *Open space*. Standards for the provision of open space vary widely, and no 'national' standards exist for common amenity space, private open space, landscaping, and children's play areas. Maintenance of such space can prove difficult, and possibly the most satisfactory method is for the space to be dedicated to and adopted by the local authority, once completed to their satisfaction.

Policy implementation

1. *Definition of 'development'*

The Town and Country Planning Act 1971 includes the requirement that planning permission is necessary for the carrying out of 'development'. The Act defines development as: *'the carrying out of building, engineering, mining or other operations in, on, over or under land, or the making of a material change in the use of any buildings or other land.'*

This deceptively simple definition is qualified in great detail by the Act itself, by subsequent subordinate legislation and other administrative procedures.

However, it can be seen that development may occur either by the carrying out of *physical* work in the provision of building etc. operations or by changing the *use* of the land or buildings even without accompanying building operations.

Two instruments are employed to provide guidance on what may or may not constitute development.

(a) The General Development Order. This statutory instrument, amended from time to time, grants permission for a range of developments, and thus removes the need for permission from the local planning authority. The principal categories included are house extensions of a limited size, temporary land use, agricultural developments, industrial development, and some works by local authorities and statutory undertakers.

(b) The Use Classes Order. This enables the Secretary of State to define what is a 'material change of use', which is done by providing in the order a list of 'classes' of use, ranging from extremely loose descriptions such as 'office' and 'shop' to detailed descriptions of certain industrial processes. If the developer's proposed change of use does not cross from one class to another, then permission for the change is not required.

2. *Acquiring permission for development*

(a) *The application*. The main categories of application are as follows.

(i) Application for full planning permission. Although there is no 'national' form, most authorities adopt the 'model' form issued by the Department of the Environment in Circular 23/72. In addition to the particulars required on the form, developers are required to supply a site plan, (in order to identify the land) and such additional drawings and information as are required to describe the development. The authority may also require further details as proofs or verification of any matters concerning the proposals.

The applicant for permission need not be the owner of the land subject to the application, but it is necessary for the owner(s) to be notified of the application. It is therefore possible for a developer to 'test the water' before making a financial commitment to the land in question. The application must also be accompanied by the necessary fees, (at time of writing, specified in Town and Country Planning (fees for applications and deemed applications) (Amendment) Regulations 1985).

The application is made to the district authority, who are required to acknowledge the application, and notify the applicant whether it is to be dealt with by the county authority.

(ii) Application for outline permission. Allows an applicant to seek approval in principle, without the financial commitment to the costs of detailed design. At this stage no more is *legally* required than the site plan plus a general description of the development – although many developers supply more detail. Permission, if granted, is then subject to 'reserved matters' which must be approved before development starts. It is possible for the authority, within one month, to require details on any or all of the reserved matters, where these can be shown to be essential prerequisites to the making of a decision.

Outline applications only apply to the erection of buildings, etc., and not to the other types of 'development' nor for material changes of use. The reserved matters may include siting, design, external appearance, means of access, and landscaping.

(iii) Application for approval of reserved matters. As the outline approval is in fact itself *the* planning permission for the development, it may be thought that dealing with the reserved matters should only amount to filling in the details. However, as the outline approval system may be used merely as a means of increasing the value on a site with a view to disposal and not as a precursor to building by the initial applicant, the application on reserved matters may involve an attempt to revise the scheme considerably. In order to avoid such conflicts, permission for reserved matters must be sought within three years from the outline permission, or the latter is deemed to have lapsed.

The reserved matters may be applied for piecemeal, or may even be the subject of successive applications.

(iv) Applications for consent, approval or agreement. Planning authorities may wish to impose conditions on a permission, and the range of matters which may be covered is totally at the authority's discretion. (This should not be confused with the 'reserved matters' consequent on outline approval.) Where application for approval on such a matter is made, no fee is payable.

(v) Application for extensions of permission. Where development has not commenced within the stated life span of the permission, and the period has not yet expired, it is possible to apply for an extension of the consent. Although a detailed application is not normally necessary, the procedure for notification of owners and publicity must be recommenced.

As there is no need to renew permission once work on the development has commenced, it may be more economical to carry out a minor amount of work on the project as a method of keeping the permission alive.

(vi) Applications for retrospective approval of contravening consent. Such applications are normally used to 'legitimise' works carried out without approval, and such action may be taken at the suggestion of the authority, in order to allow it to regulate the development or its use, as an alternative to taking enforcement action.

(vii) Application to determine whether permission is required. The complexity of the definition of 'development' has carried with it a procedure under Section 53 of the 1971 Town and Country Planning Act whereby any prospective developer may apply to the planning authority to determine whether his proposals involve 'development', and, if so, whether the proposals have 'deemed permission' under the General Development Order. This option may be attractive to developers as no fee is required for a Section 53 application; there is, therefore, the possibility of saving the cost of a full or outline application should the Section 53 determination favour the developer.

(b) *Fees for planning applications.* A system of charges for planning applications was introduced in 1981 as a revenue raising device, intended to recover between half and two thirds of the cost to the authority. A sliding scale of charges is set down in Town and Country Planning (fees for applications and deemed applications) (Amendment) Regulations 1985, and may be adjusted by the Secretary of State by Statutory Instrument. While the fee will form only a minor proportion of the capital cost of a major development, it can be expected to lead to developers being keen to negotiate further with officers of the planning authority before submitting applications.

(c) *Control of development by central government.* Successive governments have from time to time attempted to control the incidence and location of certain types of development, by both positive and negative controls.

Positive control has generally been through a system of regional policies designed to offer incentives to appropriate developments believed to be vital for designated areas, by offering grants, subsidies and tax relief designed primarily to attract industries to areas of high unemployment, and away from areas in danger of 'overheating'.

Negative controls have been implemented through the planning system, by imposing a provision that any application in respect of 'controlled' types of development is of no effect unless accompanied by the appropriate certificate. Examples have included the control of office development in London during the period 1965–79, the need for industrial development certificates for developments over a stated size outside the 'development areas' (suspended since 1982), and the current restriction on certain types of private health facilities and oil refineries.

(d) *Publicity for planning applications.* In order to further the aim of encouraging public interest in the planning process, three types of development require to be publicly advertised in a local newspaper, although the authority may use its discretion to advertise other types of development proposals.

(i) Applications involving a departure from the development plan: in this case the responsibility for advertising rests with the authority.

(ii) 'Unneighbourly' development: (the full list of these appears in the GDO, and includes buildings over 20 metres high, and other developments likely to cause noise, smell and other nuisance). The obligation to advertise rests with the applicant, and in addition a notice must be displayed on site to warn passers-by and adjoining owners and tenants.

(iii) Development in conservation areas or on listed buildings: the authority is required to publicise such proposals by advertisement and site notice.

(e) *The decision.* On receipt of any application, the authority will check that any necessary additional documents are enclosed, e.g. development certificates if required, ownership certificates and the fee; if satisfactory the application will be acknowledged. The application will also be entered on the planning register of 'pending' applications until approved or withdrawn; a second section of the register contains records of all applications, pending or determined. The registers are open to inspection by the public at all reasonable hours.

Although planning determinations are made officially by the planning authority, its function may be delegated to a sub-committee, or even to officers. The routine vetting of the application, consultation with county authorities and negotiation with developers is normally carried out by professional planning staff, although committee members may be involved in early consultations and negotiations in respect of major proposals. The result will be (normally) a report on the application to the appropriate committee, together with a recommendation which may or may not be accepted by the committee.

The General Development Order requires the authority to notify the applicant of its decision within eight weeks, or such longer time as the applicant may agree to in writing. If a decision is not given in eight weeks, the applicant has the right to appeal to the Secretary of State as if permission has been refused. Notification of the result of the determination must include a statement of reasons, if the permission is refused or made subject to conditions. Many authorities use standard lists of conditions or reasons which are generated almost automatically.

Although subsequent developments are expected to proceed strictly in accordance with the permission, there is some latitude allowed to developers to cater for unforeseen problems on site, and the subsequent issue of variations. Where developments stray to an appreciable degree from the permission, the authority may bring enforcement proceedings against the *whole* development, not merely the variation.

(f) *Appeals.* Appeals to the Secretary of State for the Environment are possible in connection with an application:

(i) for planning permission;

(ii) for any consent, agreement or approval of that authority required by a condition imposed on a grant of planning permission;

(iii) for any approval of the authority required under a development order

– where agreement, consent or permission was refused, or granted subject to conditions.

The appeal may be made only by the original applicant (there is no right of appeal for third parties *against* a grant of permission) and the appeal must be lodged within six months of the authority's decision and made on forms supplied by the Secretary of State.

The majority of appeals are now dealt with by inspectors, with the Secretary of State's jurisdiction only applying in a small number of instances.

Most appeals today are the subject of written representations, rather than through a public inquiry. As there is a statutory right for both the appellant and the authority to appear before an inspector, the use of written representation requires the consent of both parties. Obviously, there will be a large saving in professional costs to both parties if a hearing is not required. Where appeals are by written representation, both parties are required to state their positions in writing, and the appellant is allowed also to comment on the authority's statement. The inspector may make a site visit, and the decision is notified to the parties, normally including the reasoning behind the inspector's decision.

Where the appellant or the authority insist on their statutory right to appear before an inspector, it is normal for the Secretary of State to exercise his power to direct that a local inquiry should be held. Although there is no *statutory* requirement for the inquiry to be held in public, social and political pressure for open justice requires that the inquiry is a public hearing, and this is invariably the case.

The 'Inquiries Procedure Rules' require that the authority give to the appellant, prior to the inquiry, a clear indication in writing of the authority's case (recognising that the 'reasons' given in a refusal of permission or insistence on conditions may not be clear or elaborate enough without amplification). The actual procedure during the inquiry is at the inspector's discretion, but in most cases follows roughly the process used during trials in court.

Following the conclusion of the hearing, the inspector's report must be published and should include a fair summary of the evidence upon which his findings of fact and recommendations are based; and although the Secretary of State may overrule the inspector's findings (in cases where the case is not disposed of solely upon the authority of the inspector), he also must provide valid reasons for so doing, or run the risk of the decision being challenged in the courts and quashed.

(g) *Enforcement.* Where there has been a breach of planning regulations, e.g. development undertaken without permission, or undertaken outside the scope of the permission, the authority (primarily the district authority outside London, and the Borough in Greater London) has the option of considering a retrospective application, or taking enforcement action. There is no offence involved in disregarding planning regulations; the offence occurs when the developer disregards an enforcement notice.

Unless the breach is flagrant and completely contrary to the authority's policies, there will usually be an attempt at a negotiated solution prior to formal enforcement action. Interestingly, there are categories of breach laid down in Section 87 of The Town and Country Planning Act 1971, in which the authority has only four years from the date of the breach (often difficult to establish) in which to start enforcement action. After the four year period the use becomes an established one and therefore immune from prosecution. The categories are:

(i) Carrying out, without planning permission, of building, engineering, mining or other operations in, on, over or under land.

(ii) The failure to comply with any Condition or Limitation subject to which planning permission was granted.

(iii) The making without planning permission of any change of any use of any building to use as a dwelling house.

(iv) The failure to comply with a condition which prohibits or has the effect of preventing a change of use of a building to use as a single dwelling house.

All other contraventions are not subject to the four year limitation period (unless, due to an anomaly in relation to earlier legislation, the change of use occurred before 1964).

Enforcement action is started by the authority *issuing* a notice (i.e. preparation and retention in their records) and then, within 28 days, and not later than 28 days before it is to come into effect, *serving* the notice on the occupier and on any other person with a legal interest in the land. The notice will specify the steps necessary by the developer to remedy the breach, and allow a reasonable period for compliance. Only when the latter period has expired does criminal liability occur. A right of appeal exists to the Secretary of State, and the use of this facility may be attractive to developers, even on the flimsiest of grounds, as the effect of any enforcement notice is suspended pending the result of the appeal.

The penalties faced as a result of successful prosecution are: (i) on summary conviction a fine of up to £1000; (ii) on conviction on indictment an unlimited fine, plus the probability of further similar convictions if the owner or user does not then comply with the notice. If the conditions of the notice are not complied with within the time period, the authority may carry out the work and recover the costs from the persons committing the breach.

Stop notices.

The use of stop notices enable authorities to take swift action where they consider it expedient to do so. The stop notice is used as an extra component to an enforcement notice, and cannot be used unless an enforcement notice has been served. The notice must be served after service of the enforcement notice, and gives the offender at least three and a maximum of 28 days to cease the activity referred to. There is no appeal against a stop notice. Authorities must however use the facility with care: compensation may be awarded for loss or damage attributable to the prohibition contained in the notice in certain circumstances, if the enforcement notice is quashed or withdrawn, or the stop notice withdrawn. Failure to comply with the stop notice can involve fines similar to those noted above in connection with enforcement.

Future developments

In July 1985 the government published the white paper 'Lifting the Burden' (Cmnd 9571) which set out proposals intended to reduce the burdens imposed on businesses through administrative and legislative regulation. These proposals, if carried into law, will have an impact on the planning system.

1. It is proposed to introduce new legislation to permit the setting up of *'Simplified Planning Zones'* which will extend to other areas the type of planning regime already established in the Enterprise Zones (see later section on positive planning). These zones will allow the planning authority to specify types of development allowed in an

area, so that developers will be able to carry out that type of development without the need for planning permission.

2. A number of changes are planned to the General Development Order, to enable further types of development to take place without the need for planning permission.

3. A major review of the Use Classes Order has been established, and the working party set up by the Department of the Environment to examine the UCO reported in December 1985. The principal recommendations are:

– Use class I (shops) is out of date and requires major re-arrangement and expansion.

– A new general business use class should be created to incorporate existing classes I (offices) and II (light industry).

– Classes V to IX (special industrial uses) may need to be expanded, and some interchange between them may be justified.

– Use classes XI to XVIII require considerable amalgamation and expansion.

– A new residential use class is required to enable householders to carry on some business activities in their homes.

– New use classes are needed to deal with certain uses of open land. The changes in the UCO are primarily aimed at increasing the deregulatory effect of the UCO, particularly in relation to high technology industry and commerce.

4. Amendments are planned to the Town and Country Planning Act 1971 which are intended to simplify and improve the procedures, including the extension of the Secretary of State's power to award costs where the authority or others have acted unreasonably to those cases dealt with by written representations.

5. It is proposed to simplify and improve the pre-inquiry stages of major planning inquiries, in order to speed these up and improve their efficiency.

Other controls – amenity and conservation

The general principle of planning legislation is a negative one, in that powers of control are normally applied only to prevent undesirable changes in land use patterns. The general legislation requiring permission for development has however proved inadequate to deal with all of the contingencies which have appeared as society has responded to its increased awareness of the need for amenity in its surroundings. A number of supplementary controls have appeared, some self-contained, but still remaining under the general aegis of the planning system.

1.   *Discontinuance orders*

The only power which planning authorities possess to deal positively with an existing 'undesirable' but legal or established use of land is contained in Section 51 of the 1971 Town and Country Planning Act, which allows the authority to intervene to stop any use or impose conditions on a use of land. There are severe limitations to this power.

(a) It does not apply to ongoing 'operational' development, and therefore building or engineering works are unharmed by the provisions, although once the works are *completed* the authority may require alteration or removal.

(b) An order can only have effect if confirmed by the Secretary of State, who may repeal, confirm or modify the order.

(c) Compensation is payable for loss of value of the land, for disturbance of the claimant's enjoyment of it, and for the expense in complying with the order.

The compensation provision has meant that authorities have made sparing use of this facility.

2. *Tree preservation orders*

These orders may be made by the planning authority (usually the district authority) in respect of specified trees, groups of trees, or woodlands, to prevent the cutting down, topping, lopping, up-rooting, wilful damage or wilful destruction of the trees. An indication of the importance placed upon tree preservation may be gained from the fact that in addition to fines of up to £1000 or twice the value of the tree, (or larger on indictment), authorities have also sought injunctions restraining such activity, breach of which is contempt of court, punishable by imprisonment or unlimited fines.

3. *Listed buildings*

The scheme operates by requiring the owner of a listed building or buildings to seek listed building consent before demolishing, altering or extending such buildings. The basic premise for listing is the prevention of the likelihood of demolition; in view of the financial incentives that exist for the demolition of existing historic buildings, particularly in urban areas where space may be at a premium, the probability of such destruction is high, as demand for new buildings and profits is likely to outweigh any sentimental or aesthetic tendencies exhibited by developers.

The listing of a building may therefore cause great economic distress to its owner, except in those cases where the listing adds an element of social cachet.

Three main categories exist, viz:

(a) Grade I Buildings are those of exceptional historic interest.

(b) Grade II Buildings are of special interest, which warrant efforts being made to preserve them.

(c) Grade II* Buildings are those in Grade II which are considered particularly important.

Inclusion on the lists may come about as a result of updating existing lists, or through the 'spot listing' of buildings believed to be in immediate danger.

4.   Building preservation notices

These are an additional weapon available to authorities, allowing them to extend protection to non-listed buildings. The notice is served on both the owner and occupier, or by fixing the notice permanently on the building itself. The effect is to 'list' the building for six months; however, if the building is not listed *officially* within this time, compensation is payable by the authority.

5.   Conservation Areas

The listing provision may be extended to cover *all* buildings (with some exceptions) in an area declared a conservation area.

It should be noted that the buildings so listed may not all be recognisable as 'historic' in the sense of having great age; pressure now exists for the listing of comparatively modern buildings, some only twenty years old. The criteria used for listing are set down in DOE Circular 23/77.

6.   Ancient monuments and archaeological areas

The Secretary of State has the duty of maintaining a Schedule of Ancient Monuments, and the Scheduling of a site brings immediate protection from damage, as it is an offence to demolish, destroy or damage such a site. The Ancient Monuments and Archeological Areas Act 1979 gives statutory powers to allow access to the development site prior to works commencing, in certain designated areas. This provision adds statutory backing to a system in which developers are now often willing to permit such investigation by agreement.

The effect of an area being designated is to require developers to give the local authority six weeks' notice of their intention to carry out works which might disturb, flood or cover up a site in the area. The authority has the right, within four weeks of that notice, to give notice that they or a nominee wish to excavate, and may then obtain the right to investigate and excavate the site for up to four months and two weeks.

7.   Controls on advertising

In order to prevent an undesirable disfigurement of the countryside by signs and hoardings, the advertising regulations allow certain advertisements to appear without permission, e.g. election posters and traffic signs, but otherwise most advertisements require permission in the normal way.

8. *Wasteland and derelict land*

The 1971 Town and Country Planning Act permits an authority to serve an abatement notice where 'the amenity of any part of their area, or of any adjoining area, is seriously injured by the condition of any garden, vacant site, or other open land in their area' and must specify the remedial action required. Appeal is available to the magistrate's court. If the owner or occupier does not comply the authority may enter the land and carry out the works, with the costs being charged to the person who permitted the land to degenerate.

A system of grants is available from central government to aid the authority, or any person in making improvements to derelict land, the main aim being to improve areas of industrial wasteland.

Positive planning

Until now we have considered planning as a 'negative' process, in the sense that the main powers possessed by an authority lie in its ability to prevent development which is contrary to the development plan for the area. However, the development of planning law has ensured that the authority is not entirely reliant on the mercies of the private sector in promoting developments which it sees as desirable.

These 'positive' powers are conferred by statute and allow authorities to acquire land, by agreement or compulsorily, and to develop that land (these should be distinguished from other powers, e.g. of enforcement, which are largely remedial in nature).

1. *New towns*

One of the most substantial exercises in positive planning has been the creation of the new towns, under the New Towns Act of 1946 and 1965. These acts allow the Secretary of State to designate areas of land as sites for new towns. Until the new town has been fully developed, a development corporation, appointed by the Secretary of State, will act as the developer, functioning as both landowner and planner. Using central government funds, the corporation may make contracts with developers, builders, or local authorities for the provision of housing, shops, offices, factories, roads, etc., and may then let or sell the completed units.

Once completed, the assets of the new town are divided between the local authority in whose area the new town would naturally fall, and a national organisation, the New Towns Commission.

2. *Urban development*

In order to promote the regeneration of depressed inner urban areas, the 1980 Local Government Land and Planning Act makes provision for a new kind of public corporation, the Urban Development Corporation. This corporation will operate independently from the local authority and will usurp a number of the authority's functions:

(a) They will have power to make proposals for the development of land within the development area; should the Secretary of State approve the proposals, he may make a development order giving planning permission for any development of land which complies with their approved proposals.

(b) The Secretary of State may designate the corporation as the planning authority for the development area.

(c) Similar authority may be granted for the corporation to become responsible for building control.

(d) They may acquire powers in respect of highways.

(e) They may assume the powers and responsibilities of the water authority for their area in relation to the provision of sewers.

(f) Land belonging to the local authority may be transferred by order of the Secretary of State to the corporation, which has wide powers of disposal and acquisition of land.

Although there are obvious similarities between the urban development corporations and the new towns, the conditions under which the former have to operate are quite different, and there will be a need for continuous liaison between the established elected authority and the corporation if friction is to be avoided.

In addition to the powers to create the new development corporations, the Secretary of State may nominate 'Enterprise Zones', by inviting a district council, London Borough, New Town or Urban Development Corporation to prepare proposals relating to some part of their area; if approved, the area will become an enterprise zone. Such a designation has the effect of granting planning permission for types of development specified in the approved proposals (but possibly subject to strict qualifications).

It is hoped that the (limited) relaxation of planning control, coupled with financial incentives for non-domestic ratepayers, will help to rejuvenate the selected areas.

3. *Powers to acquire and dispose of land*

In order for authorities to be able to deal positively with the most urgent strategic issues, powers are available under the 1971 and

1980 legislation which allows for the acquisition and disposal of land by the authority, for the 'proper planning of the area.' Subject to compensation being payable, the authority may also acquire compulsorily if necessary.

Once the land has been acquired, the authority may enter into a variety of arrangements for promoting the desired development, e.g.

(a) Retain the freehold and employ contractors to carry out the work.

(b) Grant a long lease to a developer (subject to a ground rent) with conditions in the lease governing the way the development is to be carried out.

(c) Sell the freehold to a developer, but retain control over the use of the land through the imposition of restrictive covenants.

(d) Enter into a 'planning agreement' with a developer after selling off the freehold; this system of development is encouraged by Section 52 of the 1971 Town and Country Planning Act, which allows the authority to enter into an agreement with a developer in which the latter accepts legally binding restrictions on the use of his land in return for planning permission for the development. Such agreements may enable the authority to obtain extra 'planning gain' e.g. the provision of housing or car parking which could not be legally obtained by attaching conditions to a grant or planning permission. The issue of planning gain and the extent to which authorities may use permissions as an inducement to developers is covered in Department of the Environment Circular 22/83.

Private restrictions on the use of land

The restrictions on the use of land noted above are the result of modern statute law, and a person affected by proposals for development has only the right to object prior to planning permission being granted, or possibly to persuade the authority only to grant permission under conditions which would ameliorate whatever inconvenience is anticipated.

There are however several areas of the *common* law which may provide restrictions on the use of land. A comprehensive treatment of the provisions of land law is outside the scope of this book, but the following areas are considered worthy of some attention. Where these occur in practice, it will almost inevitably be the case that specialist advice will be required from solicitors with detailed knowledge of land law.

1.   *Covenants*

A covenant may be widely regarded as a promise to do something or refrain from doing some specified thing.

(a) Covenants running with a lease. The general rule is that the original parties to a lease, the lessor (grantor of the lease) and lessee (party receiving the lease) are bound by any covenants in the lease, through the simple fact that they have made a contract which contains the covenant(s) in question. The position may become more complex if the benefit of the lease is assigned; as many leases on land are created which may run for very long periods, it is inevitable that the lease will be assigned at some point. It is therefore important to be able to establish whether covenants remain in force, and by whom they may be enforced.

For covenants to be enforceable against assignees, they must 'touch and concern the land' in question, and not relate only in some vague way to the general condition of the lease: 'If the covenant of its very nature and not merely through extraneous circumstances affects the nature, quality or value of the land demised, or the mode of enjoying it, it falls within the definition.' (Megarry).

Therefore covenants to retain or maintain particular parts of a property, or even to add specified parts at specified times, or not to use the property or land in a particular way, will bind each assignee. Covenants requiring *personal* services would not bind an assignee, as they would not directly 'touch and concern' the land itself.

Action to enforce the covenant may be taken by the original lessor or any person to whom he assigned his reversionary interests.

The position is slightly different if instead of assigning his lease, the original lessee instead sub-leases to someone else. Should the sub-lessee commit breaches of covenant, the lessor's only recourse is to sue the lessee. This is because there is privity of both contract and estate between them, i.e. they have a legal interest in the same contract and the same estate in the land. There would be no privity of contract between lessor and sub-lessee, as there is no direct contract between them, and no privity of estate, as the estate in the sub-lease would, by definition, be less than the original lease.

Therefore if A leases to B, who sub-lets to C, who assigns to D, who then commits a breach of covenant:

A can sue B (privity of contract).
B can seek indemnity from sub-lessee C (privity of contract, or from D (parity of estate between B and D). C would have an implied indemnity from D.

(b) Covenants on freehold land. Covenants can also arise on freehold land, e.g. if A sells part of his land to B, and B covenants not to use the land for a certain purpose, then B will be bound by his promise. The problems arise when B sells the land, or if A assigns the benefit of the covenant.

For the benefit of covenants to pass to the successor in title to the original covenantee (the person receiving the benefit of the promise) there are three preconditions.

(i) The covenant must touch and concern the land.

(ii) The original covenantee must have had the legal estate in the land intended to be benefited at the time the covenant was made.

(iii) If the covenant was entered into before 1926, the successor in title of the covenantee must have the same legal estate in the land as the original covenantee. If however, the covenant was made after 1926, it is now enforceable by anyone claiming under the covenantee.

It should now be apparent that covenants touching land are for the benefit of the adjoining *land*, rather than for the adjoining owners.

Where the covenants are *restrictive* the rule is derived from the famous case of *Tulk v. Moxhay* (1848), and states that a purchaser of property upon which there is a restrictive covenant buys subject to that restriction if he buys with notice thereof, actual or constructive.

In Tulk v. Moxhay, the plaintiff owned houses in Leicester Square, and owned the open space in the centre also. He sold the open space to A, who covenanted to keep it an open space (i.e. he promised, in effect, not to build on it). The covenant was obviously for the benefit of the surrounding houses which the plaintiff kept. The open space changed hands several times, and ended up being owned by someone who had notice of the covenant when he bought the open space. The court held that the plaintiff was entitled to an injunction to prevent the defendant from building on the space, as he was bound by the restrictive covenant of which he had notice at the time of purchase.

In order for the rule to apply:

(i) The covenant must be restrictive or negative in nature.

(ii) The covenant must originally have been an *express* covenant.

(iii) The covenantee must still retain land for the benefit of which the covenant was granted.

(iv) The covenantee must not have done anything himself to prejudice the objective of the covenant.

(v) The covenant must touch and concern the 'dominant' property (i.e. the property benefiting from the covenant).

(vi) The restrictive covenant must be clear and certain.

(vii) Successors in title to the original covenantee may also enforce restrictive covenants if he can show:

- that the covenant in question was annexed to the dominant property itself, and not just for the *personal* benefit of the covenantee

OR

- that the benefit of the covenant was separately and expressly assigned to him at the time he acquired the dominant property

OR

– that there is a building scheme in existence, and the particular restrictive covenant is for the benefit of the whole scheme.

Where there is a breach of a restrictive covenant, the courts may award either damages or an injunction restraining the defendant's breach, or *may* even award a *mandatory* injunction requiring the defendant to restore the property to its original condition.

Restrictive covenants may terminate if:

(i) the party entitled to benefit from the covenant does nothing to enforce it for a long time in circumstances which would lead the covenantor or his successors to assume that further breaches will not matter,

(ii) the character of the neighbourhood changes so much that the covenant is of no value and irrelevant,

(iii) under certain circumstances the owner of land burdened may apply to the Land Tribunal for the covenant to be discharged or modified.

2. *Easements*

Whereas covenants are normally restrictions on the use of land, in order to benefit adjoining land, easements are positive rights which attach to a piece of land, and give rights exercisable over *another* piece of land. Like covenants, the rights and burdens of easements may pass down through generations of owners.

In development projects, easements become important in two ways; first, the development may not be able to proceed unless access is available across land belonging to another, e.g. for the provision of services or to give entry to the site. Second, if a developer acquires land over which someone else has rights, the developer may be unable to utilise that portion of the site unless the owner of the easement is willing to give his permission. Such permission may have to be bought.

Examples of the types of right which might exist over someone else's land would include the right to light, a right to support from the adjoining land, or rights of access for traffic or services.

3. *Nuisance*

The law of nuisance is one of the branches of the law most closely connected with the protection of the environment. The *common* law has over the past few decades been supplemented by a number of *statutes* designed to allow criminal as well as civil remedies to persons affected by nuisance.

Every *statutory* nuisance is a criminal offence which can be the subject of action by the local authority, punishable by fines which increase every day that the offence continues.

The *common law* is useful where the person offended wishes to claim damages or where the local authority refuses to act. At common law, nuisance is divided into public and private nuisance, although the same conduct can amount to both.

Public nuisance may be defined as an act or omission which causes a class of the Queen's subjects to suffer unreasonable discomfort or inconvenience or interference with their rights. Therefore the nuisance must be widespread in its effect, e.g. dust from quarrying, or obstruction of the highway.

Private nuisance is 'the unlawful interference with a person's use or enjoyment of land or some right over or in connection with it.'

Essentially, the nuisance must be continuous or recurrent in order for it to be actionable. Common examples include noise, dust and other types of pollution but may also include action for obstruction of a right of way or the blocking of a right to light.

2.2   THE FINANCIAL BASIS FOR DEVELOPMENT

Development Finance

The financing of property development must always be considered in the context of the structure of the investment market as a whole. Property development is but one shade in the spectrum of competition for investment funds, and as such is susceptible to the normal vagaries of the market place. In some financial climates property development will be a preferred medium for the deployment of investors' money, and in others it will be relatively difficult to find finance. Similarly, the attractiveness of the property development market to developers will be influenced by whatever conditions apply to the availability of those funds, in terms of the cost of the money, and whatever restrictions the suppliers of such funds may consider to be appropriate for the market at that point. The availability of funds and the conditions under which they are available are dynamic, in the sense that the parameters which affect availability can be expected to change frequently, dependent to a large extent on factors completely outside the influence of the lenders and borrowers. Examples of such influences are current and expected policies of central government, particularly in relation to the supply of money within the economy; current and future levels of taxation; the strength of the UK economy as measured by its trading position and the relative attractiveness of overseas investment; levels of interest rates set by the Treasury in support of government policy; inflation rates; costs of construction; and developments in industry and commerce in general which may have a disruptive effect on the perception of investors. Examples of the latter may include the development of new technologies such as information technology or genetic engineering, which may offer expectations of new sources of investment opportunity for the future, at the same time attracting a massive diversion of funds from other types of investment. The sale of nationalised industries to the private sector may also lead to a similar diversion of funds, or may serve to radically change the terms upon which such funds are made available.

From the viewpoint both of the suppliers and users of development finance, the most important consideration is the expectation of the future. Both rely on making profits, which are gained in essentially the same way as for any commercial transaction, by producing a margin between cost and value. In some cases this margin will be realised through a capital transaction, and in others through trading on a beneficial cash flow position. Two important considerations of the future apply in relation to two of the main sectors for development, the residential and the commercial development markets. In the former, there is a belief that most speculative housing developments will take place for owner occupation, rather than for rent. Although the picture has become more complicated over the past few years, with the introduction of alternative forms of tenure, mainly in the housing association field, these developments can be seen as reflecting current government policy in encouraging owner occupation rather than a competing market for private housebuilders. Even so, the result has been that many volume builders have been able to adjust their marketing activity to take account of this change. In the commercial area, the basis for prediction is that the end users of commercial developments – retailers, industrial organisations, commercial users – will prefer to rent their properties rather than own them outright. From the users' point of view, this allows them to have use of the capital value of their buildings for running their business, and brings the assumption that developers' calculations will be based on the receipt of rental income, rather than capital sales. A change in either of the scenarios above would bring major changes in the way in which the developments would be funded, and in the viability calculations.

While crude figures may be available for the overall size of the property funds market, there is little information on the methods by which funds are deployed on individual projects. The vehicles used for the application of funds on projects will depend on the expectations of the project, the nature of the lending institution, the perceived risks, the preferences of the parties, and on their relative negotiating skills.

The supply of finance for the property development world can be first divided into two forms: corporate finance, involving the funding of the development company itself, and project finance, where the funds are sought for an identifiable project.

Corporate finance essentially involves the company undertaking development in raising funds for its ongoing activities, not related to any particular project. There is a variety of techniques for this, ranging from the use of retained earnings, to more sophisticated methods of acquiring operating finance which may involve the issuing of shares, debentures or loan stock, together with loans on a fixed or revolving fund basis. These funds may then be applied at the company's discretion to a programme of development.

Project based funding. In contrast to corporate financing, which relies on loans being made on the security of the company's operations as a whole, project financing assumes that the funds are made available in relation to an identified project, and the land and buildings associated with the project will form the principal source of security for the loan.

Duration of loans. As noted earlier, there are three basic categories of lending: short, medium and long term, covering terms of 3–5 years, 5–10 years and 20–25 years (or much longer) respectively. The two main requirements of the developer are first, to cover the cost of acquiring the site, constructing the building and letting. For all but the largest projects this will be possible with a short-term loan, and where the project is likely to take longer than this, it is often possible to arrange for the term of the lending to be increased slightly. If the developer is primarily in business as a 'trader', i.e. one who develops and then sells out his complete interest in the development on completion, this is the only type of finance which is likely to be needed. However, if the developer wishes to maintain a long-term interest in the project, in order to participate in the extra profit to be made through the long-term growth in rental income, then the second requirement appears in the need for further long-term funds in order to clear the short-term lending, and provide a basis for continued involvement. As this funding will normally cover a period of over 20 years, it will be seen that the medium-term loan is usually of little interest to the developer.

At one time there was a clear division between the suppliers of long- and short-term funds, with the financial institutions (mainly insurance companies, pension funds and property unit trusts) supplying long-term funds, and the clearing and merchant banks supplying short-term finance. This division is now eroded, as the banks have seen the opportunity to command part of the long-term growth of income, and have become willing to participate in the equity of projects. Similarly, the financial institutions have seen the dangers in providing only long-term mortgage finance at a fixed or restricted rate, and now participate as full partners in developments, sharing the increase in income with the developer (and the concomitant risk) and also providing the short-term development finance for the projects which they intend to fund in the long term. It should be noted that the institutions are also major investors in property through their purchase of substantial shareholdings in property companies, thus gaining the advantage of income from the general activities of the companies, together with the increase in value of the shareholding, without the risks attached to the funding of an individual project.

Funding sources

(a) *Insurance companies and pension funds.* Together these types of institution provide the most important sources of funds for long-term finance. Leaving aside the non-life assurance business, these organisations exist by the acceptance of money now through premium payments on a regular basis in order to provide cash in the form of pensions and life cover at some date in the future. As their liabilities stretch well into the future, it is necessary for them to have investments which are geared towards providing income growth, with a high degree of security, rather than an immediate capital gain. To date, property has been a useful means of attaining these objectives, but must compete with alternative forms of investment opportunity. In addition to the pension schemes run by the insurance companies, there are a number of major pension funds established to serve particular industries or companies. The largest of these serve the nationalised industries such as the National Coal Board, British Steel, and British Rail, and each have assets of over £1000 million. These institutions invest around 20% of their funds in property.

Due to their sheer size and experience in the property market, they have now grown to the extent that they are able to undertake developments in their own right, without the need of a developer-partner.

The need to provide long-term 'homes' for such large quantities of cash has meant that there has over the last decade been intense competition between the funds for the right to participate in the 'prime' developments, i.e. the projects occupying the best located commercial sites, of high quality construction and finish, and able to attract the highest quality tenants in terms of their status, credit-worthiness and ability to pay the highest rents. Typical of such prime developments would be the high quality office projects in the City of London.

(b) *Investment and property unit trusts.* Unit trusts are trusts in the proper legal sense that they are governed by trustees, and for our purposes may be divided into two groups, investment unit trusts and property unit trusts. The former involve investors' money being pooled and then used to purchase shares of companies quoted on the stock exchange. These trusts do not invest directly in development, but indirectly through their shareholding in property companies. Property unit trusts, due to their tax position, are able to make a higher rate of return through direct involvement in individual projects rather than through the purchase of property company shares, but investment in these trusts is limited to pension funds and charitable bodies, with the pension funds having by far the greatest holdings.

These bodies may be contrasted with investment trusts: unlike unit trusts, which are legally trusts, these are limited companies whose activities involve investment in the shares of other quoted companies. Their shares are freely traded on the stock exchange.

(c) *Property bonds*. These exist to offer life insurance together with a direct investment in development. Ordinary investors may purchase bonds, with part of the payment being used to purchase life cover, while the majority is used for direct property development.

(d) *Clearing banks*. The clearing banks have traditionally been the primary source of short- and medium-term loans, but their attitude towards particular proposals will depend on a number of factors, such as government policy, as evidenced by instructions from the Bank of England, and the policy of the bank in relation to its preferred lending at any given time. Within these restrictions, the branch managers have a high degree of discretion in approving individual applications. Obviously, developers with an established track record with a branch will receive more favourable treatment than others, both in the availability of money and the terms of the loan. Rates of interest will range from 1%–5% above the bank's base rate, depending on the developer's record, the security being offered, and the attractiveness of the project. In addition to the interest charges, the borrower may be charged a fee for the arrangement of the loan facility.

(e) *Merchant banks*. The merchant banks are essentially entrepreneurs, living by their ability to arrange and supply finance for particular purposes, normally involving substantially more risk than that undertaken by the clearing banks. The ability to structure the finance requirements for a project to make the attracting of funds possible enables the merchant banks to charge higher rates of interest, and often to demand equity participation in the project.

(f) *Building societies*. Under present legislation, building societies are not able to participate directly in commercial development, and the major thrust of their activity is in providing mortgage finance to private housebuyers. The scale of their operation is enormous, involving some one million new loans being made each year. Recently, some societies have readdressed their role with the result that some have undertaken direct housebuilding themselves for rent and purchase, in addition to the normal activity of supplying funds to purchasers.

(g) *Major property companies.* There are now around one hundred property companies quoted on the stock exchange, and on occasion these companies may have liquidity available which is not ear-marked for immediate use, and may be loaned to another property company in exchange for a share in the proposed development. Alternatively, in exchange for such participation, the quoted company may be prepared to borrow to fund the project. The strength of the major company will usually allow it to borrow at advantageous rates, lending strength to the project's viability. Often the larger company will demand and expect to receive a majority share in the new development.

(h) *Government and EEC assistance.* A bewildering array of grants, tax concessions and other forms of aid is now available through central and local government agencies and the EEC. Most of these incentives are designed with specific purposes in mind, and are intended to alleviate local or regional problems, particularly unemployment. The range of benefits is constantly changing, and depends on government and/or EEC policy, and the level of funds available for such programmes. Most of the schemes are aimed at the end users of the facilities to be aided, e.g. tourism, agriculture or manufacturing businesses, and the funds are not usually directly available to development companies. Even in those instances where the developer can directly attract such funds, there are strict conditions attached to the grants or concessions, and the project usually has to be approved for aid *before* work can commence. These procedural requirements are normally strictly enforced and time consuming, and can slow down progress on the development considerably.

(i) *Other organisations and sources.* The net for sources of development finance can be cast very wide indeed, and it is worth mentioning some of the other non-traditional agencies. The major charitable bodies and trusts, although strictly controlled in their activities by the terms of their trusts, are repositories for substantial funds which require to be invested. The Crown Estates, the churches, and the major family estates all involve themselves in joint or solo investment in development projects, and many have substantial ongoing programmes of development. Building con-tractors anxious for construction contracts may have liquid cash available which can be used to fund projects, on the basis that they will undertake the building work, or they may be willing to fund that part of a project by agreeing to defer the normal stage payments until completion of the project, when interest would also be payable for the use of this facility. Lastly, there are a number of wealthy individuals who privately finance property development. The existence of these sources is not normally publicised, and their money would be made available through their financial advisers, merchant bankers or other agents.

Project funding – commercial projects

As noted earlier, the variety and sophistication of methods of applying funds for individual projects is limited only by the ingenuity of the parties supplying and employing the funds, plus any relevant legal restrictions. Most of these however are combinations of or permutations on the basic formats described below. Not all of these methods will be applicable or available at any given time; some methods will be in or out of favour with the market as a whole at any given point in time, only to disappear or return with a change in the financial climate or a change in fashion.

(a) Short-term finance, sale on completion. This method of using interim or bridging finance assumes that the developer uses a bridging loan (i.e. short-term loan) to cover the costs of acquiring the land and the costs of construction, and sells the completed development outright, retaining no long-term interest in the project. Unless the development is to be pre-sold to the institution taking the long-term ownership, it is likely that the interim finance will be supplied by a clearing or merchant bank. In funding one-off projects, any bank will require to see well worked-up information which will convince them of the project's viability. Assuming that this is satisfactory, the bank will then be able to make judgements on the aspects of the funding which are of commercial interest to them as bankers; these are:

(i) The size and timing of the lending. Most banks will be unwilling to lend the whole amount of the finance required for the whole of the development period; as developers do not normally wish to see their own money used for such operations, they will have to convince the bank that the proposal is *extremely* viable, or be able to offer assurances that additional finance is available. In most cases, the developer will be required to supply some element of the funding in cash, either from his own resources or through a third party. The duration of the loan will normally be the whole development and letting period.

(ii) The quality of the security being offered for the loan: normally this will be the site itself, but the bank may well require additional collateral if the value of the part completed development is below the maximum level of the loan. The bank will seek to minimise its own 'exposure' on the project, i.e. will try to ensure that it has maximum security and minimum risk on the transaction. This will be at odds with the developer's intention to try to avoid giving any additional security, particularly where this involves personal guarantees.

(iii) The details of the payback arrangements (NB – although the term 'payback' may be used to define a particular technique for financial appraisal, in which the time required to recover the initial capital investment is used to compare the viability of alternative investment projects, the term is used here in the more obvious sense). The bank will wish to be convinced that it will be able to recover its investment in the agreed time, and will wish to see reflected in the loan agreement a condition to this effect; penalties may be exacted in addition to the normal interest if the loan is not repaid on time. The conditions may give the bank the right to the first tranche of monies recovered through a sale or letting, prior to any other distribution of such income.

(iv) The answers to the questions above will to a large extent dictate the cost of the loan to the developer: projects which the bank perceives as being of high commercial risk and possessing less than absolute security for the lending will only be financed (if at all) at a correspondingly high rate of interest. The range of interest rates will be in the range of 2% above the bank's own base rate (for well secured, low risk projects) to 5% above base rate for the more speculative developments. As an alternative to pitching a rate of interest related to the bank's own base rate the loan may be indexed to the London Inter-Bank Offered Rate (LIBOR). There may also be provision in the loan agreement for the rate to fluctuate according to some prearranged formula. Normally, the developer will wish to avoid making repayments during the development period, and this will therefore entail the interest, calculated on a monthly or quarterly basis, being added to the principal outstanding (rolling-up). In addition to the interest payments, the bank may also require a fee for making the funds available, usually a percentage of the loan; this sum may be added to the loan.

The following example assumes that a developer has identified a freehold site on which he can gain planning permission to erect an office block. 100% finance has been sought and obtained from a merchant bank. No forward letting has been arranged. Details are as follows:

Acquisition costs, including legal and agent's fees	£2,500,000
Construction costs, including fees	£1,500,000
	(rate of expenditure assumed to be £166,667 p.m. – deliberately oversimplified)
Bank interest rate (interest rolled-up, added monthly)	14%
Bank's commitment fee (added to loan at start)	4%
Investment yield for scheme when fully let	6%

Expected initial rents   £400,000
Total development period   15 months (pre-contract 3
                                months)
                                (post-contract 9
                                months)
                                (letting period 3
                                months)
Selling fees   2% of value

Table 1 represents the cumulative borrowing requirements, and Figure 1 the cumulative cash flow diagram for the project.

	Borrowing Commitment		*Cumulative*
Start of Month 1	Acq. costs	£2,500,000	
	Comm. fee	160,000	£2,660,000
End Month 1	Int. for M1	31,033	2,691,033
End Month 2	Int. for M2	31,395	2,722,428
End Month 3	Int. for M3	31,761	2,754,189
End Month 4	Int. for M4	32,132	2,786,321
Start of Month 5	1st Cert. paid	166,667	2,952,988
End Month 5	Int. for M5	34,451	2,987,439
Start of Month 6	2nd Cert. paid	166,667	3,154,106
End Month 6	Int. for M6	36,798	3,190,903
Start of Month 7	3rd Cert. paid	166,667	3,357,571
End Month 7	Int. for M7	39,171	3,396,742
Start of Month 8	4th Cert. paid	166,667	3,563,409
End Month 8	Int. for M8	41,573	3,604,981
Start of Month 9	5th Cert. paid	166,667	3,771,648
End Month 9	Int. for M9	44,002	3,815,650
Start of Month 10	6th Cert. paid	166,667	3,982,317
End Month 10	Int. for M10	46,460	4,028,777
Start of Month 11	7th Cert. paid	166,667	4,195,444
End Month 11	Int. for M11	48,946	4,244,391
Start of Month 12	8th Cert. paid	166,667	4,411,058
End Month 12	Int. for M12	51,462	4,462,520
Start of Month 13	9th Cert. paid	166,667	4,629,187
End Month 13	Int. for M13	54,006	4,683,194
End Month 14	Int. for M14	54,637	4,737,830
End Month 15	Int. for M15	55,274	4,793,105
	Income on sale	£6,666,666	+ 1,873,561
	Less selling fees	133,333	+ 1,740,228

Table 1: Cumulative borrowing requirements

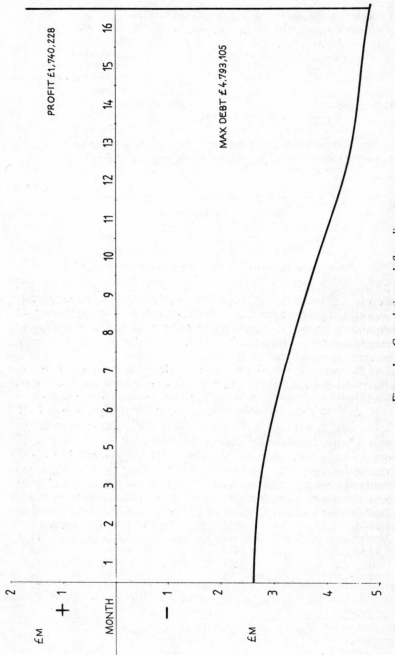

Figure 1. Cumulative cash flow diagram.

SUMMARY

A.	Income on sale on completion (Assumed fully let on completion of letting period) Valued on 6% yield	i.e. 400,000	
		.06	£6,666,666

B.	Costs		
	Acquisition costs (incl. fees)	2,500,000	
	Bank commitment fee	160,000	
	Construction cost (incl. fees)	1,500,000	
	Interest in develop. period	633,101	
	Selling costs	133,333	
		4,926,434	4,926,434

C.	PRE-TAX PROFIT		£1,740,228

(Note: profit differs from cash flow residue due to rounding-up)

The pre-tax profit is sufficient to repay the bridging loan plus interest, and leave the developer with a profit. Unless the developer was well known to the bank, or could produce evidence of a forward sale and/or letting, it is unlikely that the bank would be willing to bridge the whole costs: other sources of funds would also be required.

As the eventual purchaser will normally be a financial institution which wishes to purchase and retain ownership of the completed development for the purposes of long-term investment, it will often be possible for the developer to negotiate bridging funding from that source, at a rate of interest more favourable than that available from a bank. (In this case, the commitment fee may be dispensed with.) The only 'uncertainty' then left in the system, apart from any unseen difficulty with the cost of construction, is in relation to the letting of the project to produce the required rental income. Where there are uncertainties about the attractiveness of the project and possible rent levels, the value of the project will reduce to reflect this risk. This reduction will be reflected in the increased yield which will be applied to the projected income; the higher the yield used, the lower will be the capital value.

Using the base data in the last example, but assuming that the yield is increased to 6.5% to compensate for the uncertainty, let us assume that the developer has contracted with the purchaser to sell the agreed development (once complete and let) for a price based on that yield. The purchaser will normally have a right of veto on the proposed lettings, in order to protect his long-term interests against potentially undesirable tenants, and will have approved details of the occupation lease to be granted, particularly in respect of the permitted uses of the premises, the proposed rents, and the rent review period.

The purchase price would be calculated thus:

Rental income	£400,000
Purchase price = capital value based on 6½% yield ($\frac{£400,000}{.065}$)	6,153,846
Less costs above (£4,926,434 minus commitment fee of £160,000)	4,766,434
Developer's profit	£1,387,412

This level of profit is dependent on the developer achieving the projected rent levels; should the projected levels not be achieved, there would normally be a provision in the loan agreement with the purchaser that the amount required to redeem the bridging loan would still be forthcoming, but a formula would exist which would lower the developer's profit in compensation. The developer, however, has a considerable incentive to maximise the rental income initially achieved; a simple calculation will show that for every extra £1000 of rental income obtained on initial letting, his profit increases by £15,384, i.e.

Extra rent obtained	£1000
Capitalised on yield of 6½% (i.e. $\frac{£1000}{.065}$)	£15,384

There are limits however to the extent to which the developer can force the rents upward on first letting; in addition to the normal market resistance which would be met, a rent of much above the normal market level will reduce the scope for increases at the first review, and therefore reduce the long-term investment value to the purchaser. To compensate for the depreciation of the investment a higher yield might be demanded, thus reducing the capitalised value payable to the developer, and reducing his overall profit.

A third possible variation on the above is for the developer to identify the project and conduct outline feasibility studies, probably based upon information supplied by the potential design team members working on a no-job-no-fee basis. The planning position would be investigated during this exercise, and, based on the feasibility study, a purchase price for the existing land would be agreed (subject to contract). Armed with a well developed 'package', the developer could approach a potential funding institution and offer the package on the basis that he would be paid a fee for introducing the development and for project managing the scheme through to completion and letting. As part of the deal, a target rental level would be set which the developer would be expected to realise, and an incentive might be offered by way of a right to a prestated percentage of any increase above the target. As this would give the developer a long-term interest in the scheme, there would usually be a provision in the contract for the developer to be obliged to sell this right to income upon completion of the developer's contract, with the rental share being capitalised at an agreed yield.

Using the basic data above, but assuming a management fee payable by the institution to the developer of £100,000, and an agreement to divide any rental income over £400,000 equally between funding institution and developer, the positions of the institution and developer are as follows:

(i) Assuming rent of £400,000 achieved:

Developer receives	fee	£100,000
Institution receives	income of £400,000 p.a. therefore investment value on 6.5% yield	

$$\frac{£400,000}{.065} = £6,153,846$$

Yield to institution based on development costs

$$\frac{£400,000 \times 100}{4,766,434 + 100,000} = 8.2\%$$

(ii) Assuming rent increases to £450,000:

Developer receives	fee	£100,000

plus 50% of £50,000 = £25,000 p.a.
capitalised at 6.5%

$$\left(\frac{25,000}{.065}\right) = £384,615$$

Total income £484,615 after developer's share bought out

Institution receives   income of £425,000 therefore
investment value on 6.5% yield

$$\frac{£425,000}{.065} = £6,538,461$$

after buying out

developer $$\frac{£450,000}{.065} = £6,923,077$$

Yield to institution
based on development
costs after buying out $$\frac{£450,000 \times 100}{4,766,434 + 100,000 + 384,615} = 8.6\%$$
developer

(b) Developer retaining long-term interest The previous examples assume that the developer does not wish to retain a long-term interest in the development; where there is a desire to have equity participation in the long-term growth potential of the projects, more sophisticated methods must be employed.

(i) *Mortgage finance.* The simplest of these is for the developer to repay his short-term borrowing by giving a mortgage on the completed project to a financial institution (usually an insurance company) in exchange for sufficient funds to cover his capital outlay plus accrued interest. Two golden rules are normally applied in this type of transaction. The first is that the size of the mortgage funding is no more than two-thirds of the capital value of the completed development; this ensures, from the funding institution's point of view, that there is adequate security for the mortgage. The developer therefore has to ensure that the total development cost is less than two-thirds of the completed value, otherwise he would find it difficult to obtain a mortgage loan which would completely eliminate his short-term loan. The second rule is to ensure that the income from the completed development is greater than the repayments of interest and capital required under the mortgage agreement. If this were not the case, then the developer would be suffering a negative cash flow, i.e. paying more in instalments of capital and interest than was obtained in rent.

This method of funding lost popularity as high levels of inflation became endemic, as granting a fixed interest mortgage meant that the insurance companies were unable to participate in the rental growth, and were lending at artificially low rates. For the developer, having a low rate of interest fixed at the start of the repayment period, coupled with an inflation rate which gave great increases in rental income at each review period, was attractive – by the end of the mortgage the repayments would form only a minute call on the rental income. Institutions therefore became unwilling to grant such mortgages, and began to demand (and get) increasing equity stakes in the developments. At the same time, interest rates

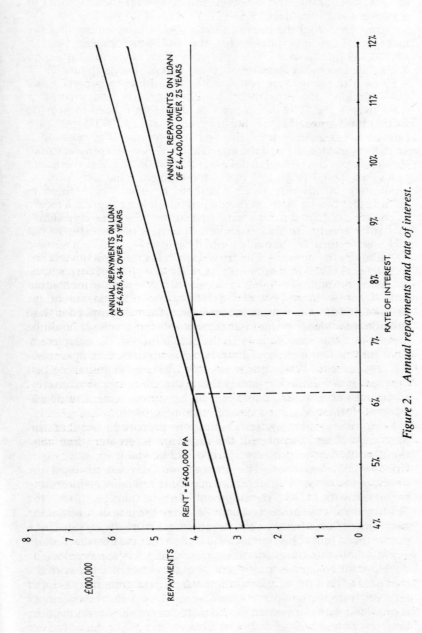

Figure 2. Annual repayments and rate of interest.

increased generally, and it became impossible for the developer to produce a viable project.

Using data from the previous examples, and assuming that the mortgage loan is available for the full development cost of £4,926,434 (in this case 73% of project value), at interest rates over 6.2%, the income is insufficient to cover repayments (figure 2).

Even if the loan were restricted to two-thirds of project value (£4.4 million), the repayments would be greater than income at rates over 7.5%. The developer would therefore need to provide further funds himself at the rate of approximately £300,000 p.a. (at a rate of 14%) at least until the first rent review. The position is actually worse than this; if the loan is at 66.67% of the project value, the developer can be said to have an equity stake, i.e. an investment of his own capital, of 33.33% of the development value in the project, amounting in this case to £2.2 million; he would be entitled to assume that this investment should provide at least as great a return as could be obtained from a 'safe' investment, e.g. blue chip shares or bank deposits. In this example not only is the investment not yielding a return, it is actually (initially at least) costing him money!

Although the position is improved when tax relief on the interest payments is taken into account (tax relief in respect of corporation tax being normally available in respect of interest repayments, but not of course in respect of capital repayments) the net of tax calculations do not improve the position in the first years enough to provide a viable investment at current interest levels. It could be argued that this analysis ignores the possibilities of the early years' poor returns being improved through growth in income at successive rent reviews. While this is possible, there is no guarantee that rent levels will improve; nor is there any guarantee that interest rates will not increase, thus negating any improvement in investment performance gained through income growth.

In summary, there are few institutions prepared to lend on this basis at present, and even if the mortgage loans were available, there would be few projects which would be viable.

(ii) *Sale and leaseback.* This method was devised to allow the developer to obtain long-term finance while retaining an interest in rental growth of the development. In its simplest form, the developer sells the project on completion to the investor, and at the same time takes a lease on the development from the investor, at a prearranged rent. This rent is calculated so that the investor obtains a reasonable rate of return on the purchase price he has paid. The developer then gains a 'profit rent', i.e. the difference between the rent paid to the investing institution and the rack rent the developer receives from the tenants to whom he sub-lets. Thus the developer is provided with permanent finance (at least for the duration of the long lease) and will probably be able to find his bridging finance from the same source. He also enjoys participation in the growth of the rental income at rent reviews. The desire of the investing institution to participate also in the growth of the project's income will however mean that a formula is devised to allow sharing of this growth. This may involve at its simplest level an agreement to proportion any income growth at rent reviews, or may be designed to allow the institution and the developer to share the rental income on a day by day basis. This latter method allows a sharing of gains made if growth occurs between formal review points, e.g. where a tenant has surrendered his lease prior to the end of his tenancy agreement, and a new tenant is found at a higher rent.

There are no fixed levels of sharing in the market place, each agreement being representative of the negotiating skills of the parties, their financial 'muscle', and the attractiveness of the project itself.

Although the sale and leaseback method brings definite advantages to the developer, there are also possible drawbacks, which are related to the existence of a long-term partner in the development. The developer is faced with a continuing commitment to the rent payable to the institution, possibly guaranteeing a minimum rate of return, irrespective of the rent levels he is able to achieve when sub-letting; his interest in the project is, by the nature of the lease, limited in time, and may be encumbered by a substantial range of obligations to the landlord through the provisions of the lease; as the institution will probably insist upon a minimum level of return, then unforeseen and unfavourable changes in the market may mean that the developer is faced with a negative cashflow at some time.

Using the base data in the earlier example, and assuming that the institution is to purchase the site and supply interim finance, and will grant a lease to the developer on completion at a rent which will give a return to the institution of 6.5% on development costs, a simple example of this method is as follows:

Rental income received by developer	£400,000
Rent paid by developer £4,926,434 × 6.5%	320,218
Residual profit rent obtained by developer	£ 79,782

If the agreement between developer and institution stated that a minimum target rent was to be agreed, and that the parties would share any excess equally between them, assume that the target rent was £400,000 and an initial rent was achieved of £450,000:

Rental income to developer		£450,000
Rent paid by developer		
£4,926,434 × 6.5%	£320,218	
Plus 50% × £50,000	25,000	
	345,218	345,218
Residual profit rent to developer		£104,782

The profit rent paid to the developer has become known as the 'top slice'. To prevent the erosion or disappearance of the top slice as a result of providing a guaranteed income to the institution plus an 'upward only' movement in the institution's income at reviews, developers have attempted to obtain more equitable arrangements for the sharing of risk and opportunity, in order to prevent the developer being totally exposed at times where part of the development might remain unlet and producing no income, or where market conditions meant that rent levels fell rather than increased. These arrangements are known as 'side by side' or 'vertical slice' agreements. In these, the parties agree to share the income at reviews in the proportion obtaining at the outset; using the figures in the last example, the proportion is calculated thus:

$$\frac{\text{Initial rent paid by developer}}{\text{Initial full rental value}} \quad \frac{345,218}{450,000} \times 100 = 76.7\%$$

At the first and subsequent reviews the developer receives 23.3%, the institution 76.7% of the new rents achieved. This system can be made simpler by omitting any reference to the sharing occurring only at rent review periods, and stating that *all* rental income is divided in the original proportions. The vertical slice method has one further advantage for the developer, in that it is possible then to value the developer's interest in the project; if the top slice method with guaranteed income to the institution is used, valuation becomes difficult, as the performance of the developer's share is unpredictable. This means that it is impossible for the developer to raise capital for further activities by disposing of his interest – except perhaps as a sale to the funding institution itself which is then in a strong position to dictate the terms of the sale.

It is also possible to add further sophistication to the vertical slice method by building in some measure of guaranteed income, at a level which would be acceptable to both developer and institution.

A predetermination of the proportions of rent attributable to the developer and institution means that there is no way for the developer to increase his share in the rental income. Thus there is a reduced incentive for the developer although in return he gains a measure of protection against adverse market conditions.

The difference between 'geared' shares, in which a movement in rental income produces a larger movement in income to the developer, and 'ungeared' or proportional agreements may be illustrated thus. Assuming that the target rental at first letting is £400,000, and that an actual first rent of £450,000 is achieved, with increases above targets divided equally:

(i) *Geared arrangement*:

At first letting on completion		
Rental income to developer		£450,000
Rent paid by developer £4,926,434		
× 6.5%	= £320,218	
Plus 50% of £50,000	= 25,000	
	345,218	345,218
Profit rent		104,782

Developer's share $\dfrac{104,782}{450,000}$ = 23.3%

Institution share $\dfrac{345,218}{450,000}$ = 76.7%

If at the first reviews rental income increases to £600,000 and the increases are to be divided equally between developer and institution:

Rental income to developer		£600,000
Rent paid by developer £4,926,434		
× 6.5%	= £320,218	
Plus 50% of £200,000	= 100,000	
	420,218	420,218
Profit rent		£179,782

Developer's share $\dfrac{179,782}{600,000}$ = 30%

Institution's share $\dfrac{420,218}{600,000}$ = 70%

Although both parties have increased their cash income, the developer's share of income has increased dramatically while the institution has experienced a small decrease. The opposite side of the coin should not be neglected, however: a drop in income through voids or adverse trading conditions could lead to the rent not being sufficient to meet the guaranteed return of 6.5% on the cost of development.

(ii) *Proportional arrangement*

Assuming that the first rent achieved was £450,000 and the

proportions at first letting are to be carried through to all further reviews:

At first letting
Rental income to developer		£450,000
Rent paid by developer £4,926,434		
× 6.5%	= £320,218	
Plus 50% of £50,000	= 25,000	
	345,218	345,218
Profit rent		£104,792

Developer's share $\dfrac{104,792}{450,000} = 23.3\%$

Institution's share $\dfrac{345,218}{450,000} = 76.7\%$

At first review, rents increase to £600,000 p.a.

Rental income to developer	£600,00
Rent paid by developer – 76.7% × £600,000	£460,200
Rent retained by developer – 23.3% × £600,000	£139,800

It may be readily seen that the developer's share increases more using the geared arrangement rather than the proportional system.

The choice of which system to use on a particular project will depend on the parties' perceptions of likely conditions in the market in the future, and the degree of security demanded in relation to the risks anticipated. Given the need for institutions to experience growth in their investments to provide for their future commitments, few institutions will now be prepared to accept arrangements which effectively produce a reducing share of income. In spite of the risks involved, they almost invariably insist on proportional arrangements, accepting that in so doing they must forego or reduce to a minimum any guarantee of return on their investment. Where guarantees *are* insisted upon, it is usually on schemes with a high degree of risk, for example on schemes which are not prelet, and on which there may be some apprehension over lettings or the rents likely to be achieved. Even here, the guarantee given by the developer may be restricted to the development period, and may disappear once the first lettings are made.

Project funding – residential projects

Relatively few of the private residential housing projects executed in the UK are undertaken by the type of developers noted earlier in this chapter; most are the product of building contractors, either operating solely as housebuilders or through a housebuilding division or subsidiary. The method of funding applied to house-building activity tends to be related to the size of the firm's output, and its desire to secure its long-term ability to produce by the establishment of land banks.

The funding requirements for residential development are postulated on the assumption that private sector housing will be made available for outright purchase and not for rent; this makes the financial calculation quite different from that employed for commercial projects. The current state of the law on the security of tenants in rented property means that building for private rental is unattractive to residential developers, as it is difficult to guarantee rent levels which would be viable in the long term, and even more difficult to obtain possession of property where the tenant is in breach of the rental agreement. Although there has been for some years pressure on governments to change the law in order to make private rental more attractive, the modifications made as a response have so far been inadequate to make more than a slight impact on the willingness of developers to participate in this form of tenure. Given the politically charged nature of the problem, it is unlikely that there will be major changes in the basic presumption in the foreseeable future.

The larger housebuilding companies are likely to organise their funding through short-term loans, often using pre-agreed overdraft facilities, and medium-term loans from merchant or clearing banks. The latter loans will probably be related to the companies' medium-term plans, and will cover the provision for the operational costs in constructing on several sites at any one time, and also for the purchase of land for building in the future. The scale on which these organisations operate means that it would be extremely difficult to organise, monitor and control the financing of a large number of sites on the basis of each having an individually agreed financing package. The medium-term loan agreement would contain pro-vision for repayment over a period of up to five years, and might be renegotiated prior to the expiry of that period in order to have a secure financing base for the future at any given time. The cost of such loans will depend on the financial strength of the company, and would be in the range of 1% above the bank's base rate, or the London inter bank rate, for the largest and most financially secure firm, to 3% over base for the slightly less well endowed organis-ation.

The slightly smaller company might pay around the same rate for its borrowings, and might also operate on a mixture of medium-term and overdraft finance, but the medium-term loans in this case would probably be tied to development of specific sites, each of which would be financed on the basis of its viability. The 'facility' or 'commitment' fee noted in connection with commercial projects would probably be demanded in these circumstances.

For the smallest company, the finance would almost certainly be linked to specific projects, each of which would be examined by the bank to establish viability, and would cost 3 to 5% over base rates. Such loans would have a currency and repayment rate linked to expected or actual sales progress.

Perhaps the greatest difference between the financing requirements for commercial and for residential projects is that in the latter case, a scheme is divided up into a number of individual units, which may be started and completed at a speed which can be altered to take account of developments in the marketplace. This allows the developer to start recovering his costs prior to completion of the whole project; it also means that the profitability of the scheme will depend on the speed with which completed units can be sold. For this reason many housebuilders will be initially cautious about starting too many houses on a large estate until the market has responded to the first batch to be offered.

Figure 3 shows the effect upon profitability of delaying the sales on a small development; in one case the sales are effected during the last six months of the 15 month project, and in the second, sales are made only after the development is complete. The difference in profitability is accounted for by the extra interest cost incurred through not making sales as soon as the units are ready. Maximising the cash flow and interest-saving advantages in this way requires a conscious effort on the part of both the construction team and the marketing team, in order to ensure that the site is planned so that the customer is not dissuaded from making an early purchase by being surrounded by the real and apparent chaos of the ongoing construction work on the later houses. The threat of intrusion by early morning use of construction plant, mud on roads, lack of finished road surfaces and footpaths will all be inhibitors to the early occupation of housing.

Although the provision of long-term finance for housing is made to the end consumer, i.e. the purchaser, and not the builder, the availability of such funds is obviously of interest to the builder, as ultimately the real demand for housing, i.e. that demand which can be satisfied through cash being available, will be determined by the funds available to the purchaser. The main source of such funds in the UK is through the building societies, although the major banks are now also a real force in this market. The size of the loan available to individual purchasers will vary according to the demand for loans and the income available to the lenders through receipts from savings and investment, as well as the security available to the lender. This security is of course the dwelling itself, and the normal procedure is for a loan to be made by way of a mortgage agreement up to a maximum percentage of the bank's or building society's

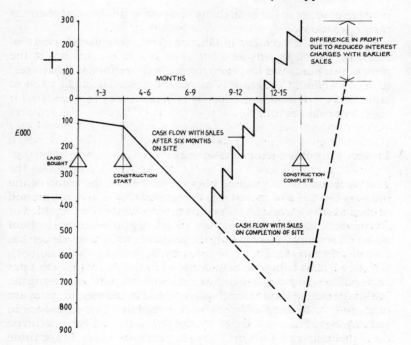

Figure 3. Cash flow on speculative residential project.

valuation of the property, usually for a period not exceeding 25 years. This means in effect that the purchaser must find a small percentage of the property value himself, through savings made for that purpose, or from the profit realised from the sale of a previous dwelling.

Major housebuilders have therefore sought to protect themselves against the difficulties which can arise through periodic mortgage 'famines' by making advance (though unenforceable) agreements with building societies that mortgages will be available for their customers (subject to the purchaser being able to convince the society that he or she is able to repay the loan – usually measured by income level) thus effectively earmarking tranches of the societies' lendable income. Not only does this mean that in difficult times sales may still proceed, but it speeds up the sale process by removing the need for the purchaser to search for funds, thus ensuring earlier sales and reducing the debt-servicing burden. In addition to the availability of funds, the housebuilder is also affected by the cost of these funds; private housing demand responds to changes in the costs of purchase in the same way as the demand for other products, and any change in the cost of mortgage finance will have an effect on the demand for housing. Companies therefore have to be alive to possible changes in the availability and cost of funds when planning their operations.

Until recently the local authorities were also a useful source of mortgage funds, usually as a lender of last resort, i.e. where the prospective purchaser had been refused a conventional loan by one or more building societies. The general financial plight of most authorities at present has reduced the importance of these loans for the foreseeable future.

Finance for public sector development

The public sector is a source of great interest to the construction industry due to its historical role as a provider of a large proportion of the industry's workload. Perhaps the most important segment of the public sector is the programme of activity provided by the local authorities, and it is therefore valuable for those designers, contractors and subcontractors who are dependent on the authorities for business to be able to understand the nature of the activity of such bodies, and the constraints under which they must operate. Although the position of local authorities as developers may appear in essence to be little different from that of others involved in the development process, the clearest starting point of divergence must be in the motives for undertaking the development role. For those in the private sector, the motives are fairly clear – the necessity to use property development to produce profits, either in the form of short-term gain, or as long-term income. In contrast, the local authority seeks to develop in order to provide a level of amenity for its area. Some decisions on the provision of amenity may be through choice, depending on the political inclinations of the ruling party, but the great majority of expenditure will be in order to discharge statutory duties in respect of, e.g. arts and recreation, tourism, cemeteries, consumer protection, education, environmental health, roads and footways, fire service, housing, planning, police, traffic, etc. The detailed responsibility for the statutory functions will be divided between the counties and districts.

Until the introduction of the Local Government Planning and Land Act 1980, the authorities had a reasonable (or so it may seem now) degree of freedom in the way in which they were able to plan and execute development plans which required the raising and disbursement of capital finance. Since then, there has been an increasing amount of control applied by central government over the amount which local government may spend on capital or revenue projects, and the way in which finance may be raised for these purposes.

Capital expenditure is now controlled through the approval by central government (Department of the Environment) of a maximum amount the authority may borrow in one year for capital projects. This approval will cover an amalgamation of almost all of the authority's project requirements, with some exceptions, e.g. police expenditure is subject to agreement by the Home Office, and some educational capital expenditure may be on the basis of individual scheme approval. The main categories within the block approval are housing, education, transport and social services, and the authority may have a limited right of virement between these heads. There is provision for this total sum available from approved borrowing to be augmented by the use of capital receipts, from e.g. the sale of council housing, and to a very limited extent some capital projects may be financed from the revenue account. In order to keep control of local government spending there has been an increased tendency over the past few years to reduce the alternative avenues for maintaining local expenditure.

Within the pre-set limit, the authority has a number of sources for acquiring the finance it requires. The main source is the Public Works Loan Board, and each authority has a quota of monies which may be borrowed from the Board. Once the quota has been exhausted, the authority may still be able to obtain permission to borrow in excess of the quota, but may be charged a penal rate for this privilege. In addition, there is the possibility of raising cash through the issue of debentures, stock, mortgages and other means as would a private sector company (with the exception that the authority cannot offer shares in itself). Although temporary, i.e. short-term loans may be used, there is some pressure from central government to ensure that the average life of the loan is not too short; ideally, the average loan period should not be less than seven years. This restriction acts upon the authorities' commercial interests as it would on a private company; they would wish to borrow at the most advantageous rate possible; temporary money is usually cheaper than long-term money, and if the economic indicators suggested that interest rates were likely to fall, the borrower would obviously prefer to borrow short-term rather than commit to a long-term rate which could prove over-expensive in the future. The normal maximum term is 60 years. As with housebuilders and other developers who have a large and frag-mented capital programme, local authorities would find it im-possible to raise and allocate loans in respect of each and every capital project; instead, the money required for all projects from all sources is pooled, and the money applied to individual schemes at a notional average rate of interest.

The cost of servicing the capital debt and meeting normal revenue expenditure is met through two main areas of income. The first is the income from rates levied on households and businesses in the area, and the second through grant aid from central government. The main grant aids are the Rate Support Grant and the Transport

Supplementary Grant, calculated and paid by central government. In addition there are specific grants which may be available to meet the costs of, e.g. slum clearance, and police. Last, there is whatever income the authority may derive from a multitude of miscellaneous activities – collection of licences, rents, trading, etc.

2.3.   MARKET RESEARCH AND MARKETING

Market Research

In the past, it was often possible for the entrepreneur to make development decisions based on the obvious fact that a particular market was underdeveloped, and with a modicum of commercial sense the development would succeed. There are relatively few development areas which can be exploited in such cavalier fashion today. In most cases, market research is a prerequisite for the confident completion of developments, and may well be necessary to obtain the funding required to initiate it. Obviously, the scale of the research operation will vary with the size and importance of the project; the market research needed to establish confidence in a proposal to convert an urban terraced house into three flats may involve no more than an examination of the local press and a selection of estate agents' handouts, while a multi-million pound shopping centre development may require months of detailed work using a questionnaire-based survey and extensive census information.

Normally, market research would be carried out to determine the state of demand for a particular type of development within a carefully defined geographical area. The most pressing need for such survey work will be in cases where the developer has no recent experience of that type of development in that area, or where the project itself will be spread over a protracted period, thus introducing uncertainty, or where market conditions can be expected to be uncertain, for example on specialised types of development.

Most development research will be oriented towards establishing the development possibilities of a particular site, rather than looking for a site to suit a predetermined project. The process must therefore start with a consideration of the national and regional picture, concentrating at first on the economic characteristics of the region or district, e.g. infrastructure, population trends, employment patterns, levels of government aid, etc. With this background information to hand, and assuming the background information itself does not negate the project intentions, the site and its immediate locality may be considered. At this stage, some of the information collected may be in the same categories as noted above, but at a more detailed level; in this way, it is possible to see whether the site locality's statistics match trends generally for the area, and, if not, whether there are reasons for this. Much of the information thus collected will be common to almost any type of development, but in order to be able to complete the picture it will be essential also to collect data on the intensity of the competition already existing for the type of development planned, together with any available intelligence on proposals for future competition. This stage is basically a data collection exercise. Following this, the study may proceed to the analysis stage, in order to fully understand the conditions and trends pertinent to the market under consideration.

The two stages above then allow the developer to address the question of what would be the response of the market to the introduction of the type of project proposed; this will be essentially an iterative process, deriving responses to questions which will test the efficacy of the proposals, and making modifications to produce the optimum project.

The final stage in the process is to make clear recommendations based on the conclusions of the study. One option here is that the proposals should be abandoned altogether, but even this must remain a *valid* outcome; there is little point in proceeding on the basis of blind faith alone (even if this has produced some spectacular successes in spite of the data, these successes are well outnumbered by the spectacular failures).

As with other forms of calcuation, the key to success in the market research operation will lie in the quality of the underlying assumptions which are made; this in turn will depend on the quality of the design and execution of the data collection phase. This may be split into two components; the examination of the geographical, economic and sociological factors in the area, and the attitudes of the consumers (personal or corporate) to the proposals.

Geographical and sociological factors

The objective of this part of the exercise is to establish the nature of the market which exists. The collection is a statistical exercise, and should be geared to producing quantitative results which will allow the calculation of the ideal size of the project, the basis for the financial appraisal, and which may also contribute towards the brief to be provided for the architectural design. Much of the material needed may already be available in published form, e.g. as census data, and as structure and local plans. In the case of the latter, there will also be available the information which formed the basis for any consultative exercise prior to the adoption of the plans. Any information which can be collected on the activities or intentions of competitors will also be useful, but for obvious reasons this is rather more difficult to collect (although an examination of the planning registers may be productive, as may informal discussion with officers of the local authority). The information thus collected may also be used to convince the funding institution of the viability of the proposals, and to persuade potential tenants that their investment in renting space in the development is justified. Should the project be one which is capable of expansion in the future, the research exercise should be kept continually updated, particularly after completion of the initial phase, in order to appreciate the real impact of the new development on the existing market.

Attitudes of consumers

Although this is often regarded as adding a qualitative overlay to the research into the area, the information collected by analysing consumer preferences is also essentially quantitative. The research may be conducted amongst all of the consumer sectors in the particular market, or may be confined to a defined sample. In either case, the objective will be to obtain a profile of consumers, their attitudes and preferences. This will enable the developer to orientate the development to satisfy the identified needs. A considerable amount of information may be gained from existing data, without the need to conduct field studies; the local authority may already have collected much of the information wanted as part of studies conducted to encourage further investment in their area. The official Census of Population, conducted at ten year intervals, will also provide data on the population in terms of age, marriage, sex, incidence of working wives, country of birth, housing statistics, etc. Care is needed in using this data, as considerable changes may occur in the economy of an area between census points. Where further information is required on the consumers, it will be necessary to conduct research based on a survey of a representative sample of the population under consideration.

Obviously the type of information collected will depend on the nature of the proposed project, but the range of consumer information which may be acquired from non-corporate consumers might include family income levels, size of family units and occupations, education levels, age and sex of respondents, shopping patterns, etc. Where the proposed development is housing, the questions would also include the characteristics which the occupiers found particularly attractive and unattractive about the existing provision. For industrial or warehousing developments, potential occupiers might be asked about their preferences for design features such as eaves or storey heights, loadings, sprinklers, heating and insulation, as well as more basic information on the need for specialised labour, or availability of raw materials and transport. Having demonstrated the need for carefully designed and executed market research as a basis for establishing confidence in the success of a project, it is necessary to introduce a note of caution: first, because research into markets and consumer preferences is a highly specialised and expert process, and cannot be safely undertaken without considerable experience and knowledge of the appropriate techniques, and second, because there will almost inevitably be considerable gaps in the picture produced by the research, due to a shortage of information. It is invariably uneconomic for a developer to collect *all* the information needed as a 'one-off' exercise, and *all* market research will need to rely to an extent on generally available (and therefore out of date) information. The purpose of this caveat is not to negate the need for the research, but to point out that the developer, in making decisions based on such work, needs to be aware of the shortcomings of the studies, of where such problems lie, and the sensitivity of the project proposals to such inaccuracies.

Sales and promotion

The promotion and selling of a completed or proposed development may be considered as the reverse side of the market research coin. If the research into the desirable features of a development proposal has been thoroughly undertaken and the findings carried through accurately into the final design, there should be little possibility that the project will be unattractive. However, even the best-conceived developments will require some effort on the part of their promoters if they are to be successfully sold or let.

It is almost impossible to give guidelines on the size and cost of the marketing and sales campaign which will be needed for any particular development; even on relatively small-scale projects, it may be necessary to budget for what may seem initially to be an unreasonable amount of effort and expense. However, the initial research into the project should have given some indication of the likely strengths of the project in terms of its attractiveness in comparison to the competition, and on this basis it should be possible to provide a reasonable budget allowance for promotion and selling which would form part of the overall financial calculations. The next question is how this allowance should be apportioned between the different vehicles for promotion which exist. The costs of disposal (discounting for the moment legal costs) may be considered to lie in two areas: making the potential clients aware of the project, and persuading them to purchase at the most advantageous price. Although a crude division may be made between these two areas, they do have a considerable influence on one another; a successful promotion campaign will increase customer awareness of the product and will hopefully make an advantageous contract easier to achieve, while a misconceived campaign will make it difficult, if not impossible, to achieve a contract at any price.

Media for promotion

(a) Newspapers and magazines
A huge range of publications is available to the prospective advertiser: popular and quality newspapers, local newspapers, free local and regional papers, academic and professional journals, plus specialised magazines for almost any trade or business in existence. The advertising managers for all of these will have ready explanations for the choice of their publication as the best promotional medium. Many of the enquiries which result from any campaign will be from sales people on rival publications anxious to sell advertising space. In general, the better daily newspapers, with audited circulation figures and a verified breakdown of reader types, will form the best 'core' for the promotion of larger types of development. Even here, however, it is better to be selective about the timing of the advertising and the location within the paper. If the paper has a regular property page or series of features on property matters, it is preferable to use those days on which the features or pages appear, as many people in the property business will purchase only them, to read the specialised matter. Likewise, it is preferable to use either the specialised pages, or the other prime positions – either the front or back pages, in particular the top corners, or alternatively where it may be assumed that the advertisement will be near interesting editorial material.

Where the building is of such a specialised type that the expense of national daily papers cannot be justified, it may be more sensible to place advertisements in the specialised trade press. There are dangers in assuming that a blanket coverage in both general and specialised press will bring results; the greater likelihood is an overlapping of readership with a concomitant redundancy factor.

It is always difficult to judge the success of any press campaign; although attempts should be made to trace the source of an enquiry. It is quite possible that many enquirers may have seen the promotion some time ago, and may not recall its origin.

(b) Direct mail
There is now a large number of organisations which specialise in supplying lists of individuals and organisations within defined categories of size, location, type of business, etc. These lists may be used effectively to direct mail shots to the type of people who may be assumed to be interested in the project for disposal. Owing to the huge amount of such direct advertising today, it is essential that the message is expressed in as simple and direct a style as possible. Short, concise messages may help the message to be absorbed before the recipient has an opportunity to throw it into the waste

paper bin. It is also important to use only those firms who can demonstrate that their lists are regularly and accurately updated, otherwise a large number of mail shots will be wasted.

(c) Posters
Posters or billboard types of advertising can be effective provided that the design of the material and its location are carefully thought out. The most obvious location is at or near the site or building itself, or in other prominent locations where the material may be seen by a large number of people. Sites such as railway stations, prominent hoardings at major road junctions, on buses and on the Underground may be suitable. As with other printed material, it is essential that the message is readable quickly: the display must not be so cluttered that the essential details are lost.

(d) Television and radio
Until a few years ago there was relatively little use of TV and radio for property advertising, due in large measure to the expense involved. The proliferation of commercial radio and the arrival of a second commercial TV channel have meant that these objections are reduced, although it is still true that these media have only been used for major campaigns – for promoting major buildings, for selling speculative housing and for the promotion of areas for development, e.g. the new towns or regions with special development problems.

Allied to television is the use of teletext – information which can be accessed by direct transmission or via the telephone lines, and received on special TV sets. This service has been slow to take off and find acceptance in the UK so far, but it seems likely that in the near future there will be a substantial increase in its use. Already there are a number of experimental systems in private use, connecting firms of estate agents to allow them to expand the range of property on offer in any one agent's portfolio. Increases in this facility may also be generated by the current proposals to change the monopoly on the conveyancing of buildings.

Managing the promotion and sales

It is relatively unusual for the property owner to have a programme of disposals consistently large enough to justify the retention of an in-house team of a size able to organise all the aspects of the disposal programme. These types of team tend to be concentrated in the local or regional authorities, to support their programme of promotion of the area as a whole, or in the larger firms of speculative housebuilders, for whom the employment of an in-house team is viable because of the concentration of sales in one area or site for a predetermined period. A developer with a single property or a relatively modest programme will usually employ an estate agent to handle the promotion and sale.

There are certain advantages to be gained through the use of estate agents, and some of these will apply even when the client has his own in-house team. These advantages may be summarised as:
(a) Specialised expert knowledge
Many agents specialise in particular types of property, for example, factories or housing, and should therefore be able to offer an expert view of that market or a particular sector of that market. Local agents or the regional offices of national companies will have developed a detailed knowledge of the market and its peculiarities in their particular locality. Even when a national firm of agents is employed for the disposal campaign, it will often be useful for them to employ the help of a local agency if the national firm has no base in the area in which the development is situated. In such a situation the experience of the national firm in handling large and complex developments may be complemented by the detailed local knowledge and contacts possessed by the local firm. The ability to apply specialised knowledge, based on experience of selling similar developments in the area, means that the agent can usefully be appointed as a member of the development team at an early stage, in order to input information and advice on design, siting and other features which may improve the marketability and profitability of the scheme.
(b) Selling ability
It was suggested earlier that the disposal process could be regarded as having two main components, promotion and persuasion to buy at the most advantageous price. Neither of these two complementary activities may be regarded as fields for the enthusiastic amateur; both require expertise which cannot readily be acquired without a fair degree of specialisation. The ability to negotiate and close a sale at the most advantageous terms is one which may be reliably offered by most reputable agents, for the simple reason that their income and viability depends on this ability; if there is no sale, the agent does not obtain a fee (unless the developer is an unusually generous example of the species!)

The appointment of an estate agent as the developer's *agent* implies contractual terms which may or may not be spelt out in the written contract with the estate agent. It is therefore necessary for the developer to be quite clear in his own mind whether he wishes to grant an agency contract, or form some other more loose arrangement. If an agency contract is intended, the agreement should clearly spell out what the terms of the engagement are to be, how long the agency will last, how it may be determined, whether retainers are to be paid, what level of commission is payable and under what circumstances, whether the agreement is for a sole or joint agency, whether the developer has a right (without penalty) to employ additional agents, and whether a 'no-sale-no-fee' deal is to obtain. Unless these and other issues are clarified and recorded prior to the signing of the agency agreement, there will be considerable scope for argument and misunderstanding later.

The alternative to appointing agents formally is for the developer to make approaches to one or more estate agents with the offer of commission being dependent upon the signing of a sales or lease agreement with a party introduced by that agent. This would not constitute a formal agency agreement normally, although care should obviously be taken in framing this type of arrangement also. There is little advantage in developers trying to comprehensively cover the market by making this type of offer to every agent in the market (or, for that matter in formally appointing a large number of agents), as each agent will quickly become aware that he is in competition for the business with many others, and is as a result unlikely to expend much time or effort. There is a concomitant danger that if a large number of firms are all trying to sell the same development, potential customers will inevitably be approached by a number of agents, and may justifiably feel that the developer is anxious to be rid of the project. This can raise two ideas in the potential customer's mind; first, that there may be something wrong with either the scheme or the developer, and second, that the developer, in view of his apparent anxiety, will be willing to sell or lease at a lower price.

Whether agents are formally appointed or the looser arrangement is employed, it is essential, when a number of firms is used, for the developer to keep accurate records of any introductions or appointments made, in order to remove any doubts over who actually introduced the buyer, and to provide information on the relative merits of the agents used, for future projects. The solicitor used by the developer should be asked to keep in touch with any agents employed, and should be asked to informally 'vet' any promotional literature prepared by the agents prior to circulation. As well as keeping the solicitor informed of any developments in the 'package' being offered, in which case he will be able to react more quickly should an agreement be reached, this liaison will help to avoid any inadvertent misrepresentation of the particulars of the site or of any conditions attendant on its disposal and use.

2.4 FINANCIAL APPRAISAL

The financial appraisal of development projects is in essence no different to that undertaken for any other kind of commercial undertaking, with the costs of the venture being calculated and deducted from the value of the project in order to decide whether an adequate return can be made to compensate for the risks involved. The return may be in the form of a capital profit on sale, or by way of a continuing income which is in excess of the ongoing costs of ownership. For public sector projects, the return may not be in the form of a profit margin, but in the provision of some higher level of amenity; but even here, it will often be necessary to make comparisons between the costs of the project and some arbitrary measure of value, e.g. in comparing the costs with the yardstick set by government for that particular type of building.

The difficult part of development appraisal comes in determining the values to be used for the many variables involved. It is useful to examine these variables here, in order to determine their nature and the degree to which they may influence one another.

Cost of land

This may be determined either by the price which is being asked in the market, which will normally be pitched above the level at which the owner expects to realise a sale, in order to allow for a negotiating margin, or by the amount which a potential vendor could afford to pay, after taking into consideration the other potential costs of development. The latter method of determination is probably the most important, as no purchaser is likely to pay more for the land, irrespective of asking price, than the amount which can be demonstrated by deducting all other costs from the expected value. This is known as a residual valuation of the land, and is one of the most common techniques used in development appraisal, and may be demonstrated by the simple calculation

A = value of project on completion
B = building costs (including profit allowance)
$A - B$ = maximum costs of the land.

The method may also be used to calculate either of the other two variables, providing the land value is known.

In addition to the price paid for the land, other ancillary costs of acquisition must be taken into account. These will normally be the legal costs in acquisition, including any stamp duty payable, plus any fees paid to an agent for identifying the land. There may also be costs of development which should fairly be allocated as purchase costs, for example the site may be encumbered by restrictive covenants or easements which need to be removed (if possible) in order that the development possibilities are not restricted.

Costs of construction

The major component of construction cost will normally be the sum paid to a builder for carrying out the actual construction, and this will in turn depend on the size, type and complexity of the building, together with some factors not directly associated with the building itself, for example the tendering climate, predicted inflation, and type of building contract used. In simple development appraisal calculations, it will be the tender price (plus any contingency sum deemed appropriate) which will be used in the appraisal. This may be adequate where the construction period is short and the building simple, but where there are expected to be substantial fluctuations due to inflation, it may be necessary to introduce a greater degree of sophistication into the calculations. In some cases it may be safe to ignore inflationary increases, as it may be the case that any increase in costs due to inflation will be compensated for by a similar increase in value of the completed job. However, as there is unlikely to be a direct relationship between construction cost and project value, it would be unsafe to proceed on these lines. Added to the cost of construction will be the fees paid for professional design services. Traditionally, these fees have been based on a predetermined percentage of building costs, according to the scale of fees laid down by the professional associations. Although many professionals abide by these fee scales, which in some cases are mandatory on the members of a professional body, there has been of late a greater element of competitiveness amongst professionals, which can lead to lower fees. Using 'standard rates', architects' fees are around 6% of building costs, quantity surveyors' about 4%, and structural engineers' about 2% (for new work, and depending on the complexity; for rehabilitation work, the fees for architectural services will be higher). Simple repetitive projects will benefit from fee abatement for repetition, and may attract fees at around 5–6% of construction cost, while large, complex and heavily serviced schemes, e.g. a large hospital complex, will require additional consultants and may produce fees as high as 15–18% of construction cost. To these fees will be added the cost of planning and building control consents.

Short-term finance

As may be seen from the previous section, there will be few projects undertaken in which the developer's own finance is used; in most cases short-term borrowings will be used to fund the development period. Even where the developer's own money is employed, an allowance should be made for financing costs, in order to allow for the opportunity cost of not using the cash elsewhere. The short term funds are likely to cost in the region of 2–5% over base rates, and the actual terms will have to be negotiated before the development starts. The other variable associated with borrowings is the period over which they are to be applied. There are normally three periods which have to be considered here: the time from the initial land purchase to the start of construction, the construction period itself, and the period from practical completion of the building works until the project is let or sold, and producing revenue or capital income. The cost of land will normally have to be funded from acquisition until sale or letting, and this is therefore easily calculated. If it may be assumed that the construction costs will occur evenly through the on-site period, it is simple to allow for interest by basing this on the whole construction cost for half of the building period, plus the whole of the construction cost for the whole of the sales/letting period. Even though most of the professional fees are normally paid early in the development, as they are a small proportion of total cost, the error will not be great if an even distribution over time is assumed. Where the construction cost is not evenly spread, e.g. on a long or phased project, it will be necessary to carry out more accurate projections in order to arrive at the interest costs. This is covered later in a consideration of the cash flow method which can also be used to take into account the fact that most contracts allow for a retention sum which is released half on practical completion and half on expiry of the defects liability period.

Area of the building

For buildings produced for rent, the income is usually calculated by reference to the useable floor area. In most buildings, there will be areas which are not 'useable' space, and on which no rental income will accrue. It is part of the skill of the designer and developer to ensure that this area is kept to the minium. The type and configuration of the building will determine the likely areas; e.g. old buildings with thick internal walls and many internal subdivisions may have only around 60% of their gross floor areas as rentable space; in tall buildings the need for fire escape routes, lifts and common access corridors may reduce useable floor space to a similar level.

Rent levels

Estimates of likely rental income should be realistic and based on what the market is likely to be willing and able to pay for the development. In the boom period of the early 1970s, there was a tendency to assume that rents would continue their inexorable course upwards, and this led to many developments being undertaken on the basis of completely unsupportable projections of income. At that time there was relatively little research into rent levels, but over the last decade there has been an increasing amount of published information available on market trends and expectations of rent levels for various types of building in different parts of the country. These surveys are published frequently by some of the larger firms of surveyors and estate agents, and similar information for the private housebuilding market is published by the larger building societies.

Where no such information is available on similar developments, it will be necessary to undertake the type of detailed market study described earlier in order to have a sufficient level of confidence in the income likely to be produced, and in the viability of the project.

The income levels used for viability calculations should be the net income, i.e. the residual income after deducting the expenses of managing, maintaining and insuring the completed development. The lease or rental agreement will define the responsibility of the landlord and the tenant for the ongoing costs; in many cases the tenant will be responsible for most of the outgoings, but in large or complex developments with multiple tenancies there may be considerable costs involved in maintaining common areas, and in collecting rents and arranging for new tenants at the expiry of leases or due to premature surrender. In such cases it might be prudent to allow a deduction from gross rents of 2–3% to produce a net figure to be used in the feasibility calculations. Assuming that a reasonable estimate can be made, the figure used should be the current level rather than an allowance for what the property may realise on completion; not only does this discourage a reliance on an overestimate of what the future may bring, it also provides a measure of conservatism in the calculation and thus greater security than a calculation built upon predictions.

Pre-contract, building and letting periods

The primary reason for attempting to estimate the length of these three periods as accurately and realistically as possible lies in the fact that until the development is complete and let or sold, interest charges will accrue on the monies borrowed to carry out the development. The length of time required before construction work commences will depend on the difficulties likely to be experienced in assembling the parcels of land needed for the project, the delays in obtaining planning permission, which may necessitate an appeal to the Secretary of State, the time needed to develop the design and prepare sufficient production information to allow a proper start on site (while it may be possible to start without a full set of working drawings, the risks entailed in not allowing sufficient design time should not be underestimated; this is explored further in section 3.4 dealing with procurement systems). The actual construction period can be more easily estimated, based on experience of contract (and actual) periods for similar buildings. Again, it is important to be realistic and allow some measure of contingency period, to allow for possible overruns outside the design team's or contractor's control. Finally, it is necessary to estimate the time needed after completion of the works for tenants or purchasers to be found, and for the time needed for any tenants' fitting-out to be done.

The tenancy agreement should be quite explicit about the date for occupation, and the time from which rent will be payable; it may be necessary to allow a rent-free or reduced rent period in which such work may be carried out, and where this is the case, these periods should be clearly recorded. Although it may be tempting to assume that purchasers or tenants may be allowed to complete such work while the main contract is in the completion stages, this runs contrary to the normal conditions of the building contract, in which the main contractor has a right to sole possession of the site for the duration of the contract period. Many contractors will not wish to have others working on the site at the same time, for obvious reasons of security and obstruction, and if the main contractor does agree for the sake of goodwill, he may have a justifiable claim to extra time and money if his work can be shown to have been interrupted by others.

It may appear that a safer course would be to attempt to pre-let the project either prior to work commencing or while construction work is under way, and it is true that finding funding for the scheme may be easier if the developer can show that he has already secured a forward sale or letting. However, in a buoyant market, where rent levels are justifiably expected to increase prior to completion of the project, it may be more sensible to wait until nearer the end of the works before seeking occupants, in order to realise a higher level of initial rents. In this case the developer must accept greater risk in return for an anticipated increase in profitability. Where a pre-letting or forward sale is seen as desirable and is achieved, it should be remembered that the income for the scheme is then fixed; care must in that case be taken to ensure that the costs of construction are carefully controlled, as any escalation cannot then be compensated for by seeking a higher income. In any event, it is prudent to ensure that the construction costs are clearly defined before agreeing terms for forward rental or sale.

Margin for profit and risk

As in any other speculative venture, the property developer will require a margin to cover the profit he wishes to make and provide a reward for the risk undertaken. Again, the simple commercial rule will apply, that the riskier ventures will only be pursued at a commensurately high rate of return. Indeed, it may not be possible to obtain funding for a risky proposal unless it can be demonstrated that a high rate of return is likely. As any major project involving forward commitment of resources for several years is likely to find itself at risk on a number of the variables, the profit margin must be high enough to compensate for this. The simplest way of expressing this is as a percentage of either the *cost* of the development or the *value* of the completed project. As it is obviously necessary for the development cost plus profit percentage to equal development value, if the project is to be viable, it may be demonstrated that the profit margin as a percentage of cost is arithmetically related to the profit as a percentage of value.

The actual percentage required will depend upon risk, competition, availability of development ventures, and margins obtainable on other types of investment; it can only be determined on a job-by-job basis. For the purposes of initial calculations, it may be safe to work initially on a mark-up of 25% of development cost (equivalent to 20% of development value).

Costs of disposal

These may be incurred in one or both of two ways. If the project is to be retained by the developer and let to one or more tenants, then it is likely that this operation will be handled by an estate agent experienced in the letting of such property. If, on the other hand, the developer is building with a view to sale at the end of the construction period, it will be necessary to find a purchaser. In the case of lettings, the fee to be paid will depend on the size (value) of the project, and on whether the agent acts alone or shares the commission with another agent. A normal fee for sole agency would be 10% of first year's rent, rising to 15% if more than one agent is involved. For a very large project, a reduction might well be negotiated, on the basis that a large project requires little more work than a smaller job, in spite of the increased value.

For arranging a sale of the development, the fee would be in the order of 3–4%, with a corresponding reduction in the case of a very large project. Where one firm of agents acted alone for the developer in the whole process, i.e. site finding, letting, and finding a buyer for the completed and let development, then further reduction in fee levels could be expected due to the volume of business and the economics to be expected in the continuity thus granted to the firm. Any additional costs in promoting the development for sale or letting, for example in the preparation of posters, direct mail shots, or other media advertising, would be in addition to the fee paid to an agent. The costs involved in this operation would be dependent on the developer's and his advisors' perceptions of how difficult it was likely to be to sell or let.

Investors' yield

As noted earlier, the market for commercial property development is founded at present on the basis that occupiers of premises prefer to rent rather than buy, in order to free capital for use in their businesses. Taken alongside the need for financial institutions to find homes for investments which will lead to long-term income and growth, the result is a market for the ownership of such completed developments which is quite separate from their occupation and use. This market must compete with the other investment opportunities for investors' funds, and the returns (yield) must relate to what is available in other sections of the investment market.

In times of high inflation, the most attractive element of property development is the potential for income growth, due to frequent rent reviews. It is the potential for rental growth which is likely to be the greatest determinant of the initial yield required by a purchaser of a completed development; where expectations of growth are high, the initial yield demanded may be low, and vice versa. The initial yield required may vary from as low as 4–5% for high growth potential, e.g. new buildings on prime sites, to over 15% for older, poorer quality projects with less potential. The importance of the yield used in the development calculations lies in its use in calculating the capital value of the project. This may be demonstrated by example: suppose that the net income from a completed development is £1000 p.a., and that the yield is 6%. As the yield is the annual return which would be gained from the investment, then
$6/100 \times$ capital value = £1000

$$\text{Therefore capital value} = {}^{£1000}\!/_{.06} = £16,666.67$$

It may also be easily seen that a small variation in the yield used will make a large difference to the capital value (and hence to the profitability of the scheme on sale).

Costs in use

The criteria noted above relate in the main to the initial cost of the project. However, for both investor and end user there are continuing costs associated with any building. The investor will be faced with costs as part of his covenant as landlord, and in connection with any upgrading or repair which is required in order to attract new tenants at the expiry of the lease. The end user will be concerned with the costs of his covenants as tenant, and with his costs in occupying the building; of these latter costs, those associated with energy usage are perhaps most important. The developer will also need to take account of these costs in relation to the attractiveness of the property to tenants, as this will reflect in the rent levels which may be obtained, and thus will influence the overall profitability of the project. While it is possible to calculate with a reasonable amount of precision the cost of constructing a building, the calculation of the running and maintenance costs is more complex: this requires the ability to predict, well into the future, values for the life of materials, the cost of alternative design solutions, costs of repair, and the cost of money.

In the UK, scant attention has been paid in the past to the need for decisions on building design to reflect more than an optimisation of initial cost. This may be attributable to a number of factors such as: the actual difficulty in performing the calculations and determining the values to be used for the variables; the apparent lack of interest shown by many clients; lack of initiatives by government in increasing client awareness of the issue; the lack of any credible input in the education of designers to make them aware of both the problem and the means by which it might be tackled. There is at present some indication that the issue may assume greater prominence in the future; the greatest impetus seems to have come from the rise in energy costs in the last decade, coupled with levels of failure and 'routine' maintenance costs on new buildings which have become unacceptable to many building consumers and investors. The techniques which may be used are beyond the scope of this book, but for a comprehensive study of this area, see *Building Design Evaluation – Costs in Use* by P. A. Stone, published by E.& F.N. Spon.

Example of appraisal

The following example will demonstrate the interrelationship of the factors noted above.

Assume that a developer wishes to construct an office building of $1000m^2$ gross floor area, of which $800m^2$ will be available for letting. In addition there are ancillary construction costs of £40,000 in laying roads and sewers to the building. The construction costs are estimated to be £600/m^2. Professional fees are estimated to total 13% of construction costs. Short term finance is available at 16%. The rent expected is £300/m^2 p.a. net. The developer wishes to see a return for risk and profit of 20% of development value. The precontract period is expected to be six months, the building work is estimated to take 15 months, and a period of three months has been allowed for letting. The developer intends to sell the completed and fully let development to a financial institution, and it is anticipated that an initial yield of 7% will be required. Within these fixed parameters, the value of the site may be established.

1. Capital Value of Project

Initial income = £300/m^2 × 800m^2 =   £240,000
Yield required by financial
institution = 7%
Therefore capital value = $\dfrac{£240,000}{.07}$ = £3,428,571

2. Project Costs

(a)   Construction costs:
       1000m^2 @ £600/m^2 =   600,000
       Roads and sewers =   40,000

                                          640,000

       Professional fees – architect, QS,
       structural and services engineers
       – assume all-in @ 13% =   83,200

                                          723,200   723,200

(b)   Short-term finance:
       on total construction costs for
       half building period
       723,200 × ^{16}/$_{100}$ × ^{15}/$_{12}$ × ½ =   72,320   795,520
       on total costs at end of
       construction period, for whole
       of letting period
       795,520 × ^{16}/$_{100}$ × ^{3}/$_{12}$ =   31,821   827,341

(c)   Allow contingency sum, say
       5% of total to date
       827,341 × ^{5}/$_{100}$ =   41,367   868,708

(d)   Disposal costs:
       Letting fee @ 15% of first year
       income
       15% × 800m^2 × £300 =   36,000

       Selling fee for finding purchaser
       for completed and let project
       4% × 3,428,571 =   137,143
       Advertising/promotion costs, say   5,000

                                          178,143   1,046,851

3. *Total costs, excluding land*   1,046,851

4. *Add developer's profit*

  @ 20% of development value
  $^{20}/_{100} \times 3{,}428{,}571 =$ 685,714 1,732,565

  Capital value =   3,428,571
  Costs and profit (excl. land) =   1,732,565
                1,696,006

Therefore maximum site acquisition cost based on rents and costs in two years = £1,696,006.

In order to convert a site cost based on values two years hence to current levels, this figure must be multiplied by the present value of £1 in 2 years at 16% interest. This figure may be obtained from the valuation tables, or calculated from the formula

$$PV = \frac{1}{(1 + i)^n}, \text{ where:}$$

 i = interest rate as a decimal, in this case 0.16
 n = number of years.
 PV £1 : 2 years @ 16% = .7431629
Therefore site acquisition cost now = .7431629 × 1,696,006
           = £1,260,409

but this figure must include the costs of acquisition – agent's fee, stamp duty, solicitor's fees – say 4% of land cost.
Therefore maximum site value now
= $^{100}/_{104} \times 1{,}260{,}409 = $ £1,211,931
 This is the maximum figure the developer could afford to pay for the site without reducing his profit or other costs.
 The calculation may be checked by recalculating the developer's profit using this figure for land costs.

1. Capital value as above   3,428,571
2. Costs:
  Construction, fees, short-term
  finance on same, contingency,
  disposal costs, as above   1,046,851
  Land cost, inc. acquisition
  costs   1,260,409

Short-term finance on land cost for whole development period		
1,260,409 × 16% × 2 years =	435,597	
	2,742,857	2,742,857
Developer's profit		685,714
As % of development value	$\dfrac{685,714}{3,428,571}$	= 20%
As % of development costs	$\dfrac{685,714}{2,742,857}$	= 25%

This profit margin may be demonstrated by examining the profit to the developer assuming that the project was retained, rather than sold on completion.

Income = £240,000 p.a.
Costs:

Construction etc. as above	1,046,851
Land cost, incl. acquisition	1,260,409
Finance on land cost	435,597
	2,742,857

In the same way that the investor's yield was expressed as the ratio of investment income to development value, the *development* yield may be expressed as the ratio of income to the developer's costs, i.e.

$$\text{Developer's yield:} \ \frac{240,000}{2,742,857} \times \frac{100}{1} = 8.75\%$$

The profit margin may also be shown to be the difference between the yield to the developer and the yield to the investor, expressed either as a percentage of the developer's yield or the investor's yield, i.e.

$$\text{Profit as \% of development yield} \ \frac{8.75-7}{8.75} \times 100 = 20\%$$

(which equates to the profit margin calculated on development value)

$$\text{Profit as \% of investment yield} \ \frac{8.75-7}{7} \times 100 = 25\%$$

(which equates to the profit margin calculated on development cost).

This simple appraisal contains a number of inaccuracies, which on a project with a short development period might not cause any anxiety, but could have a considerable impact on a larger and more protracted scheme. The inaccuracies relate to the times when the costs arise, and the way interest charges accrue on those costs. In the example, the largest source of possible error is in the timing of the payments connected with the construction period. It was assumed that the certificates were of equal value, and equally spaced, and not subject to a retention fund; this allowed the assumption that interest could simply be charged on the whole construction cost for half the construction period (or vice-versa). In practice, certificates are unlikely to be of equal value, as on most projects the curve of cost against time is 's' shaped, and around 60% of construction cost arises after the mid-point. In addition, there is normally a retention fund, the last of which is not usually released until at least six months after completion. This means that the linear assumptions in the example overestimate the amount necessary to be allowed for finance charges on construction costs. In contrast, because the professional fees were merged into the overall construction cost prior to the calculation of interest, the interest charges arising on those items will have been underestimated, as approximately 75% of the professional fees will be paid prior to construction commencing. Fortunately, on this small project the inaccuracy will be small, but on a much larger scheme the cash difference will be considerable. The third error may lie in the way interest is calculated. The interest rate was stated as 16% p.a., but it would be unusual for only simple interest to be charged. In the example, the only large cost on which interest accrues is the cost of the land, and the interest on this was calculated as compound interest (through the use of the PV tables to discount to the present value). However, in practice, compound interest would also arise on the construction costs (which might to some degree offset the overestimate of construction cost interest noted above). It is also possible that the short-term loan might be on the basis that interest charges were added to the sum owed at periods of less than 12 months e.g. quarterly or even monthly. If this were the case, then the compounding would occur at more frequent intervals, and the true annual rate of interest would be markedly higher than that stated.

On a project of modest cost and time scale, particularly projects taking less than 12 months from start to finish, little harm might be done by the inaccuracies, as they would be small and might tend to cancel each other out. On a larger scheme, covering a number of years, and particularly where phasing of handover (and therefore income) was involved, there could be major implications for the viability of the project. If the interest charges were underestimated, the developer could find himself at the limit of his borrowing agreement before the scheme was complete, and might find considerable difficulty in extending this without incurring penal charges from the source of finance; in the event of the extra funding being available, the developer's profit margin would be eroded by

Table 2: Cash flow diagram

Month	TYPE OF COST Construction cost	Fees	Disposal fees and costs	Total costs start of month	B/F from previous month	Sub-total	Interest at 1.24451% p.m. (Compounds to 16% p.a.)	Total indebtedness at end of month
2		29,120		29,120		29,120	362	29,482
3					29,482	29,482	367	29,849
4					29,849	29,849	371	30,221
5					30,221	30,221	376	30,597
6		33,280		33,280	30,597	63,877	795	64,672
7		1,300		1,300	64,672	65,972	821	66,793
8	15,000	1,300		16,300	66,793	83,093	1,034	84,127
9	15,000	1,300		16,300	84,127	100,427	1,250	101,677
10	20,000	1,300		21,300	101,677	122,977	1,530	124,507
11	24,000	1,300		25,300	124,507	149,807	1,864	151,672
12	34,000	1,300		35,300	151,672	186,972	2,327	189,299
13	40,000	1,300		41,300	189,299	230,599	2,870	233,468
14	40,000	1,300		41,300	233,468	274,768	3,420	278,188
15	64,000	1,300		65,300	278,188	343,488	4,275	347,762
16	64,000	1,300		65,300	347,762	413,063	5,141	418,203
17	62,000	1,300		63,300	418,203	481,503	5,992	487,496
18	52,000	1,300		53,300	487,496	540,796	6,730	547,526
19	45,000	1,300		46,300	547,526	593,826	7,390	601,216
20	40,000	1,300		41,300	601,216	642,516	7,996	650,512
21	35,000	1,300		36,300	650,512	686,812	8,547	695,360
22	30,000			30,000	695,360	725,360	9,027	734,387
23	44,000		178,143	222,143	734,387	956,530	11,904	968,434
24					968,434	968,434	12.053	980,487
25								
26								
27								
28	16,000	1,300			17,300			
	640,000	83,200	178,143		901,343		96,442	

DEVELOPMENT SOLD END MONTH 24

Note: income received at start month 25 could generate interest during period 25–28; not allowed for in this example

Capital value of development	£3,428,571
Outstanding debt prior to sale	£980,487
Final certificate + fee payments	17,300
Contingency sum	41,367
Profit and risk @ 20% of value	685,714
	1,724,868
	1,703,703

Max. acquisition cost in 2 years
Therefore site value today
= 1,703,703 × .74316 (i.e. PV of £1, 2 yrs, 16%) = £1,266,124 (incl acquisition cuts)
Less acquisition costs $^{10\%}/_{104}$ × 1,266,124 = £1,217,427

Summary

1.	Construction cost, fees & disposal	£901,343
2.	Contingency	41,367
3.	Interest on 1	96,441
4.	Land and acquisition costs	1,266,124
5.	Interest on 3	437,580
		2,742,855
	Development value	3,428,571
	Profit	£685,714

Profit as % value = 20%
Profit as % cost = 25%

the extent of the underestimate. On the other hand, if the financing charges are grossly overestimated, a residual valuation undertaken to find the maximum bid for the land will be underestimated, thus reducing the developer's ability to compete in the market for the land. Again, there could also be penal charges by the bank for organising a loan which was not totally used (the money having been committed by the bank for the project, the bank may not immediately be able to find a customer for the money, and may demand compensation).

These problems may be overcome by the use of the *cash flow* approach to appraisal. The greatest difference between the cash flow approach and the simple appraisal is that in the former, the timing of cash inflows and outflows is noted, and the effect of financing charges can be accurately determined. The periods for calculating each component of cost and its finance charge can be varied to suit the project e.g. on a monthly, quarterly or annual basis.

Using the basic data on the previous example, but assuming an 's' curve of construction costs (figure 4), and itemising in more detail the incidence of costs and income, the cash flow would be as noted in table 2. It has been assumed that as part of the short-term funding agreement, interest will be charged on the outstanding balance at the end of each month, and that the construction contract has a 5% retention, released half at practical completion and half at the end of the defects liability period. All costs are assumed to occur at the beginning of the month in which they arise, and interest is charged for that month also.

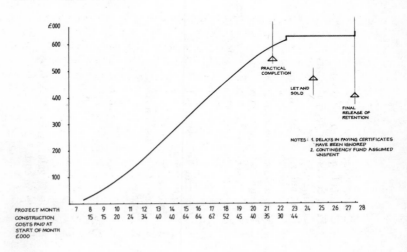

Figure 4.   Construction expenditure curve.

It may be seen that the money available for the purchase of the site has increased from £1,211,931 in the simple residual valuation to £1,217,427 in the cash flow example. The same basic system of calculation may also be used to show the increase in profitability on the scheme, assuming that the amount paid for the site remained unchanged, or the increase in expenditure possible on construction should the other figures remain unchanged.

In the example above, there has been some simplification in the assumptions used; no account has been taken of the delays which may occur in the payment of certificates, and it has been assumed that the professional fees for the on-site supervision element of the service can be spread evenly over the period. Any inherent error in these assumptions is likely to be minimal in relation to the other costs. A more substantial criticism could be levelled at the fact that in the time between the end of month 24, i.e. the date of sale and receipt of income, and the arrival of the final release of retention and payment of fees, the project cash flow is positive, with the indebtedness having been removed.

It could reasonably be argued that this positive flow could be used to generate income, and that this would reduce the overall debt during the project. While this may be true, considerable caution needs to be exercised in building this element into the feasibility study. First, in order to compare like with like, it would be preferable to assume that the receipts could be invested at the same rate as was being charged for borrowings – an unprovable assumption, and second, depending upon the developer's tax situation, it is likely that only income net of tax would be receivable against the interest charges.

While all but the most modest developments will show a positive response to the accuracy obtainable using a cash flow approach, there are certain types of project where a simple residual valuation is not appropriate, and is likely to be misleading and possibly disastrous. These will be the schemes where the progress from inception to design to construction is not linear, in the sense that there may be a need for some parts of the scheme to lead or lag behind other components, e.g. where there is a requirement for phased handovers, or delays in obtaining part of the land required. Similarly there may be a reasonable anticipation that certain of the basic assumptions may change, e.g. interest rates, yields, rents or inflation, on a protracted project. The simple residual model is unable to cope with changes in the basic parameters, but with the cash flow method it is relatively simple to build in these changes when they are expected to occur. For the same reason, it is possible to juggle with the parameters and their timing in order to find the optimum combination for the scheme. The types of project which would most obviously benefit from this approach are speculative housing, multi-client offices or warehousing, multi-occupant retail centres, etc.

Table 3: Net terminal value method

Month	Cost for month	Interest till sale at 1.24% p.m.	Cost of item on completion
1			
2	29,120	1.32906	38,702
3			
4			
5			
6	33,280	1.26491	42,096
7	1,300	1.24936	1,624
8	16,300	1.23400	20,114
9	16,300	1.21883	19,867
10	21,300	1.20385	25,642
11	25,300	1.18905	30,083
12	35,300	1.17444	41,458
13	41,300	1.16	47,908
14	41,300	1.14574	47,319
15	65,300	1.13166	73,897
16	65,300	1.11775	72,989
17	63,300	1.10401	69,884
18	53,300	1.09044	58,120
19	46,300	1.07703	49,867
20	41,300	1.06379	43,935
21	36,300	1.05072	38,141
22	30,000	1.03780	31,134
23	222,143	1.02505	227,707
24	Total at end of 24 months =		980,487
25			
26			
27	17,300	1.0	17,300
28			————

Capital value of development		3,428,571
Outstanding debt prior to sale	980,487	
Final certificate + fees	17,300	
Contingency	41,367	
Profit and risk @ 20%	685,714	1,724,868
Max. acquisition cost in 2 yrs		1,703,703

Site value today = 1,703,703 × .74316   = £1,266,124
Max. land bid   = £1,217,427

A quicker and slightly simpler approach to the calculation of the cash flow is to itemise the individual amounts of expenditure and calculate the interest on each item for the whole period until the project is free of debt, i.e., in this case, on the sale of the project. The end result is the same, but doing away with the need for repetitive calculation of each month's interest saves time. The disadvantage lies in the fact that it is not possible to identify the total indebtedness at each point in the project. This technique is known as the Net Terminal Value method.

Table 3 shows this method of calculation applied to the example above.

A third method of approaching the problem of accounting for the fact that costs are outlayed over a period of time and thus represent differing values is to use Discounted Cash Flow techniques. In this method, each item of cost is discounted back to give the present value; this calculation is the reverse of the previous methods above, where costs were projected forwards by allowing for interest, and the land value found by discounting the value in two years. Table 4 shows the DCF method applied to the previous example. The answer is the same for all three cash flow methods (minor differences due to rounding-up errors may be ignored), and in terms of speed of calculation the last method is probably the fastest (at least for manual calculation – the use of computers means that with appropriate software, even more detailed and sophisticated approaches are possible very quickly). The major disadvantage of the last two methods is that while they may give the speediest answer, they do not identify the level of total debt at any particular time, and therefore give less flexibility in carrying out variations in the calculations.

Changes in the variables

In the introduction to this section, certain variables were seen to be important to the feasibility studies. In preparing the examples above, assumptions were made about the value of these variables. While a reasonable amount of research may give confidence in the accuracy of these assumptions, it is inconceivable that in any development there will not be changes resulting either from inaccurate assumptions or from changes in the underlying market conditions. The expectation of these changes was allowed for in the calculations by building in a contingency sum, and by pitching the requirement for a profit and risk margin at a level which provided an adequate return for the uncertainty inherent in a development which was to take place over a protracted period. One area of uncertainty which causes consistent anxiety is the incidence and level of inflation. Although the levels of inflation in recent years

Table 4: DCF method

Month	Cost for month	PV £1 at 1.24% p.m.	Present value of cash flow
1			
2	29,120	.98771	28,762
3			
4			
5			
6	33,280	.94003	31,284
7	1,300	.92848	1,207
8	16,300	.91706	14,948
9	16,300	.90579	14,764
10	21,300	.89466	19,056
11	25,300	.88366	22,357
12	35,300	.8728	30,810
13	41,300	.86207	35,603
14	41,300	.85147	35,166
15	65,300	.8410	54,918
16	65,300	.83067	54,243
17	63,300	.82046	51,935
18	53,300	.81037	43,192
19	46,300	.80041	37,059
20	41,300	.79057	32,651
21	36,300	.78085	28,345
22	30,000	.77126	23,138
23	222,143	.76178	169,223
24			
25	(3,428,571)	.74316	(2,547,989)
26	41,367	.74316	30,742
27	17,300	.74316	12,857
28	685,714	.74316	509,598

Site value now =   £1,266,131

Less acquisition costs = $\frac{100}{104} \times 1,266,131$

Max. land bid = £1,217,433
(the small difference between this and previous calculations is due to rounding up errors).

have fluctuated widely, it would be safe to assume that for the foreseeable future inflation is likely to continue at levels which may cause some disruption in the marketplace. The question is then how much (if any) allowance should be made in the calculations for this factor. The answer may depend in part on the developer's intentions for the scheme; if the scheme is being provided for long-term investment purposes, then no great dangers may result in using the best available current information on rent and cost levels, as any short-term fluctuations will be smoothed out over the life of the development. For a developer wishing to sell his interest in total on completion, it will be more important to carry out detailed research into the likely movement of the variables in the short term, as there will be no possibility of using the long-term position to compensate for inaccuracies in the assumptions. It should be noted that it is dangerous to assume that any inflationary pressure on an element of cost will be balanced by corresponding increase in value; while in *some* circumstances there may be *some* relationship between the current costs of providing developments and the resulting value, there is absolutely no guarantee that there *will* be such a relationship, or that if such a relationship exists it will hold good for the development in question. Other market forces outside the cost of provision are just as important in determining value, and may well outweigh a simple consideration of cost.

In summary, the prediction of the levels of variable is difficult, and the success of a scheme is likely to depend in large measure on the effort made to identify the correct levels to be used. Perhaps the simplest and most effective solution is to obtain the most accurate *current* estimates for costs and value, and to use those levels in the feasibility study; the relationship between current cost and value is understood and viable in the current market, and given the difficulty of predicting the future, these relationships are as likely to produce a credible feasibility study as a prediction of the future. However, as markets become better understood, and as methods of prediction improve, it may become possible to offer more sophisticated models for projecting future values; there has been considerable improvement in this area in the last decade, and it may be one of the benefits of the information technology revolution that accurate information, coupled with improved methods of calculation, will remove some of the speculation which is at present inherent in the development process.

Notwithstanding the difficulty in prediction, it is essential for any developer to be able to ascertain where the greatest areas of risk lie in the feasibility calculations. This may be done by analysing the effect of changing the variables, and noting which of them have the greatest capacity for disruption. This technique is called *sensitivity analysis*.

As the name implies, the technique allows the identification of those variables which will have the greatest effect on the financial outcome of the scheme. A crude measure of sensitivity may be gained by merely examining the comparative magnitude of the variables in the initial assumptions – in the example it is obvious that a 10% change in the cost of the land will have a greater effect than a 10% change in the level of professional fees. For some of the other variables, however, e.g. interest rates and yields, the changes will have to be calculated in order to ascertain the project's sensitivity to them. In the example above, the developer required a margin of 20% to cover his profit and risk (as a percentage of development value). Table 5 indicates the percentage erosion of or addition to this margin as a result of a 10% variation in a selected number of the variables. In calculating these changes it is assumed that the other variables remain unchanged, except for those subject to a knock-on effect from altering one of the variables. By using this technique, the developer is able to establish which variables have the greatest effect on the profitability of the scheme, and on which he should spend the greatest amount of time in research.

Table 5: Changes in developer's profit margin (as % of development value)

Variable	Assumption +10%	Assumption −10%
Construction cost	−10.3	+10.3
Rent	+32	−44
Interest rate	− 9	+ 8
Land cost	−25	+25
Investor's yield	−38	+38

In common with most sensitivity calculations, the construction cost, land cost, rent and investor's yield will be the factors to which the profit margin is most sensitive.

Other, more sophisticated variations on this type of calculation are possible. One could, for example, calculate how large a variation in any of the variables would be necessary to completely eliminate the profit margin, and then make an estimate of how probable a variation of that magnitude would be. While this sort of calculation may appear crude, it does give an indication of how much attention must be given to the assumptions made.

An extension of the first approach to sensitivity would be to try a selected number of changes in each of the variables to which the scheme appeared to be most sensitive; in order to limit the number of permutations, values for the most optimistic, pessimistic and likely levels of the variables could be inserted, and would then indicate to the developer the likely range of differences which could be experienced.

In considering sensitivity so far, predicting the likelihood of a particular value occurring has been assumed to be part of the art or experience of the developer. Although outside the scope of this book, it is possible to move from a subjective to an objective view of this likelihood by the use of probability theory. For a detailed review of the use of this technique in development see C. Darlow (ed.), *Valuation and Development Appraisal*, published by the *Estates Gazette*.

3. Preconstruction Process

3.1 SYSTEM REQUIREMENTS

The 'traditional' model of the construction process in the UK has been built upon a number of simple assumptions about the nature of client bodies and the way in which they will choose to have their buildings produced. In this model there are clients who are generally assumed to have little or no knowledge of the construction industry, who will automatically approach an architect in order to begin the process of procuring the development in question; the architect, in conjunction with other consultants chosen by him (but contractually responsible to the client) will then fully design the scheme and seek tenders in competition, the tenders being based on full designs and full Bills of Quantities. The contract for the construction works will be one of the standard forms prepared by the Joint Contracts Tribunal, and the works will be subject to the supervision and certification of the architect.

While this approach may have served the industry and its clients well for the two decades after the Second World War, there have been in the last three decades such marked changes in the environment in which buildings are procured that the simple assumptions must now be questioned. Amongst others, there are perhaps three features of the last thirty years which combine to subject the traditional model to critical scrutiny. The first is the increased level of inflation and high interest rates in this period, which has meant that clients have been increasingly interested in the financial progress of their schemes, with delays bringing large penalties in interest charges; the second, the increased exposure of construction clients to the experience of developing in countries outside the UK, particularly the USA; and third, the changes in attitude of the participants who serve the clients, i.e. the designers and contractors, who have been forced to respond to the changing needs of the client base – often with the greatest reluctance.

In order to establish some sense of order in what may appear at first sight to be a seemingly haphazard series of responses to an equally random series of demands from a vast spectrum of project promoters, it is useful to approach the analysis from the assumption that what is being considered is a *system* which is established in order to meet a client's needs.

In doing so, it is necessary first to consider what a system is, and what are the essential characteristics of a system.

One definition of a system is: 'Any entity, conceptual or physical, which consists of interdependent parts. Each of a system's elements is connected to every other element, directly or indirectly, and no sub-set of elements is unconnected to any other sub-set'. Used in the context of property development, this implies that for a successful outcome (successful from the promoter's viewpoint) all of the component parts of the operation must be identified, and arranged in such a way that the process as a whole is optimised for the benefit of the promoter or client. This implies in turn that it is *not* necessarily the case that each of the *component* parts of the operation is optimised – some degree of sub-optimisation of some of the components may be acceptable or even necessary to achieve success in the project as a whole. It may be easily seen from the outline of the approach that the 'traditional' method of building procurement cannot hope to satisfy all the possible system requirements. This is not to say that the traditional approach is without value; indeed there may be many projects where the traditional method provides the optimum solution. However, in these circumstances the use of the systems approach allows the user to derive the organisational requirements to which the traditional model may provide a solution.

Open and closed systems

Closed systems are those in which there is no contact or exchange between the system and its environment. The environment in which

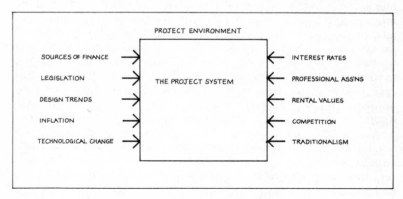

Figure 5.   Project and environment.

the system operates may be considered for our purposes as those elements, not being part of the system itself, which can produce an effect in the system. An open system contrasts with a closed system by its ability to be influenced by changes in the environment. This concept of an open system, able to make exchanges with its environment, is important in relation to the establishment of a project system. Any development which involves design and construction must of necessity be influenced by a huge range of factors outside the project boundary. Some of the major environmental influences to which a project may be forced to respond are noted in figure 5.

This environment will have an effect on the optimum design of the project system in two ways: first upon the project system itself, e.g. by influencing what may be built through the planning process, and secondly through having an effect on the client's own business, which will then be reflected in the constraints which the client has to place upon the project. Many practitioners in both design and construction seem quite prepared to ignore the fact that the client has to operate his business in an environment which may be quite foreign to those involved in construction; this usually operates to the detriment of both, as the client fails to achieve the optimum solution to his needs, and the designers and contractors consequently fail to acquire a fully satisfied client.

The system must also have an objective, clearly framed and communicated so that all participants in the process are aware of it. This is not to suggest that the objective once defined is immutable; this would be contrary to the initial proposition that the open system is susceptible to the influence of the environment. Neither is it suggested that the objective may be subject to continued fundamental change, but rather that the objective will be the subject of development, with such development being communicated with as much clarity as the original. (There is perhaps one exception to the initial suggestion of the last sentence; that is where the ability to adapt to constant, unpredictable and fundamental change is one of the system objectives – this may be demonstrated in particular types of building where it may be important to be able to make fundamental design changes up to a late stage in the process; in this case the organisational system must be designed to allow this, although this may result in cost penalties – an example of sub-optimisation of the (cost) sub-system in order to achieve the overall objective.)

On development projects the system objective may be demonstrated by the client's brief, i.e. the client's description of what is required from the completed scheme. The derivation of the brief and its importance are considered later in this chapter.

It follows therefore that the focus of the organisational effort in procuring buildings must lie in the determination of the system's objectives, and their relationship with the environment; communicating these objectives and ensuring that they are seen as compatible with the objectives of individual participants; anticipating the need for modifications in the system; ensuring that adequate communication takes place between the sub-systems; and ensuring that a feedback mechanism is built in to allow monitoring of the performance of the sub-components and the overall performance of the system.

3.2   CLIENT TYPES

It was suggested earlier that an understanding of the environment in which the client operates was essential to the formation of a system for executing the project. Although an individual client's needs may depend on the nature of his business, a great deal may be gained from an understanding of the characteristics of generic types of client body; i.e. there are likely to be fewer differences within the generic group than there are between the groups. One benefit of examining client groups as opposed to individual clients may lie in the increased level of service which may be provided to an individual client as a result of understanding the nature of the group; it will often be the case that a designer or contractor can give advice to a client based upon experience gained through operating with other clients with similar problems, and indeed this may be the reason for a client awarding the commission in the first place. While it is normal for contractors or designers in construction to identify as 'the client' the person or organisation which gives instructions and pays the bills, the real focus for decision making on the project will often be much more diffuse than this. On a simple project, e.g. the construction of a house extension for a private individual, it ought to be fairly straightforward to identify the householder and his/her needs, to derive a brief and execute the project (leaving aside such minor complications as whether husband and wife can actually agree on the size, shape and colour of the building, and whether the planners and building control officers then require something completely different). On a more substantial development, say a major town centre redevelopment undertaken as a partnership between the local authority, a pension fund, and a developer, which will be used partly by the local authority as offices, partly as public open space/amenity areas, and where the greater part will be let as retail and office space to the open market, there will be a multiplicity of interests which will lay claim to the right to establish the project objectives, and the way in which these should be interpreted. The difficulty which arises here, and often on much more straightforward projects also, is in establishing who *is* the client?

Returning to the earlier suggestion that the client is recognisable as the body which takes decisions and pays for the result, we may look rather more closely at whether this implied level of authority actually exists in practice, or whether the ostensible client is merely an agency for whichever organisation is establishing the 'ground rules'. Where the latter is the case, it is useful to know whether the client is experienced in interpreting the requirements of his own environment, or whether there are dangers in assuming that the client knows his own business well enough. The latter risk may appear most often in public sector projects, in which there will often be complex rules governing the amount and flow of finance from central government, the nature of the building design, and the procurement system which may be used. But this does not rule out a similar situation in the private sector, where the nature of the end user of the building and his requirements, as well as the dictates of the suppliers of finance, may be better understood by the experienced property manager, specialist designer or contractor than by the client. In both these circumstances, the sensible client will recognise the virtue of having a high level of informed advice available; but this does not mean that this client or any other will welcome the news that his business is understood well unless the input is accompanied by a high level of diplomacy!

The extent to which the client's discretion may be limited may be demonstrated by example. A considerable proportion of the industry's public sector housing orders now come from the Housing Association movement, and although the client system described below is unique to the movement, the general principles may be found in many parts of the public sector.

Housing Associations are usually run under 'charitable' rules, and their activities are subject to compliance with such rules (usually under the Industrial and Provident Societies Acts). They are also run under the general scrutiny of the Housing Corporation, which as well as supplying most of the loan finance for the Associations' activities has a remit from central government to police Associations' work. The Housing Corporation also sets detailed constraints on the technical content of the housing provision which it finances, as well as a detailed procedure for the processing of schemes in terms of approvals at various stages. The form of procurement used is subject to control, as is the form of contract and the details contained in the appendix to the standard form of contract. Housing Associations are usually given dispensation to operate in designated geographical areas, in order to prevent competition between Associations for the same properties, and their development programmes will be circumscribed by a funding programme which allows a set amount of property acquisition, plus a fixed amount of cash to translate these acquisitions into building projects. The actual amount which the Association may spend on each acquisition is governed by the valuation of the land or buildings supplied by the district valuer (an officer of the Inland Revenue) – the Association is not allowed to pay more than this valuation. The amount which may be spent in total on acquisition, building works and professional fees is *usually* limited by an upper limit known as the Total Indicative Cost for the scheme (based on factors such as size of accommodation and geographical area, and subject to updating at intervals). There are also rules on the way in which contractors and professionals may be selected, and on their payment. In addition, the Association must comply with the same requirements for planning and building control approvals as any other developer.

As not all Associations are large, sophisticated bodies which can afford to maintain in-house development experts, it is necessary for any organisation seeking to service a Housing Association to become familiar with the ground rules governing its development activities; failure to do so is likely to lead to a substantial amount of abortive work, for which there is little possibility of gaining reimbursement.

This familiarisation will also prevent moments of frustration, when decisions are awaited on matters for which a third party approval is necessary.

By comparison, it may appear that private sector developers have a relatively easy life; but the comparison is meaningless unless the other complications in the private sector client's life are considered also. In any case, many of the control mechanisms noted above are mirrored in the private sector, albeit in different forms; companies are controlled by the provisions of the Companies Acts, and the availability of funds for their activities is controlled by the general restrictions on finance imposed by competition in the marketplace and legislative constraints on or incentives towards the provision of development funds. The ability to include certain features in a scheme may be constrained by the financial institution's views on the marketability of such features. The scheme will also be influenced by the developer's perception of what the end user is likely to find appealing in the completed project. It is true, however, that in general the private sector operator is likely to have considerably greater discretion over the form and content of his scheme, simply because the project is being developed as a speculative venture, which by definition must contain an element of risk, and it is for taking that risk that the developer may expect to receive a profit.

Therefore, in order for the project team to formulate any kind of *project* system it is necessary to have an adequate understanding of the client system and the environment in which it operates, from which it derives much of its form. It is obviously impossible for any individual or organisation to have a detailed knowledge of each client type, but the need for an understanding of the client does lead to the establishment of a vocabulary in which the necessary information may be framed.

The client field for construction may be classified by using three main divisions, each of which is considered briefly below.

Public clients

These may include any organisations which are publicly owned, and which may raise finance, either by borrowing from government sources or through a government mandate to borrow in the open market, and expend such monies on development or construction. As in the Housing Association example, there will be a strong element of public accountability present in their approach to development, which will be evidenced by a multi-layered approval system, and a generally bureaucratic approach. Finance is likely to be available on a year by year basis, with only a limited facility for roll-over from year to year. The year by year approach to funding often leads to absurdities, as when a project may be delayed for much of the financial year due to conservatism in relation to the organisation's budgets as a whole, followed by a crash programme of activity near the end of the financial year when it is realised that the budget is going to be underspent unless a fast start is made on the project. In such circumstances it may be impossible to ensure that the client obtains the best possible service in terms of economy, but from the client's viewpoint the need to spend is probably more important than absolute value for money, for the simple reason that next year's budget is likely to be set in relation to the amount spent in the current year; an underspend this year implies a reduced budget next year.

Where there is scrutiny by an elected body as well as by officers, as in a local authority, it will be necessary to have a reasonable understanding of the dynamics of the relationship between officers and members; it is not at all unusual for development projects to be used as political 'footballs' and an understanding of where the real influences on decision making lie may prevent the ball from leaving the pitch too often. In these circumstances there is great merit in the appointment of a project coordinator from within the client body, appointed with the powers to liaise across all necessary departments (as recommended by the Wood report in 1975 and adopted by many public bodies).

Individual (personal) clients

These are relatively scarce in the construction industry today, and are usually people who require a purpose-built house. While individuals have a large degree of freedom in their decision making, they are not free from constraint; if mortgage finance is required, then the bank or building society will wish to ensure that the property provides security for the loan, and this may rule out the worst excesses that the client may wish to incorporate. Otherwise the only constraints which will apply are the normal development control functions.

This category may be enlarged to include the sole proprietor of a business. Even in this case it is advisable to undertake a careful analysis of the business and the manner in which it operates, as the disinterested and analytical observer may form a picture of the operation which is different (and perhaps on occasion more accurate) than that supplied by the proprietor. Indeed it is not at all unlikely that the first real analysis of the business will occur when the owner wishes to expand, and wishes as part of the expansion to add to or adapt his premises. Initial assumptions by the owner over what capacity for expansion exists in the present premises and where additional space might be best sited may be validated or refuted by such a study. It would be sensible here also to take some advice from the workforce (if possible), as their perceptions of how the business activities are ordered may be quite different to those of the proprietor. In any case, some of the information required may only be obtainable from the workforce, and this sort of liaison may be encouraged or even demanded by the proprietor.

Corporations

Such organisations may range from a size similar to the sole proprietor to the largest multi-national, and encompass, sometimes within the same company, a wide range of organisational types, functions and objectives. Again, a thorough understanding of the nature, form and purpose of the organisation is essential. One of the most fundamental difficulties which may arise is similar to that noted in relation to the public sector body; exactly where does the real decision making power lie? It might be thought that the ultimate source of authority would lie in the board of directors, but in practice many companies are subsidiaries of larger organisations, sometimes located outside the UK. Even where the company has a sophisticated approach to development, and has appointed an in-house project manager or coordinator, it may be difficult to establish the limits of that individual's authority. Human beings are sometimes (understandably) reluctant to admit that there are limits to their authority, particularly where this limit is patently below the level needed to exercise proper control of decision making. This may lead to the project team being misled over the parameters being applied to the scheme, and thus to a great deal of abortive work. Where the corporation is large and the project proposed will be used by a number of parts of the organisation, it is necessary to understand fully how these components relate to one another, and to the priorities of the organisation as a whole. It cannot be assumed, for example, that a department's perception of its own importance is reflected at a higher management level; even when this is established it will still be necessary to consult with these components in order to gain a complete picture of the client and his objectives in order to define the project system's parameters in the project brief.

Once a sufficient amount of investigation into the client system and its environment has been undertaken, it will be possible to attempt to enshrine the constraints thus identified in the project system itself. However, this cannot be done as an isolated exercise; a system of feedback must be established to ensure that the development of the project system does not, through its gestation, become an end in itself. There must be continual cross-reference between the proposals for the project system and the client system in order to be certain that the developing project system continues to reflect and match the needs of the client.

3.3 CLIENT FUNCTIONS

The degree to which a client will become involved in a project depends mainly on two factors.

1. Whether the client is a 'naive' client, i.e. one who has not built before, or who builds so infrequently that no experience or expertise in the process has been acquired; or whether the client is a regular developer, and therefore has the knowledge, ability and confidence to order the project in the way which best suits his interest. Added to this criterion is whether the client at this time has resources available in-house which can be devoted to the management of the project.

2. The nature of the organisation structure of the client body, whether this is concentrated centrally or is diffuse, and what level of authority is granted to the part of the organisation which will be acting as the client for the project.

Where the client has considerable experience in development, it will be possible for the client's representative to have a high degree of informed involvement, which will mean that less reliance need be placed upon the client's principal advisor; the converse is also true, that where there is little experience of managing development projects, the client will need to delegate considerable authority to an agency (project manager, surveyor, architect, or contractor) to manage the scheme on his behalf.

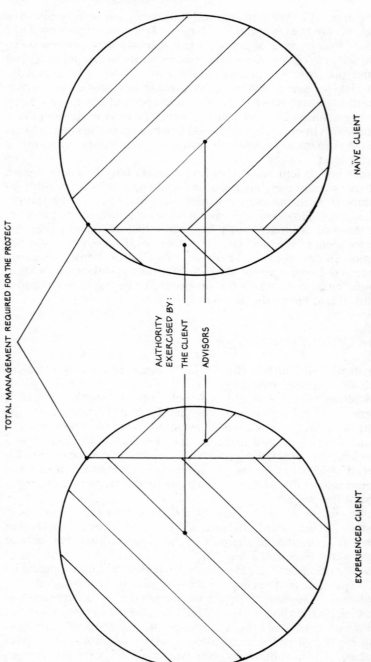

Figure 6. Authority exercised by client.

These two possibilities may be illustrated diagrammatically as in figure 6.

One difficulty which can ensue occurs where the client organisation has a centralised system which does not easily allow for the delegation of the necessary authority for the project, to either the individual nominated to be the focus for decision making or to the principal external advisor, and does not provide for short lines of communication to compensate for the lack of delegation. In this case neither the client representative nor the advisor is likely to be able to make the decisions necessary to progress the scheme in a satisfactory form. This situation is illustrated in figure 7.

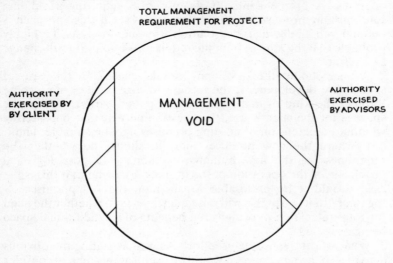

Figure 7.   Poor communication and lack of delegation.

The management void will result in the client's needs for the project being incompletely stated, the design team will be faced with a high degree of iteration and abortive work before an acceptable design is produced, and even then there will be a lack of confidence in whether the result can be truly said to represent the client's needs. At a later stage in the project, there will be problems in obtaining approvals for the myriad of minor matters which require resolution. Only by good fortune will those associated with the project escape criticism for the result.

Assuming that the client has been able to nominate a focus within the organisation, and that the person has access to whatever personnel are needed within the organisation to form a team to consider the project, it will usually be necessary to carry out a preliminary feasibility study to ensure that the company has a reasonable basis for pursuing the project further. Amongst the questions which need to be answered at this stage are:

1. Is development actually needed? Where the project is being undertaken for rent or sale, there would appear to be an obvious answer – yes – to the question. But even in these circumstances there may be an alternative solution, e.g. to invest the funds earmarked for development elsewhere, for instance in purchasing shares, government securities, or other speculation. Where the scheme is being pursued for use by the client, the answer may not be so obvious. It was suggested earlier that, prior to any decision to build, the client should undertake a careful analysis of his objectives, including a review if necessary of the way in which the business operates. A problem initially diagnosed as requiring a building solution may produce a quite different answer if this approach is taken. Even if building *is* the solution after such analysis, it is highly probable that the *kind* of building required as a solution will change as a result.

2. Where should the development take place? In the case of speculative development, the answer to this question may come through the kind of market survey described earlier. Where the space is for the client's use, the question may involve considering whether an extension of existing premises may be suitable, and if not, where the new premises may be sited, and whether the remoteness of the new buildings is thought to pose logistical problems for the operation of the business as a whole; if this is the case, would it be preferable to abandon the old premises altogether? In its turn, this will raise questions as to whether the need for total relocation outweighs the benefits of the additional space being provided.

3. What will the space be used for? As well as stating the obvious activities in the new space, it would be useful at this time to consider operating methods as a whole, and whether the revision of the spaces allocated to parts of the business could usefully encourage revised methods of e.g. production, information transfer.

4. What are the important cost parameters? As well as the obvious question of how much the client can afford to spend, consideration should be given to whether the client would be best to choose a low capital cost/high maintenance building or vice-versa, what grants or other incentives are available (and under what conditions), and whether it is desirable to build-in features to the scheme which may be surplus to the client's needs but would increase the value of the property on the open market should the need for sale arise. These factors can only be resolved through a detailed knowledge of the client's financial affairs, including his taxation position.

5. How quickly is the development needed? Many clients, particularly naive clients, have little appreciation of the lead times necessary for the provision of building developments. In particular, there is always a tendency for the precontract period to be

underestimated. While there are a number of procurement systems available which can reduce overall development and construction times, the client needs to be aware that there is almost certain to be some trade-off necessary between the saving in time and the increased risk to quality and cost. In this respect, the trade-off is no different to that which would occur in any other sector of manufacturing industry or commerce.

Once the client's team has been able to find acceptable answers to the above questions (where they are not able to formulate accurate responses without external advice, they may be able to pose the question with greater precision than would otherwise have been the case) the team will be able to progress to the next stage in the operation, the provision of a detailed statement on the parameters to be satisfied by the team which provides the building. This statement should provide information both on the requirements for the development itself, and the procedures which are essential to the client during the provision. This process is known as the derivation of the client's brief.

The brief

In practice, it would be unusual if not impossible for the brief to be prepared without considering the system to be used for procuring the building. The form of the brief and its contents will depend to some extent on whether it is being used within a particular procurement process. Indeed, it may not be possible (or desirable) for the inexperienced client to formulate a brief for a development without obtaining professional advice, and it is relatively unusual for a *complete* brief to be made available to the design and/or construction team without some help from the team in posing the questions to which the client will respond. In extreme cases the client may only have the haziest notion of what he requires from the development, and the briefing process may only be really under way once the client has been presented with a number of sketch options from which he may recognise a building solution which appears to meet his desires. It is also relatively rare for the brief to be determined all at once; more often it is produced as an iterative process, with interaction between the designer and the client in order to offer potential solutions to the problems as initially perceived, and with repeated attempts to close the gap between the evolving solution and the system requirements as yet unsatisfied.

For convenience, the choice of procurement options is left until the next chapter, and at this point it is assumed that the client is able and willing to consider a logical assembly of the important areas on which the design and construction team will require information. In considering the brief, no assumptions are implied as yet over

Figure 8. Outline plan of work.
Plan of work diagram 1

Stage	Purpose of work and Decisions to be reached	Tasks to be done	People directly involved	Usual Terminology
A. Inception	To prepare general outline of requirements and plan future action.	Set up client organisation for briefing. Consider requirements, appoint architect.	All client interests, architect.	**Briefing**
B. Feasibility	To provide the client with an appraisal and recommendation in order that he may determine the form in which the project is to proceed, ensuring that it is feasible, functionally, technically and financially.	Carry out studies of user requirements, site conditions, planning, design, and cost, etc., as necessary to reach decisions.	Clients' representatives, architects, engineers, and QS according to nature of project.	
C. Outline Proposals	To determine general approach to layout, design and construction in order to obtain authoritative approval of the client on the outline proposals and accompanying report.	Develop the brief further. Carry out studies on user requirements, technical problems, planning, design and costs, as necessary to reach decisions.	All client interests, architects, engineers, QS and specialists as required.	**Sketch Plans**
D. Scheme Design	To complete the brief and decide on particular proposals, including planning arrangement appearance, constructional method, outline specification, and cost, and to obtain all approvals.	Final development of the brief, full design of the project by architect, preliminary design by engineers, preparation of cost plan and full explanatory report. Submission of proposals for all approvals.	All client interests, architects, engineers, QS and specialists and all statutory and other approving authorities.	

Stage	Purpose	Action	Personnel	
E. Detail Design	To obtain final decision on every matter related to design, specification, construction and cost.	Full design of every part and component of the building by collaboration of all concerned. Complete cost checking of designs.	Architects, QS, engineers and specialists, contractor (if appointed).	**Working Drawings**

Any further change in location, size, shape, or cost after this time will result in abortive work.

Stage	Purpose	Action	Personnel	
F. Production Information	To prepare production information and make final detailed decisions to carry out work.	Preparation of final production information i.e. drawings, schedules and specifications.	Architects, engineers and specialists, contractor (if appointed).	
G. Bills of Quantities	To prepare and complete all information and arrangements for obtaining tender.	Preparation of Bills of Quantities and tender documents.	Architects, QS, contractor (if appointed).	
H. Tender Action	Action as recommended in NJCC *Code of Procedure for Single Stage Selective Tendering 1977.*	Action as recommended in NJCC *Code of Procedure for Single Stage Selective Tendering 1977.*	Architects, QS, engineers, contractor, client.	
J. Project Planning	To enable the contractor to programme the work in accordance with contract conditions; brief site inspectorate; and make arrangements to commence work on site.	Action in accordance with *The Management of Building Contracts* and Diagram 9.	Contractor, sub-contractors.	**Site Operations**

K. Operations on Site	To follow plans through to practical completion of the building.	Action in accordance with *The Management of Building Contracts** and Diagram 10.	Architects, engineers, sub-contractors, QS, client.
L. Completion	To hand over the building to the client for occupation, remedy any defects, settle the final account, and complete all work in accordance with the contract.	Action in accordance with *The Management of Building Contracts** and Diagram 11.	Architects, engineers, contractor, QS, client.
M. Feed-Back	To analyse the management, construction and performance of the project.	Analysis of job records, Inspection of completed building. Studies of building in use.	Architects, engineers, QS contractor, client.

* The publications *Code of Procedure for Single Stage Selective Tendering* (NJCC 1977) and *Management of Building Contracts* (NJCC 1970) are published by RIBA Publications Ltd for the NJCC.

whether the design will be executed by a design team in private practice, or by contractor-led designers, or through any other option. What *is* assumed is that the system will imply the use of designers of some sort, irrespective of their location in the procurement system.

The brief's contribution to the design

To a large extent, any building design may be considered to be a personal and therefore subjective statement made by the designer in interpreting the client's needs into a built form. The design solution will therefore be one of a range of possible solutions constrained by the designer's perceptions of the system boundaries defined by the client. It is essential therefore to eliminate sources of error which could arise if the boundaries also were to be stated in a subjective and therefore imprecise manner. This is not to imply that the boundaries stated by the brief need be static; even the most objective and carefully researched brief contains the possibility for errors and omissions, and the briefing process can logically be considered as evolving rather than static; the process can be characterised by a series of interactions, with solutions being tested for effectiveness at each stage of development. The process will continue until the solution satisfies the client requirements. The evolution process and the interactions between client and designer are well described in the RIBA 'plan of work' as noted in figure 8. Although this plan of work was evolved as a systematic method for the coordination of design and construction using the 'traditional' method of procurement, it is a good example of the nature of the interaction between designer and client, and also where the process of briefing should end. The plan of work itself clearly states that the plan is an outline of the approach, and that the plan should be modified to suit the project in question. It should not be assumed that the progress from stage A to D will be protracted, although on a major, complex scheme it is likely that this will be the case. On more modest schemes, it is possible to coalesce stages A and B into C or C and D.

As well as outlining where in the design and construction process the briefing takes place, the plan also makes it clear that the derivation of the brief must be brought to a halt at some point; in this case it is the point at which the client has accepted a design scheme on which the detailed design for the project may be based. Although it is quite possible for the client to continue to modify the scheme and its parameters, the plan of work alerts the client to the fact that after the agreement on a scheme which appears to be an acceptable interpretation of the brief, the detailed design work which follows is expensive in labour terms, and as a consequence the client could be faced with an extra charge for any abortive work which follows; this is justified on the basis that the designer is expected to work for the fee scales recommended by the professional institution, and these fee scales are calculated on the basis of the 'average' amount of commitment at each point in the plan of work. Probably the most important section of the brief in terms of the design will be the study known as the *user requirement study*.

The user requirement study is undertaken to identify the purpose for which the building is required, including both human-environmental and functional aspects, and to use this information to define the design problem. For some 'standard' types of building or sections of building, there may already have been information published which makes recommendations for the design standards which would otherwise have to be sought from one-off studies. Similarly, some of the information may be strictly controlled by codes of practice or legislation. In the former case, it will be necessary to distinguish between the type of study which needs to be made because the client's needs *are* unique, and the study which will merely 'reinvent the wheel'. There is some merit in clients persuading designers not to try a new variant on accepted methods merely to achieve a new design solution as an end in itself – unless that very aspect is one consciously encouraged by the client.

The variety of building types and complexities makes it impossible to set down any definitive classification for the information which should be sought at this stage, but it is possible to establish a series of *objectives* which could be reached. These objectives may be seen as a process which begins with a statement by the client on:
1. which people will use the building (if any);
2. what purpose the building will be used for;
3. what sort of organisation structure the client will use in uniting 1 and 2.

The statement may then be augmented by a detailed investigation of each of the sections in it.

The information needed may be supplied by collecting data already available in the client organisation, e.g. on manufacturing space and personnel per machine, storage requirements for different levels of production, present and future use of particular technology types, etc., or by observation where the data is not available or believed to be unreliable. This may be elaborated upon by discussion with the people who will use the new facilities, or where the building is a speculative venture, by the market research described earlier. There are distinct advantages to the client in preparing as much of this kind of information as possible prior to the first interaction with the designer; it will in most cases speed the process of inception, as it will to some extent accelerate the learning curve for the designers on first acquaintance with the client, and where the investigatory work is complex and outside the reasonable scope of the standard fee scales, it may avoid the need for additional design fees. It is unlikely however that the client will be able to anticipate the full range of investigation needed for the design process, even where the client is experienced. Nor should any slight shortfall in client's information be seen as a criticism of the client's endeavours; requests for further particulars by the designer may result in a better solution than might be achieved otherwise.

Having satisfied the need for information, the skill of the designer may now be employed in *interpreting* this by considering how the facts may be arranged to define the problem in design terms. The facts may be ordered to define the space standards required for the people and their activities, and to indicate how they may be interpreted in a building form.

The interpretation stage is one which also requires the client's participation; it is necessary to check whether the interpretation meets the client's intentions: the process becomes a loop, with continual feedback between designer and client. Once this series of iterations appears to be producing consistent results, it is possible to move to the end of the briefing stage, with the client being asked to adjudicate on specific recommendations made by the designer in the form of a scheme design, or a number of alternative scheme solutions. Once agreement has been reached, the briefing process should come to an end, and the project may move towards the detailed design stage. (The standard conditions of engagement for architectural services require the architect to obtain specific approval from the client before proceeding to the next stage.)

This does not imply that all design decisions must be firmed-up at the end of scheme design; this stage only provides the outline decisions on the design, to be used as a basis for the detailed work which will still require client's input in decisions on points of detail.

The briefing process may be illustrated diagrammatically as in figure 9.

In parallel with the investigation of functional solutions to the design problem, the designer must interpret the client's requirement in terms of cost. Even on the most simple building, this must embrace wider aspects of cost than merely the capital cost of construction. Where the client's stated intention is to produce the building at the lowest initial capital cost, it would be irresponsible of the designer not to point out the future implications of such a decision, or to design the building without reference to costs in use.

In considering the preferred balance between initial and operating costs, there are considerable difficulties in arriving at a quantifiable solution. These difficulties may be classified as, first, problems in evaluating an extremely complex mixture of variables, ranging from the effects of orientation of the building upon energy consumption, to predictions of the life span of materials, components and equipment. The second problem arises from the

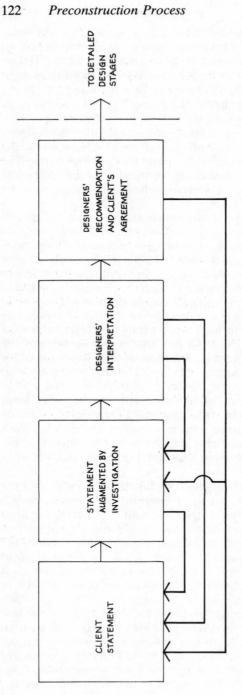

Figure 9. The briefing process.

apparent reluctance of professional advisors and their clients to take seriously the issue of life cycle costing. In spite of conscious promotion of the concept over the last two decades, there has been little acceptance of the need for this type of approach. Few designers have received anything other than a perfunctory reference to the issue in their education and professional training, and the combination of a lack of expertise and client ignorance provides a situation where, with the exception of the cost of energy, there is little consideration of the problem. The techniques for dealing with cost in use calculations are essentially based on discounted costs as used in the earlier feasibility examples, and with the aid of microcomputing facilities there is little valid excuse for the avoidance of this issue.

Whichever approach to costs is used, the evolving design will require to be tested against the cost brief in parallel with the functional studies, a cost plan being agreed as an integral component of the scheme design; at this stage the estimated cost of the scheme should also be frozen, and become a fixed design parameter. An exception to this rule may arise where the nature of the design brief makes it clear that one of the client's objectives is to have as much flexibility as possible in making design changes up to as late a stage as possible. Where this is a stated objective, it should be clear to the client that such a criterion has its own set of consequences in terms of cost, time and quality. Such situations may arise where the client's business is subject to volatility in levels and types of competition, and where the client needs to be able to respond quickly and effectively to changes in market conditions in the period between inception and completion of the project.

The brief's contribution to the procedure

In addition to the elements of the client system which have a bearing on the design of the building, there will be complementary factors which will dictate the *conditions* under which the procurement of the development proceeds. Some of these will also have a bearing on the actual design solution. They may be summarised under the following headings:

1. *Timing*

The most obvious factor of importance in timing is the speed with which the building is required, and the degree of realism attached to the client's expectations. While the UK construction industry has been severely criticised for its performance in terms of speed in comparison particularly to the USA, it has been shown that with the correct combination of client input and determination, and the correct selection of designer and construction systems and people, it is quite possible to achieve comparable performances in the UK. Therefore, if speed is considered to be of paramount importance, the client must be prepared to select and brief his team accordingly, and to apply the same standards of judgement to his own performance in the supply of information and timely decisions. In addition to the overall project time target, there may be constraints on the timing of intermediate stages of the procurement process, e.g. in order to have information available for approval at board meetings, or to coordinate with the activities of other parts of the organisation in other countries.

Where the development is a part of a larger programme of, say, relocation or restructuring of the client's activities, there may be absolute deadlines for completion of the project or stages of it, to allow the essential parts of the client's business to continue without interruption. Where this is the case, it is imperative that the client carries out sufficient planning studies in depth to allow the design team to accept these constraints as part of the design process. In such circumstances the timing may be the most important criterion, and may determine which options for design and construction are available, as well as defining the ideal procurement system.

2.   *Cash flow*

This could be considered as a sub-component of timing, but it may be useful to consider the cash flow as a criterion in its own right. The importance of cash flow may have an effect in two ways; first as a determinant of the flow of the *project*, as in a phased development, where the income from an early phase is required to fund later stages, or second as a planning and monitoring device, where predictions on cash flow may be necessary to maintain the confidence of the funding institution. In both cases it may be necessary to test the design solutions against whatever criteria exist for the flow of funds.

3.   *Decision making*

Reference has been made to the effects upon the project of different degrees of authority concentration. The client should make the chain of decision making clear as part of the brief, and the client's advisors should be informed unequivocally of the level of discretion given to the client's coordinator. Where decisions must be referred further up the organisation, or in the case of public sector projects to a committee or government department, the time factors involved should be stated with as much accuracy as possible. An example of the disruptive effects of not stating these constraints would lie in the situation where competitive tenders are sought for a main contract, and the tenderers are required to keep their offer open for acceptance for a stated period. If the time required for the client's adjudication is longer than the period stated, the lowest tenderer is under no obligation to keep his offer open. The client may approve the tender sum only to find an immediate demand for an increase; the client is then faced with accepting this or retendering.

4.   *Reporting formats*

The client, particularly the public sector client, may have requirements for reporting in a particular format and at particular times. Where this is the case, the requirements must be made clear at an early stage, as the collection of the data to achieve the format may be a constraint on the way the contractual documentation is prepared, i.e. the documentation may need to be structured to allow the retrieval of information in a particular way, particularly in respect of progress information on cost and time. The basis for monitoring and reporting systems is considered later in this chapter.

3.4   PROCUREMENT SYSTEMS AND STRUCTURES

In the last section an attempt was made to identify some of the characteristics of the client system which could have an influence on the design of the ideal system for the procurement of the project. As well as identifying some of the parameters which would form the brief for the project, it was suggested that the degree to which the client structure allowed delegation of authority to those in charge of the project would have a strong influence on the success of the scheme. If sufficient authority was not available, either to the client's manager or to an external advisor, then a void in the management requirements would result.

The need for removal of this void may be demonstrated by the range of tasks which must be performed in any project, particularly major, complex projects. In addition to the definition and performance of these tasks, there must be management of them, through an integration and control mechanism. The degree to which the tasks are specialised activities, only able to be undertaken by independent organisations, will depend on the nature of the project itself. In functional terms, any building project will resolve itself into three main areas:

1. the client functions – briefing, monitoring/control and occupation;
2. the design function – embracing all aspects of the design, irrespective of where or by whom the design is executed;

3. the construction function – which may include an element of the detailed design.

In practice, the areas which have come under the greatest scrutiny have been 1 and 2. The management and integration of activities in the construction function have received comparatively little criticism, as to a large extent the construction function has been a highly integrated one for some considerable time. Where there has been debate on this function, it has tended to be over how much it needs to be integrated with the design function, or into the process as a whole.

Discussion on the ideal procurement system for building projects should be viewed against the background of an industry in which the primary vehicle for procurement is what has been referred to earlier as the 'traditional' model. This system still accounts for the majority of construction projects in the UK and in those countries where the construction industry has followed UK influences.

As many of the alternative procurement systems have appeared as a reaction to the deficiencies of the traditional model, rather than as a conscious attempt to derive the ideal system for each occasion, it is useful to examine this system in some detail.

The traditional system

The traditional system is based on specialisation in the fields of design, quantification and construction. By the end of the eighteenth century the role of the architect as an independent designer of buildings was well established; at the beginning of the following century, the general contractor in roughly his present form had appeared, together with the embryo quantity surveyor contributing, through Bills of Quantities, a common format for contractors to price work in competition. This has evolved into a process, upon which the standard forms of building contracts with quantities are based, as follows.

Client with a building need
↓
Client briefs architect
↓
Architect considers brief, advises on other consultants required
↓
Design team led by architect prepares scheme, gets client's approval
↓
Design team prepares detail drawings, specification and B of Q.
↓
Contract documents prepared and sent to contractors for tenders

↓

Contractors price documents, send tenders to client

↓

Design team reports on tenders, makes recommendation

↓

Client enters into building contract with (usually) lowest tenderer

↓

Contractor manages construction operations, completes contract

The assumption and normal practice is for the architect, quantity surveyor, engineers, and any other consultants or specialist designers to be separate, independent practices, with separate contracts for their services between themselves and the client. The architect is assumed to be the head of the design team, and is responsible in general for the quality of the design provided (although the individual designers still retain their responsibility in contract and through the common law for the service they provide). The contractor is directly responsible for carrying out the construction work, and for the activities of any subcontractors he may employ, including the work of specialist subcontractors nominated by the architect (although the nominated subcontractor may also have provided a warranty directly to the client).

In theory, the contractor's price should be a lump-sum, fixed price, as the bills of quantities should be an accurate representation of all the work which is required to complete the project. In its turn this assumes that all the detailed design work is complete before the bills are prepared.

The contractual system may be shown as in figure 10.

One of the most obvious oddities here is the mismatch between the contractual system and the communication system. For example, the client is in direct contract with the contractor, with whom he has no rights of communication or instruction under the contract, and the architect is expected to control the other members of the design team, without having any contractual influence or authority over them.

Before discussing the failings of this system, it is useful to record its benefits.

1. The system has been used in its present form for several decades, and is well understood in the UK and in those countries which have adopted UK practice.

2. If the design has been properly completed prior to billing, the client should have a high level of confidence in the contract price being the same as the final account. (Although there may be escalation due to price fluctuation, this may be ascribed to a commercial decision of the client to accept the risks of inflation; if the client wishes these risks to be carried by the contractor, it is possible to require the contractor to do this in the invitation to

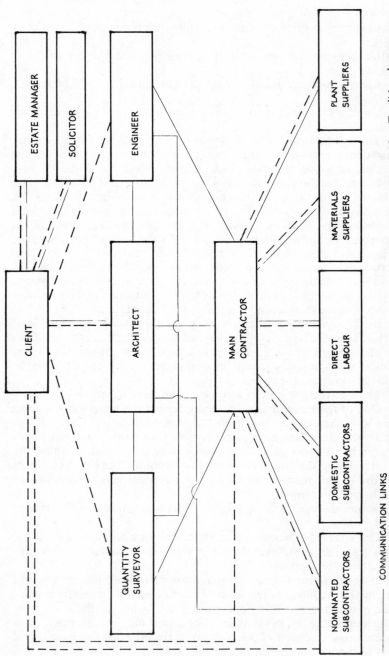

Figure 10. Traditional system.

tender. In this case, the tender price will reflect the contractor's estimate of likely price increases. Unfortunately, few contractors are asked to do this on contracts much over one year, and therefore tenders on a long-term fixed price are likely to overestimate the effects of price rises.)

3. It is possible to introduce as many specialist designers as are necessary into the design operation, and the architect has considerable freedom to use these specialists in the evolution and development of the design; as these appointments will probably be on standard fee scales, there should be sufficient remuneration to the designers to supply an adequate service.

4. The architect is also able to consult specialist installers and component manufacturers at an early stage, in order to ascertain their requirements while developing the design; these may be integrated into the construction process using the nomination procedure. These suppliers and subcontractors may be selected by negotiation or through competition ahead of tenders for the main contract.

5. The drawings and bills of quantities provide a common basis for obtaining and comparing tenders.

6. Should the client require changes during the course of the project, the contract provides for this, and also for a means of valuing such variations by comparison with similar items of work in the bills.

7. The presence of the quantity surveyor should allow a high level of cost planning during the design stages, and monitoring during the construction phase, using the priced bills of quantities.

The main criticisms of the traditional system are as follows.

1. The system has a poor reputation for overall speed, due to the fact that the design and construction systems are 'end-on', with no parallel working. As contractors tender on bills based on fully worked out design, the whole of the design needs to be complete prior to tender. The extra time required for end-on working will have an effect on the cost of the scheme due to the additional interest charges incurred on land cost, fees and interim payments.

2. The use of a number of independent specialist designers with no contractual obligations to one another implies the need for a high level of integrative management. Unless this is supplied by an informed client with a high degree of authority over the project, the onus for management lies with the architect. There is therefore a built-in conflict of responsibility for the architect; the architect is not only expected to be the principal designer, but also to supply the integrative effort needed to make the dispersed members of the team act together effectively. Not only is there difficulty in exercising objective judgement in this situation, but it must be questioned whether there is any basis for management being exercised at all. It has been suggested that the aptitudes and skills

necessary for the two main functions under discussion – design and management – are so different that it would be unreasonable of a client to expect to find them residing in the same individual or organisation, except in outstanding cases. Even if this were held to be an exaggeration, there is little doubt that the development of management and commercial skills is not a priority in the education and training of architects. Should any of the specialist designers be unhappy about the organisation of the project, there is a strong inhibition about bringing this to the notice of the client; not only is the architect seen as the primary link with the client, but the architect's recommendation or patronage may have obtained their commission in the first place, and there will be an understandable reluctance to 'rock the boat'.

3. The ability within the system to involve specialist subcontractors in aspects of the design at an early stage has generated two separate but linked problems. First, there is conflict of interest for the subcontractor. His initial appointment is made through the architect, and it is to the architect that he will look for future work. The primary contractual responsibility is to the main contractor, who may feel unable to exercise sufficient control due to the privileged position of the subcontractor in relation to the architect. Many contractors have been quick to exploit this situation, and to seek extra remuneration and extensions of time based on the failure of nominated subcontractors. The second is the increasing tendency for architects to abdicate from their responsibilities for design by attempting to involve nominated subcontractors on even the most simple and mundane elements, for instance on relatively straightforward electrical and mechanical installations. The result is that the client pays twice for this element of design, once in the architect's fee, based on a percentage of the total cost of the job, and again in the fees charged for the design work by the subcontractor, disguised in this case as part of the subcontractor's overhead charges. There have been a number of explanations offered for this: for example, that practices are now approaching commissions with an increasing commercial stringency (at least as far as their own profitability is concerned); and that they are trying to reduce the increasing burden of design liability and the escalation in professional liability actions. Whatever the cause, the result is an increase in the fragmentation of the process, and a further diffusion of responsibilities, without the concomitant increase in the management input which would be necessary in compensation.

4. The system relies for part of its efficacy on the design being fully developed prior to billing. The capacity of the contract to allow changes during the construction phase was originally intended to allow the client to change his mind (at his cost) without voiding the contract. However, there has been an increasing tendency for the quantity surveyor to be required to commence (and complete)

billing before the design is completed. This involves the quantity surveyor in inspired guesswork in taking-off quantities from incomplete or non-existent drawings, and leads to a situation where the quantity surveyor is *de facto* responsible for much of the specification also. Where this presents problems is when the design detailing is different from the assumptions made in the bills. This then provides an element of disruption to the contractor's planned progress on site, followed by claims for extensions of time and extra payments. As well as causing extra payments to the contractor, the delays incur additional interest charges for the client. If the variation orders on an average job were examined, the vast majority of them would be for changes in design originating with the design team, rather than changes introduced by the client. It is debatable how much of this inefficiency is caused by the organisation of the design, and how much by pressure from clients on the designers for an early start on site, ignoring advice by the design team on the consequences of not allowing sufficient time for design development.

5. The normal practice is for the design team to be appointed on the basis of the standard conditions of engagement issued by their respective professional institutions, and thus on standard fee scales. There is therefore little competition on fees, although a tendency towards it is growing. There is little comprehension on the client's part of what is actually contained in the standard conditions, and there is little in these which actually promotes the level of coordination and management needed in design and construction.

6. The system assumes a complete separation of design and construction phases. This has been recognised and criticised since the Emmerson Report in 1962, but the problem is comprehensively ignored in the traditional method. The problems which stem from this are varied. First, there is the increased difficulty in managing a system where the contractual responsibilities are diffused. Second, there is the operational inefficiency arising from the contractor's being excluded from the design phase, and therefore being unable to aid the development of the design in a form which would recognise the problems of 'buildability'. (It is fair to point out here that many designers are sceptical about the value of the contractor's contribution at the design stage, even though this is one of the major benefits claimed for some of the alternative procurement systems). The third is the exclusion of the designer from the construction phase. Although the architect is responsible for supervising the contractor's performance on site, the standard forms of contract give no discretion to the architect in determining sequence or method of operation. Many architects experience frustration when, after trying to evolve a design which takes account of the operational difficulties on site, the effort is ignored and the project is built in what appears to be an inefficient sequence. (The

contractor's view on the value of the designer's advice probably mirrors that of the architect in respect of the contractor's contribution to design.)

7. It could be argued that the traditional system is totally unsatisfactory for most large and complex projects, where a large range of specialist design input is required, unless special provision is made for injecting into the project the management skills and structures which are conspicuously absent in the traditional format.

The criticisms resolve themselves into three components:

(a) that the system itself is flawed (need for integration, none provided);
(b) that the system is open to abuse (over-use of nominated subcontractors; too many design variations);
(c) that the system has been employed too frequently on projects for which it is not suited.

The remainder of this section is devoted to those systems which have evolved to meet the shortcomings noted above, or which have been designed to offer a more viable alternative.

Variations on the traditional system

In order to remove some of the drawbacks of the traditional system, a number of variants have been introduced.

Two-stage tendering

This system was introduced in the 1960s to try to overcome the total divorce of design from construction. Typically, the design team is set up in the same way as before, and when sufficient design development has been done, a notional bill of quantities is prepared in which the work items are fully described, and approximate quantities attached to them. Selected main contractors are then asked to tender upon this notional bill, and may also be asked for their proposals for the management of the construction operations. These proposals may also include suggested changes to the design detailing or strategy. The successful contractor is then appointed and becomes a full member of the team, under the general direction of the architect, and may give advice to the design team on features of the project which could be altered to give greater speed or economy. Once the design is fully developed, a full bill of quantities is prepared, and priced on the basis of the rates in the notional or approximate bill. Where new items appear which have not already been priced, these are negotiated using comparable rates in the original bill. This produces a price for the project which is incorporated in the contract. The contract is then executed by the contractor under the supervision of the architect as before.

The advantages are:

1. The contractor is able to make technical contributions, including using proprietory construction methods where these are appropriate.

2. The contractor may be involved in the selection of nominated subcontractors, thus avoiding some of the problems associated with the division of loyalty noted above.

3. Where the project is large or complex and the design solution may not be derivable without specialist construction advice, e.g. on a large, congested inner city site, or where substantial preformed components are required, or where there are severe sequence problems.

4. It is possible to make a start on site before all the design work is completed, as the contractor can be involved in the scheduling of design work to suit the accelerated programme.

Disadvantages are:

1. The system still does not allow the contractor an involvement prior to crucial design decisions being made; considerable development may have taken place using the original design strategy, and it may not be possible to alter this without losing time and incurring abortive design fees. The contractor may also feel inhibited in making far-reaching suggestions, due to the need to cooperate with the design team.

2. Many designers are sceptical about the value of the contractor's contribution to the design, and a full appreciation may only come after the event when the contractor is faced with the need to resolve problems on an *ad hoc* basis. Designers may also feel that the contractor's suggestions imply criticisms of their design decisions, and may therefore not cooperate fully.

3. The nature of the tendering process, based on a mixture of bill items, overheads and contractor's proposals, may make comparisons of tenders difficult, as like is not being compared with like, e.g. one contractor may have based his proposals on using pumping for concrete placement, while another may wish to use a number of tower cranes.

The system is an advance on the traditional system in bringing a higher level of integration into a fragmented process. It also benefits by exposing the design team to the management skills of the contractor, and may tend to give some management stimulus to the process of design, even though the contractor is in a subordinate role. The scepticism and possible resentment of the design team may require a strong involvement by the client's coordinator to reap the full benefits available, although this is unlikely to prove a problem in those cases where early selection of the contractor is made on the advice of the architect.

Continuity contracts

These have been evolved to avoid the necessity for repeated tendering where a client has a programme of work; resources may be used more economically where continuity is available, producing a programmable flow of work for the contractor, and savings in cost and time for the client. In most cases, the traditional split between design and construction responsibility is maintained. Continuity contracts may be classified under three main headings.

1.   *Ad hoc continuity contracts*

Where a client has one contract under way on site, and is satisfied with performance, and a further similar contract is envisaged, the contract bills may, by agreement between client and contractor, be used to negotiate the second contract. In these circumstances, the contractor will have priced the original contract on the basis that it is a one-off, and he is under no obligation to negotiate on the basis of the original. When agreement has been reached, the second job may be established as a separate contract (or possibly as a variation to the original contract).

2.   *Term contracts*

In these, the contractor is appointed to carry out all of the work allocated to him over a fixed period, often 12 or 24 months. The contractor's price for each job is based on a master document, usually a schedule of rates comprising descriptions of all typical operations. When a particular job is identified by the client, a specific order is placed for it, and the contractor invoices at regular intervals. Term contracts are frequently used for repair and maintenance works, usually of low individual value.

3.   *Serial contracts*

These are often used where a client intends to construct a number of buildings of similar types, and wishes to obtain economies of scale and savings in the overall time by omitting repeated tendering. The approximate number of projects is stated in the master bill, and the serial tender is in effect a standing offer to carry out a number of projects on the basis of the tender documents. It is important here for the tender documents to be as accurate as possible, as any error will be repeated several times. The designs for all of the projects will not be finalised at the time of tender, but the design team must be at an advanced enough stage to allow confidence in the accuracy of the tender document. As soon as the design work on a particular scheme is finalised, this may be translated into a firm tender for that scheme, and a separate contract signed.

Advantages of continuity contracts:

1. Early selection of the contractor and collaboration through a number of jobs should produce a better working relationship, and a useful level of construction input.

2. Early information on the costs of designs should allow more reliable cost planning across the series.

3. Contractors' costs are reduced, through economies of scale and the opportunity to plan a workload, and the client can expect to benefit through lower prices.

4. Time savings may be made in the production of information for individual contracts.

5. The client gains a measure of protection against volatility in the market, but must accept the risk of market conditions turning against him during the course of the contracts. Similarly, the client must accept whatever predictions the winning tenderer has incorporated in his tender about market conditions.

Disadvantages of continuity contracts:

1. If the market for building work declines during the contract, the client may pay more than if the contract had been tendered separately.

2. A delay or poor performance by the contractor on one project may have a knock-on effect on successive projects.

3. A mistake in the master document will be magnified by the number of projects.

4. If proprietary methods are employed in the design specification, a contractor may find himself in a monopoly position, due to his increased knowledge not being available to other contractors, and may be able to dictate terms on future contracts.

5. Great care must be taken in the selection of the contractor as an error will be reflected in poor performance on a large number of projects. Ideally the contractor should be selected on capacity to perform (assessed by interview, examination of resources, inspection of previous work, and by references) as well as on price.

6. The client needs to be absolutely certain that he can predict accurately the number of projects to be carried out, otherwise there may be claims for loss of profit. This cannot be effectively avoided merely by writing the tender documents so that only a loose indication is made of the size of the batch of projects overall; if this is done the contractor's price will reflect the lower degree of commitment, and his inability to plan with confidence.

Continuity contracts have found their greatest use on public sector contracts, for repair and maintenance work, school building, and similar applications where a high volume of repeat business can be assured. Few private sector clients have been able to make effective use of these methods, except in some maintenance situations.

Use of multi-discipline design practices

Although not a procurement system in its own right, the use of a multi-discipline design practice may serve to remove some of the difficulties in integration using the traditional system. The typical multi-discipline practice will embrace all of the primary disciplines in construction – architecture, engineering, quantity surveying – plus either in-house experts in some of the less often used professions, e.g. landscape architecture, acoustical engineering, or ready access to these disciplines in other practices. The fact that one organisation may be appointed to carry out the whole of the design operation should imply a greater facility for efficient coordination of the design work; communication lines should be shorter, and a single source of responsibility for design can be identified. In reality, the success of such an approach will depend on the organisation structure within the practice. If the practice is organised merely on the lines of discipline specialism, without any effective cross-disciplinary management, then the benefits will be slight, as the design leader will still be acting also as the coordinator for design. However, some multi-disciplinary practices are now clearly structured internally to avoid this problem, with specialist staff in e.g. job programming and coordination being appointed as in-house 'project managers' to ensure that the teams set up for each project are able to operate effectively. Two drawbacks may exist in using such practices; first, that few practices could reasonably claim to be equally skilful in every aspect of their service, although this may be compensated for in practice by the increased efficiency of a team which is experienced in working together for the same company objectives; and second, that some of these practices are large, and clients may feel distanced from the principals in the practice, when compared to contact with conventional, smaller practices. The use of such organisations is unlikely to improve integration with the client body, or with the construction phase (except perhaps where the practice also offers an all-in project management service to control each aspect of the scheme). Nor should it be assumed that these practices need be restricted to acting in relation to the traditional procurement system. They have been touched on here as a method of removing some of the inconsistencies of the traditional system, but could operate equally effectively in other procurement systems.

Cost reimbursement systems

In considering the following range of alternative procurement arrangements the generic title 'cost reimbursement' is used to differentiate them from the traditional system, which has been described as 'lump sum fixed price'. This differentiation is a useful shorthand description, but neither title is totally accurate. We have already seen that the traditional system may be neither lump sum nor fixed in price by the time the final account is prepared, due to the effect of variations and fluctuations. Neither is it correct to assume that the tender represents a fixed price; in practice the tender will comprise preliminary items, unit rates, PC and provisional sums and profit margins, and within this list those items listed as PC and provisional sums will be finalised at the discretion of the architect, and the cost of these will be reimbursed to the contractor, with a percentage addition for overheads and profit. Therefore in reality, the contracts placed under the traditional system will represent a mixture of fixed price and cost reimbursable items.

One other frustration for anyone seeking to establish any classification of systems in construction is that there are huge semantic problems stemming from an inconsistent use of terminology; in the context of this section, the reader should beware of the use of loose descriptions to represent discrete and different forms of organisation, procurement, tendering and contractual methods. In spite of the inaccuracies noted above, the grouping of the following systems under the heading of cost reimbursement serves to indicate a common difference from traditional contracts, in that in the traditional system, the contractor tenders to execute the works at a price fixed in advance and accepts the risk of poor estimating. In cost reimbursement, the client agrees to pay the net cost of the work to the contractor, and here the *client* accepts the risk of the initial estimates being exceeded, but benefits if the final account is lower than the estimate. In addition to the net cost, the contractor is paid a fee to cover overheads and profit; the means of calculating the fee will depend on the variant in use.

The method of remuneration highlights one of the main reasons for a client being willing to use these methods; the fee payment is divorced from and removes the need for the contractor to make profit on the work items executed. The basis of appointment is assimilated to that of the other professionals, and the contractor is expected to perform as a professional construction manager in cooperation with the other members of the team, thus removing one of the barriers to integration and management of the design and construction continuum.

One additional problem in analysing these alternative systems, which is related to (or possibly a cause of) the semantic problem is that there are no industry-wide standard forms of contract; each company and probably each contract will be run on its own unique variant of the system. A strong case could be made for *not* providing standard forms: even though they might introduce a greater common understanding, it is likely that the ability of the industry to offer a flexible response to needs would diminish, as evidenced by criticisms of the JCT standard forms.

1. 'Cost plus' contract

This is the simplest version of the cost reimbursement contract, and might be used where the works are very unusual or experimental, or are required as an emergency service, the usual characteristic being that the works cannot be determined accurately in advance. The contractor is paid his costs for labour, materials and plant, with a fee to cover overheads and profit, either as a percentage of the total net cost, or as a lump sum. There is little incentive for the contractor to be efficient except perhaps where the fee is a lump sum; here any increase in cost will lead to a reduction in *percentage* profit margin. This system cannot be recommended unless the job is so urgent and unique that no other method can be found; except in such extreme situations it is difficult to see how the benefit could outweigh the risk to the client.

2. *Fee contracting*

Fee contracting systems originated around fifty years ago, and the most prominent promoter so far has been Bovis Construction. Fee contracting should be carefully differentiated from the simpler cost plus method; although both are forms of cost reimbursement, the difference lies in the degree of sophistication of the reimbursement method and in the level of protection which may be achieved for the client.

In the fee system, there is also a difference in the level of management expertise which is distributed across the design and construction system. There is a shift, too, in the balance of authority and in the interrelationship of authority which is NOT necessarily reflected in the conditions of appointment of either the designers or the contractor.

The system operates thus: The client's architect is appointed and briefed in the traditional manner, and such additional consultants as are necessary are appointed. The design team under the architect's direction prepares scheme designs in the usual way, and at around this point the contractor may be appointed. This initial appointment is made either through negotiation with one contractor, or on the basis of competition. In the latter case, the appointment normally follows a presentation by pre-selected companies, who will offer their proposals for method of construction, programme, expected constraints, suggestions for modification of design, cost control mechanism, reporting and fees. The fee proposals will include the required percentage fee, with details of which site and/or head office costs are to be included in the fee, and which are to be reimbursed as part of the prime cost of the contract. Once appointed, the contractor and the client's quantity surveyor will agree on the estimated prime cost (EPC) for the project. (In some variants, this may be done as part of a negotiation prior to a firm appointment.) The client, architect, quantity surveyor and contractor will agree on the EPC and programme, and the latter will usually contain details of the contractor's requirements for the supply of information. The design team will produce working drawings as usual, and it is possible for construction to start as soon as the first drawings are available. The design, as it is developed and produced in working drawing form, is checked against the budget to ensure that the EPC is adhered to. Where design decisions imply adjustment to the EPC, this is communicated to the client and an adjusted EPC agreed between contractor and quantity surveyor. In parallel with the design development a means of financial control must be devised. This may be a conventional bill of quantities, priced by agreement between contractor and quantity surveyor, or some simpler format. The pricing of such a document is regarded as a means of budgeting, and not as a set of firm prices. While the contract is on site, the contractor organises and carries out the works under the direction of the architect, using an agreed combination of direct and subcontract labour. Where the architect wishes to use nominated subcontractors, these will be selected and appointed by agreement.

During the course of the works, the contractor will be paid his net costs of materials, labour, plant, subcontract costs and such site overheads as have been agreed as lying outside the scope of the fee, together with a proportion of the fee pro rata to the value of the work executed to date. This may be subject to an agreed retention. In order to ensure that the contractor's claim for reimbursement is fair, the quantity surveyor has access to the contractor's books and records for the project. Should there be a justifiable escalation or reduction of costs during the course of the contract, the EPC will be adjusted accordingly, during and at the end of the contract. The final fee payable to the contractor will be the agreed percentage of the final adjusted EPC, *not* the final cost.

Where the final costs are less than the final EPC, the client reimburses only the final cost, but the fee percentage is based on the EPC; where the final cost exceeds the EPC, the client still pays the costs, but the fee remains based on the EPC. In the latter case, the contractor's profit margin decreases as a percentage of turnover, although the monetary value is unchanged. The contract may contain safeguards against the contractor being inefficient or profligate with labour or other resources, and usually allows the possibility of deduction of liquidated and ascertained damages after certification by the architect.

Advantages of fee contracting:

1. The contractor is involved at an early stage and can advise on the speed and cost implications of design decisions.
2. Parallel working on design and construction can reduce overall time, and thus reduce the client's interest costs.

3. The period required for the preparation of tender information may be reduced considerably or eliminated.

4. The system contains a high capacity for allowing change without the financial penalties involved in fixed price contracts.

5. There is the capacity for the client to make informed choices on the costs of different speeds, either at the start or during the currency of the project on site.

6. Although the contractor is not overtly employed to manage the design process, his involvement at an early stage places demands on the design team to produce information to accord with the overall programme which has been agreed between the contractor, client and designer. In effect, the interface between design and construction gains an integrative input.

Disadvantages of fee contracting:

1. The quality of the design may suffer if pressure is applied to obtain what may be an unrealistically early start, as time for design development may be limited.

2. Where the contractor is appointed on a fee basis contrary to the advice of the designer, ensuing resentment may lead to a breakdown of the integrative effort implied by the system.

3. Where the fee contractor is selected by tender, it is difficult to compare like with like, as the tenders will be on the basis of different methods.

4. The client will not know the final cost until the building is complete, and final invoices collected. This can lead to serious difficulties for clients for whom public accountability is important.

5. In a period of escalating costs, the client may pay more for the cost increases than under the fluctuations provision of the standard forms of contract.

6. Where the contractor is inefficient in carrying out the works, it may be difficult for the client to withhold payment for this amount due to the problems in quantifying the liability.

3. *Management contracting*

The first 'pure' management contract to be carried out in the UK was completed in 1972, and the system has been regarded by the contractor, Bovis, as a natural extension of its fee contracting system. Prior to its adoption in the UK, management contracting had been used in a similar form in the USA since the 1940s, and still is in that country. Although the evolution from fee contracting means that in many respects the operating system and its parameters are similar, there are some essential differences.

Perhaps the most fundamental difference is that in management contracting, the contractor does not carry out the construction work directly; while fee contracts may be executed using a mixture of direct and subcontract labour, the essence of the management contract is that the work is carried out by a series of subcontractors, and the expertise of the management contractor is employed in defining the subcontract packages, in ensuring that there are no gaps in responsibility between them, and that the programme requirements for production information from the design team are met, and in selecting, appointing and controlling the subcontractors on site. The appointment process for management contracting is identical to that for fee contracting, as is the preparation of an EPC and detailed precontract programme. The fee is usually a percentage of the EPC as before, with explicit agreement on the site and head office overhead costs to be borne by the client as a prime cost, and those to be reimbursed within the agreed fee percentage. During the precontract stage, the contractor will provide advice on the comparative viability of design solutions, and will establish an overall management system for the project. In parallel, work will proceed on defining the work packages, and early discussions held with those likely to be appointed for the most critical subcontracts. For most of the packages, the subcontractors will be appointed by competitive tendering, using traditional methods, e.g. on drawings and bills of quantities. The appointments will be made by agreement with the design team. The contractor is responsible for monitoring, controlling and paying the subcontractors.

Cost monitoring and control during the construction phase are on a similar basis to that obtaining in fee contracting, with the EPC being adjusted as necessary. There are great attractions to contractors in becoming involved in management contracting; due to the method of remuneration, the risks involved are much lower than for traditional contracts, both in terms of a guaranteed return of costs (assuming the client stays solvent!) and in the reduction of the risks associated with the employment of direct labour. As a result most large and medium/large firms now offer a management contracting service; although only a minority of contracts are procured on this basis, it is predicted that there is considerable capacity for growth is predicted in this area.

As in fee contracting, the contractor's involvement during the design stages encourages a greater integrative effort, which is taken further than in fee contracting; in employing the management contracting system, the client is making a clear statement that he expects the contractor to take the lead in the overall management of the process, and even though the contractor may not have a contractual responsibility to control the design team, there is little doubt that this is the end result. (Some variations *do* also provide for the contractor to assume responsibility for design management.) It could be argued that in fee contracting the contractor's influence on the design stages is less overt, and probably less effective.

In essence therefore, the management contractor is engaged to supply professional construction management skills, and has no direct involvement in *physically* executing the works; the contractor is expected to work alongside the other professionals, with equal professional status. In both fee and management contracting as described above, the risk of cost exceeding the estimate is carried mainly by the client (with only a small risk to the contractor in deductions for inefficiency, percentage profit margins reduction, and LAD). In both these systems, and in others noted later, it is possible for the client to pass at least some of the risk back to the contractor. This can be achieved by setting a target cost, and sharing increases or savings between client and contractor in a pre-determined proportion. Where this is done, the system is sometimes referred to as a *target cost contract*.

The target may be set for the EPC as a whole, or for selected elements which the client sees as the risk areas to be reduced. The philosophy behind the system is that where the final cost exceeds the estimate, it is probable that at least part of the increase is due to inefficiency on the contractor's part; conversely, where the final cost is below the estimate, at least part of the saving will be produced by the contractor's efficiency. It is logical therefore that the client and contractor should share the risks. The risk shares may be in any pre-agreed proportion, and the cost target may be agreed between the contractor and the client's quantity surveyor, or may be stated in the tender documents if competition is desired.

While the system may offer an element of incentive to efficiency, there are drawbacks. First, the contractor has a greater vested interest in the financial outcome, as his profit is affected, and it may be difficult to provide impartial professional advice while having a financial interest in the result. Second, the need for accurate measurement of cost against target involves the production of a detailed financial control system, usually a full bill of quantities; this need may negate the savings in time which could be achieved if less detailed control were employed. It also extends the period needed prior to contractor selection. Finally, because of the extra element of risk, the contractor's profit requirement will be increased in proportion to the extra risk introduced.

A variation on this system known as the 'value cost system' was used for around sixty years by the LCC and GLC for housing contracts in London. In this, the contractor was paid 3% of the final valuation, augmented or reduced depending on the extent by which the final valuation was over or under the target. In extreme cases, this could lead to the final fee being a negative amount, where the contractor had to refund money to the council.

Separate trades systems

This generic term may be used to describe systems which are similar in form to managing contracting, but in which the subcontracts are placed directly with the client, and are organised and managed as a professional service. This is not a new concept in the UK, being common in Scotland and the north-west of England during the first half of this century.

The two main versions are distinguished by whether the management function is carried out by the contractor (construction management) or by the principal designer (alternative method of management (AMM)).

Construction management

This is yet another term which suffers from being used by different people to refer to different types of service. In the current context, the term is used as in the Building EDC publication 'Thinking about Building', to describe a management service provided by a fee-based contractor, with the trade subcontracts placed directly with the client. This should be differentiated from the American usage, where construction management is a 'process by which the owner engages an agent to coordinate and communicate the entire project process, including project feasibility, design, planning, letting, construction, and project implementation, with the objective of minimising the project time and cost, and maintaining the project quality' (J. A. Adrian, *Building Construction Handbook*, Renton Publishing Company Inc.). The American usage approximates more closely to the system of project management in use in the UK, considered in the next chapter.

As defined by the Building EDC, construction management may be considered a further refinement of management contracting, in which the client assumes a greater share of the risks by having direct contracts with the subcontractors. The construction management company supplies only a professional management service, and is totally disconnected from the physical performance of construction operations. The company contracts with the client to give a clear management lead to the design and construction operations, and is paid a percentage of the construction cost. It is possible for either the client or the contractor to accept the cost and time risks, and the fee will reflect the level of risk and service to be provided.

At this level of professional involvement, the integration between client, designer and construction operations should be high; effectively, the construction manager is operating as a 'professional client' and even where the manager is not carrying the time and cost risks, he acts as a single source of authority over the project, subject only to client veto.

One of the problems in examining procurement options offered as alternatives to the traditional model is that there are no industry-wide standard forms of agreement. Although this makes it difficult to make authoritative statements on the extent of the services provided, it does mean that the procurement system may be tailored to suit the needs of the client.

Alternative method of management (AMM)

In this system the client contracts directly with the subcontractors who execute the work, but in contrast to construction management, there is no involvement of a general contractor. Instead, the management function is undertaken by the architect, who coordinates not only his own and other specialists' design work, but in conjunction with the quantity surveyor selects the subcontractors and coordinates their activities. The work on site is directly supervised by the site architect/manager, who effectively replaces the site agent in the traditional process.

The process begins with briefing and appointment of a design team in the conventional way, and the scheme designs are prepared and approved. The design is then developed to the point where there is sufficient production information for work to begin. In conjunction with the quantity surveyor, tenders are sought for the first subcontractors, either by negotiation or by competition, and the elements of production information required later are developed while site work progresses. There may be a need for the appointment of a general builder to provide some central services on site – unloading, making good, clearance, etc.

This system aims to tackle the problem of design and construction fragmentation in a different manner from construction management or management contracting. In the latter, the integration is achieved by the application of more management to the process; in the AMM, the integration is achieved by reducing the number of participants through the removal of the main contractor. Specific construction expertise is not employed, and the architect is expected to supply this. It is claimed that any lack of relevant experience can be compensated for through the shortened lines of communication between designer and tradesman/trades foreman. The presence on the site at all times of the job architect and his or her daily contact with the workforce should certainly reduce the number of mistakes made in communicating the design intention, and it is easy to see how such daily contact with production should sharpen the designers' skills in producing 'buildable' design. Nevertheless, it cannot be denied that there will still be a conflict of operating objectives, with the management of design and the operational design being undertaken by the same person or organisation (as noted in criticism of the traditional process). Advantages centre on the higher degree of coordination made possible by reducing the number of participants, and on the ability to have design and construction working in parallel. This should reduce overall time and therefore reduce the client's interest costs, while the higher level of direct supervision should reduce the incidence of substandard work.

The disadvantages are that the client's commitment is open-ended on cost and time (unless a target cost is introduced); the client's involvement with the project must be greater, in order to retain some independent control; the client must also have a high degree of confidence in the architect/manager, and given the normally low level of education and experience in management of most architects, this must limit the number of such contracts which can be undertaken with credibility. In addition, the responsibility for any failures in performance in terms of time, cost, design or supervision may be difficult to determine (although this criticism has also been levelled at the traditional system, at fee and management contracting, and at construction management).

Single source responsibility systems

In the systems described so far as alternatives to the traditional method, an attempt has been made to introduce a greater level of integration into a fragmented process, either through supplying an additional management input, or, in the case of the AMM, by making a reduction in the number of participants to be managed. The next category of systems examined also attempts to reduce fragmentation by reducing the number of participants, but in a more fundamental manner. As before, there are sufficient areas of similarity in these systems for them to be confused, and the confusion is understandable when the differences may well lie in the detail of individual contracts, rather than in the fundamentals.

Design and build

There have been a number of names used for systems in which all or part of the design is the responsibility of the contractor, e.g. 'design and construct', 'develop and construct'; for our purposes these variations are ignored in favour of the generic name.

In attempting to differentiate 'design and build' from the other systems offering a single source responsibility, it is assumed that such an arrangement occurs when the contractor is able to offer a service to design and build any type of building. Design and build is not new; prior to the nineteenth century it was common for 'architects' to offer to design and construct buildings, and also for master craftsmen to offer the same service. In the USA the provision of design and build is also common, by both contractors and architects.

The system commences with the client either identifying a need for a building, and deciding on the basis of his own expertise to approach a design and build company, or first seeking advice to clarify the nature of those needs.

Assuming that the client is able to make a reasonable assessment of need and thus be in a position to provide a brief, the selection may be through negotiation with one firm, or by competition. Where competition is desired, it is necessary to provide details of spatial and layout requirements, and if possible develop these to scheme design stage, preferably with the foundation and site layout also established. A performance specification is also needed. Using this information, each of the tenderers will submit their proposals for satisfying the brief, the contract period required, and an analysis of the contract sum in sufficient detail for the client to be able to ascertain the costs of any changes which might be made. Where the client wishes to stipulate the contract period and maximum contract sum, the competition will be on the design proposals only. It is possible to introduce further sophistication into the system, with the tenders being initially only for the design development, following which the accepted and developed design may be the subject of further contract. Once the client has decided to accept a tender, the successful firm then goes on to develop the design and construct the building.

It is more likely however that the client will require advice on how to draw up a brief, and it is preferable for this information to be supplied by an experienced construction professional. This service may cease on the provision of tender information, or may extend to cover advice on the selection of the successful bidder, or further to give a watching brief on the project until completion, including advice on standards being achieved, pricing of variations, and handover.

In order to avoid the criticism that a contractor-led design and build service is likely to be biased towards construction efficiency rather than design quality, a variant has been developed in which the client appoints a designer, usually an architect, to provide the scheme design and performance specification, and the design build company is expected to translate this scheme design into built form. The initial designer may drop out after providing the outline design, or may be retained to 'police' the contractor's interpretation as the design is developed and built. A standard model for design build contracts has been produced by the Joint Contracts Tribunal in the form of the 'Standard Form of Building Contract with Contractor's Design' (1981). This form contains provision for the consultant appointed by the client to act as the employer's agent, but with fewer powers of instruction and control than the supervising officer in the 'traditional' forms of contract.

Advantages of design and build:
1. The system offers greater scope for integration of the design and

construction phases, as the design development and construction are carried out by the same organisation, leading to an overall reduction in time, and subsequent saving in client's interest costs.
2. The client is offered a single source of responsibility for the project, which shortens lines of communication and allows easy identification of responsibility for failure.
3. Parallel working on design and construction is facilitated, as this may be planned and integrated within one organisation.
4. The client is offered greater security for his financial commitment, at an early stage. The only changes in the scheme for which the client is responsible are those introduced by the client. Any design changes arising through design errors or omissions are the responsibility of the contractor. This in its turn should allow faster construction through less disruption to the building work.
5. Although the costs of design are built into the package, the higher integration should lead to less detailed production information being required, and the design cost element will be lower than for a system based on the employment of independent designers.
6. Competition offers the chance of obtaining economic pricing, and alternative designs.
7. A relaxation in the code of practice for architects now allows them to be principals in construction organisations, and this may allow architects to assume more senior positions in design and build companies, with a concomitant increase in the priority given by those organisations to design quality. A complementary advantage is that designers working in this environment will be working closely with those responsible for construction, and the designers' appreciation of construction methods and problems will increase, leading to more 'buildable' and economical design.
   Disadvantages:
1. In spite of the changes referred to in 7. above, the majority of design and build organisations in the UK have a construction background, and their work has had an orientation towards construction, rather than design. As a result, it has not been noteworthy for design quality. For clients to whom good architectural design is a priority, there may be difficulty in selecting an organisation in which the design is not sub-optimised in favour of construction.
2. Although the design and construction should be well integrated, there is still a difficulty in the interface between client and contractor. Where the client is inexperienced in building, professional advice is essential. While this may ease the problems in communication, it raises in its turn the need for yet another party to be integrated into the system, with a need for a clear definition of the professional's authority limits and communication lines.
3. Variations in design and construction methods make tender comparisons more difficult.

4. It may be difficult to identify design elements in tenders which could cause future maintenance problems, due to the limited design information available with the tender.

5. Savings in design costs may be offset by the need to employ additional professional expertise to prepare the briefing document and tender information, and to police the design development and work on site.

6. The design and build company is not an independent advisor to the client, and the company's aims will not be the same as the client's.

Package deal

In many cases the terms 'design and build' and 'package deal' are used interchangeably, and it is true that in some cases it may be difficult to distinguish between the two services. The term package deal simply implies that the contractor supplies everything that the client may need to provide a building. Package deals are unlikely to be used for all types of building, and the service is concentrated upon clients requiring 'simple' buildings, often involving a proprietary system with a high level of standardisation and prefabrication. These elements of simplicity and standardisation are the main points which distinguish the package deal from design and build, the latter usually implying a higher 'bespoke' content. Package deals tend to be marketed directly to the potential clients rather than through consultant firms, and tend to appeal to those clients desiring fast and economic building provision, without design 'frills'. The dealer may also undertake to find a suitable site, e.g. to maximise the use of investment grants, and frequently concentrates his business on new development areas for this reason. The acquisition of planning and building control consents will often form part of the service, which may also extend to finding and arranging finance for the project.

The system operates in this way. A client with a building need approaches one or more package dealers and obtains their proposals on building form, cost, time, and, where appropriate, finance. Further negotiations with one or more will then take place to enable the client to make a judgement on the technical and financial qualities of the proposals, prior to selecting the favoured company. After entering into a contract, the package dealer completes the design work and constructs the building. Payment may be by stages or by lump sum, or a combination of both. There is no 'standard' for this kind of service.

Advantages:

1. Many of the advantages noted for design and build are applicable, particularly those which centre on a higher level of integration, and a single source of responsibility.

2. The client may obtain an even more comprehensive service with package deals, e.g. in site finding, financing.

3. The use of proprietary building forms reduces design and construction time, and hence lowers the client's interest charges and allows the building to be used sooner.

4. Examples of previously completed buildings may be seen; the inexperienced client does not need to struggle to visualise the building from drawings. Where the system has already been used, there should be an assurance that the problems associated with prototypes have been eliminated.

5. Prefabricated components may be instantly available, thus reducing construction time and allowing a fast start.

6. The total cost of procuring the building is finalised at an early stage.

7. The design cost component is much lower than for bespoke building.

8. Mass production of components allows the client to benefit from economies of scale.

Disadvantages:

1. In spite of 4. above, there have been failures amongst proprietary building methods.

2. It may be difficult for the client to vary the design, either at an early stage or while the project is in progress, due to the level of standardisation; even where variations are technically possible, there may be penal charges levied for them. (It could be argued here that this is actually an advantage, as it encourages the client to ensure that his requirements are properly thought out at the start.)

3. Package deal buildings are not noted for their aesthetic qualities, and the range of designs available is limited.

4. If the client wishes to gain an independent technical assessment of the package deal proposals, or obtain assurance that the specification is being adhered to on site, he will need to appoint an advisor for this purpose, incurring additional cost and complicating the lines of communication.

The turnkey system

The term 'turnkey' has found greater use in the USA and in the Middle East than in the UK, and there may be little difference in practice between the turnkey approach and some examples of design and build or package deals. The essence of the system lies in the name; the implication is that all the client has to do in procuring buildings this way is to commission the project, pay the bills and turn the key in the door of the project at the end.

What *does* distinguish the turnkey system is the deliberate attempt by some contractors to offer the fullest possible service, excluding the need for the client to deal with any party other than the turnkey contractor. As well as land acquisition, feasibility, design and construction, the deal may include short-term and permanent finance, commissioning, letting, sale or leaseback, plus recruiting and training the staff who will operate the fully completed and equipped building. The extent of the contractor's influence over the project means that the choice of contractor is critical, as the client may have only a limited discretion over changes once the system has commenced operation. The principal advantages over the other methods are the concentration of control over the project, and the high degree of coordination and control which may be exercised by making all aspects of the project the responsibility of one party.

The BPF system

Towards the end of 1983, the British Property Federation, an organisation set up to represent the interests of private sector property owning and development companies, presented their proposals for a radically new method of procuring buildings – the 'British Property Federation System for building design and construction'. The need for the new system was derived from criticism of the traditional system noted earlier, i.e. separation of design and construction, an outdated contract system, lack of consideration of construction problems by designers, separation of client from contractor, inadequate briefing by clients, split responsibility in the event of failure, general slowness and poor value for money. The system was designed by a working party of the BPF, without consultation with the industry, as it was thought that any consultation would lead to dilution of effort and delays. The result is a 99 page manual containing one of the most carefully thought out new processes seen by the industry in modern times. Whether the system will be adopted by a significant number of clients, or whether history will judge the scheme merely as a symptom of malaise in the industry remains to be seen.

The new system has been designed to change attitudes and to alter the relationships between the professions and contractors, so that each has the motivation to manage his own affairs efficiently and with vigour, and to cooperate with others. The system also attempts to remove overlaps in the services provided, particularly between architects, quantity surveyors and contractors, and to redefine the risks undertaken by each party, so that the commercial success of each more accurately depends on his own efficiency, rather than the ability to blame others. A further deficiency identified is the lack of awareness of real costs on the part of all concerned. The overall intention of the system is to produce good buildings more quickly and at lower cost.

Although the manual is a detailed description of the process, roles, and responsibilities inherent in the system, the authors have taken pains to point out that the object has been to create a framework which can be flexible, and may be tailored to suit individual projects; slavish adherence to a predetermined, rigid procedure is to be avoided. The main features of the system are:

1. The separation of the main components into clearly identified roles; a *client's representative* is made responsible for the overall management of the project – this may be a project manager, architect, surveyor or engineer, or an employee of the client organisation. Some of these responsibilities may be carried by the *design leader*, the person or organisation responsible for the pre-tender design and for sanctioning the part of the design undertaken by the *contractor*, who in turn is responsible for post-tender design and carrying out the construction. Post-contract supervision is carried out by the *supervisor*, a person or firm appointed to ensure that the drawings and specification are adhered to. The supervision functions may be undertaken in total or in part by the design leader, with his terms of appointment modified to include this service.

2. There is no place in the BPF system for the independent quantity surveyor, as the use of bills of quantities is considered to cause over-detailing and unnecessary work by designers and contractors, with the bill actually dictating the volume and detail of the design. Cost targeting and control is the duty of the client's representative and the design leader, the latter being free to employ (at his own cost) additional consultants if he feels it necessary. Any taking-off which is required for tender preparation is left to the contractor, whose tender breakdown takes the form of a *schedule of activities*, related to the *priced programme*, priced by the contractor in as much detail as he considers necessary, and on which stage payments are based (but only for stages which are fully completed).

3. The separation of tasks into clearly defined roles means that there is a clear but *planned* level of fragmentation in the process; this is overt and recognised, with provision being made for the increased integration necessary through the appointment of the client's representative, who assumes the responsibility for the elements of scheme management carried by the architect in the traditional process.

The operation of the system is as follows:

1. *Concept*

The client with a need to build examines the alternative courses of action possible and establishes whether building is the most viable alternative. A client's representative is appointed to assist in establishing the brief and the cost plan for the project.

2. *Preparation of the brief*

The design leader is selected, and appointed for this stage only, on the basis of a lump sum fee and a design programme; the brief is further developed by the client's representative with the assistance of the design leader, ending with a complete statement of the client's requirements for the project, and the time and cost constraints, in sufficient detail to allow development of the architectural design, and to make application for planning permission. The design leader is required to confirm that it is possible to build the building within the brief, and time and cost restraints. During this stage, the client's representative should advise on how much of the design work is to be done by the design leader, and how much by the contractor. Anything not designed by the design leader will be designed by the contractor. At the end of stage 2, the client's representative will have established the primary control documents for the project, i.e. a master programme and master cost plan.

3. *Design development*

At the beginning of this stage, the design leader quotes for the work to be carried out by him for this and the remaining stages, and is appointed on a lump sum fee for each stage. (This should include design work to be carried out by other consultants which the design leader wishes to appoint at his own expense, although the system can cater for a client wishing to retain the right to appoint and pay separately for other specialist designers.) An extra fee may be paid as a bonus for satisfactory completion of the design leader's work. The design leader's fee is incorporated in a priced design programme covering stages 3 and 4, payable monthly as stages are completed. The main task in this stage is the translation of the brief into drawings and specifications. The master programme and cost plan may be updated as the design is developed, but the design leader has no mandate to alter either the time or the cost parameters without a specific instruction from the client's representative.

4. *Tender documentation and tendering*

After planning permission is obtained, the design leader produces tender documents, i.e. clear, unambiguous and comprehensive drawings and specifications. As anything not designed by the design leader (and his co-designers) must be designed by the contractor, it is essential that the tender documents clearly designate those elements to be designed by the contractor, and the performance limits applied to those design elements.

Each tenderer supplies a priced schedule of activities *with* the tender; this will include a programme, and the construction methods to be used. The system recommends that tenders be on a fixed price for contracts up to two years, with only a single index used to calculate fluctuations for periods over two years. If the lowest tender is within the cost limit, or over by an acceptably low margin, the designer may receive his bonus; if not, he may be required to redesign at his own cost. After selecting a winning contractor, but before signing a contract, the contractor may be required to supply a more detailed schedule of activities, on which stage payments may be based.

5. *Construction*

The function of the design leader during this period is to be limited to sanctioning the elements designed by the contractor as complying with the specification, and to assess variations. The management of this phase is carried out by the client's representative. The client may appoint a supervisor to check whether the contractor is constructing as designed and specified. It is vital here that the demarcation of responsibility between design leader, client's representative and supervisor is clearly recorded and understood. The contractor is responsible for carrying out the works, and for providing and coordinating whatever working drawings are required, including obtaining statutory consents for the works designed by him. Stage payments to the contractor are for the activities in his schedule, but payment is only made when the stage is fully complete. In the case of disputes during the construction phase, these are to be resolved by *immediately* referring them to an independent *adjudicator*. The manual to the BPF system lays down these procedures in great detail, and includes check lists for activities, and model pro-formas for payments, fluctuations, designer selection, schedules, etc. The contract form recommended is a modified Association of Consulting Architects (ACA) form, (which has been subject to criticism for being biased towards the client). Standard forms of appointment for the client's representative and design leaders are to be available shortly.

The system as a whole is a brave attempt by a major client grouping to introduce a procurement system which will meet the needs of its constituents. It is too early to assess whether the system will be adopted widely, or whether resistance by clients, designers and contractors will deny the initiative a chance to develop. Early indications are contradictory; there have been many criticisms levied from designers who feel that their traditional leading role is being eroded, and that competition on fees is likely to reduce the professionalism of their service; from contractors anxious about the extra workload in preparing tenders without the aid of a bill of quantities, and fearful of the extra responsibility of undertaking design work, with its attendant long-term liability. Some of the concern may be well founded; in any completely new and untried system there will be teething problems until the players understand the system, and the inconsistencies are removed; much of the criticism however may be ascribed to the inherent conservatism of the industry, and an unwillingness to change. On the other hand, the increase in the rate of development of alternative procurement systems in the last decade may have improved the climate for the adoption of radical solutions, particularly in the current economic climate, where neither designers nor contractors can afford to be too hesitant to react to initiatives, particularly when these come from clients.

Future developments

Given the increased interest in the last decade in alternative forms of procurement, and an increased willingness on the part of the industry's practitioners to participate in these developments, it is unlikely that the initiatives will dry up in the foreseeable future. It could be argued against this statement that many of the initiatives have appeared as a survival mechanism to allow professionals and contractors to maintain their workload and profitability in a time of recession, that any increase in economic activity will see a return to traditional methods, and that the current ability of clients to insist on their own preferences will disappear. This may be true to some extent, but denies the effect that experience of different methods may have on established attitudes. A safer prognosis might be that the need to demonstrate a flexible response to clients will leave designers and contractors with additional marketing and operational tools at their disposal, and will allow them to be used as the occasion demands. Also, the experience of the industry's clients during the period when they are dominant is likely to have a lasting effect on them; many will be unwilling to revert to traditional practices even if a supply-dominated industry returns.

It is unlikely, in spite of the initiatives noted earlier, that the traditional system will disappear in the immediate future; on the contrary, the inertia in the system, particularly in the public sector, suggests that the traditional model will be used on the majority of projects for a considerable time.

Public accountability

As noted in the consideration of clients, strictures apply to the public sector client which are additional to those on clients in the private sector. This is not to suggest that there are no elements of public accountability faced by the private client; indeed the increasing level of social and fiscal awareness in relation to public (quoted) companies means that these organisations are at increasing pains to ensure that their actions are seen to be responsible. Whether applied to the private or public sector, accountability is often at odds with the most efficient use of money and other resources. The manifestation of accountability most often appears in the guise of the prevention of corruption, and in the need to justify decisions on the basis that they deny the possibility of a corrupt use of funds. There are however other areas of accountability which are of equal importance, and of these probably the most important is obtaining good value for money. Unfortunately, in construction procurement this is a most imprecise quantity, and subject to judgement more on the basis of opinion than of fact.

In the context of the public sector, the predominant requirement is an early definition of the cost to be committed, and an assurance that this sum is the lowest possible. This has tended to result in the use of the traditional model, which appears to offer early and accurate definition of cost, in the form of a tender gained through competition on an equal basis, without the subjective element which could result from comparing contractors' alternative proposals. In spite of experience which suggests that tenders are rarely equal to or higher than the final accounts in traditional contracts, the system offers the advantage that it is familiar even to the lay members of an authority, and has received the seal of approval through precedent.

Any use of an alternative procurement method must not only overcome the resistance stemming from conservatism and inertia, but be capable of satisfying a series of conflicting requirements in the public sector. This is well demonstrated by examination of the conflicts within the public body. Consultants and contractors operating for public bodies usually receive their instructions from officers (i.e. salaried staff) of the authority. They in turn are answerable to their section or directorate heads, who in turn advise and are instructed by elected members. The power of the elected members is constrained by the political acceptability of the proposals, not only within the authority, but in their relations with central government, whose ministers in their turn cannot act too far outside the limits acceptable to parliament. These layers of discretion may apply in general to the derivation of policy to be employed, or may apply in situations where schemes are subject to individual approval. A further inhibiting factor is the increased attention given by the media to decisions which are outwith the normal practice of authorities. Unusual or experimental practices are liable to be reported and commented upon by local (and occasionally national) newspapers, and by the construction press.

It is not surprising that officers responsible for individual schemes are reluctant to suggest alternative methods; not only is there the perceived conflict between accountability and real value, but the

	PROCUREMENT SYSTEM	Client/project parameter						
		Shortest overall time	Lowest overall cost	High level of competition possible	Flexibility	Complex projects	Design quality	Single source responsibility
	Traditional	1	2	4	5	4	5	2
	Traditional – two stage	3	3	4	5	4	4	2
Cost reimbursement	Cost plus	3	0	0	5	1	2	2
	Fee Contracting	4	4	3	5	4	4	3
	Management Contracting	4	4	4	4	5	4	3
Separate contracts	Construction Management	4	4	4	4	5	3	2
	AMM	4	4	4	4	3	4	3
Contractor's design	Design Build	4	5	4	2	2	3	5
	Package Deal	4	5	4	2	1	2	5

The above analysis uses the author's rating of ability to satisfy client/project parameters on scale 0–5 where 0 = no capacity, 5 = good capacity.

(There is insufficient experience of the BPF system as yet to make reasonable judgements and it has been omitted from the table.)

additional obstacle of educating and persuading the layers of authority that alternatives might be more efficient. The persuasion must be accomplished against the certain knowledge that any failure in the 'new' system will be used to full political advantage by the opposition party, and will be subject to considerable publicity. Given the other limitations of fixed annual budgets, design constraints, delays in approval and 'crash' starts to projects, it may be judged by the authority that its manpower resources are better spent in following the traditional model, with all its deficiencies, as efficiently as possible, and actually getting schemes approved and built, rather than spending abortive time attempting to promote more value-efficient methods. This level of suboptimisation in the system would perhaps be acceptable if it was planned and recognised as the most practical option; in many cases however it may be seen as merely a useful way of evading a complex issue.

3.5   THE DESIGN TEAM

Introduction

From any viewpoint, the role of the designer of buildings is probably one of the least understood and most criticised. Some of the criticism, whether from the client who cannot understand why his building is late, or from the contractor who sees the designer as a hindrance to a close businesslike relationship with his client, may be justified, but many of the barbs directed at the industry's consultants are based on prejudice and misunderstanding. Before considering the main participants in detail, it is useful to reflect on the background to design systems as they exist today.

Many of the current systems have evolved from practices existing in the middle ages; for major buildings of that period, it was common for a master mason to 'design' the building, although the term would not have the currency it has today; he would also organise the supplies of labour and material, and deal with the problems of constructing the building from day to day. The client would meet the bills for labour and materials directly, and might supply his own 'watchdog' in the form of a surveyor or clerk of the works. The centuries immediately prior to the industrial revolution provided a stimulus to the emergence of the architect, due in large measure to the interest in classical forms, and their adoption in Britian during this period. The demand for buildings of all sorts during the industrial revolution, and the increase in engineering skills which derived from the need for buildings and transport facilities, saw the emergence of the engineer to give an identifiable separate service, although not in the modern 'professional' sense.

By this time it was relatively common for building contracts to be let to general contractors, and embryo quantity surveying skills were developing. Although the development of distinct services was emerging, it would be erroneous to assume that these were offered as discrete services; often one person could combine a number of roles. The identification with specific roles led to the formation of specialist associations or clubs, and these developed into a means of promoting a sense of professional identity.

The result of increased insistence on the recognition of separate and distinctive skills, coupled with the specialisation needed to accommodate the demand for an increasing variety and number of buildings up to the start of the First World War, led to an acceptance of the division of roles and responsibilities which is still with us. The supplementary charter of the Royal Institute of British Architects in 1887 held that architecture and membership of the Institute was inconsistent with being involved in providing buildings for a profit; architects could not be builders or developers. The primary function of the architect was that of an artist, using artistic skills in the design of buildings. The mass of basic and mundane building provision was not to be the province of the architect; this was left either to the speculative builder, or, for industrial buildings, to the engineer. The focus on artistic design meant that for many prestigious buildings, the architect was forced to rely on the engineer for the design of the structure. The lead given by the architects in divorcing themselves from contracting was followed by the RICS in 1907, when the rule prohibiting members from employment with contractors was introduced. Bowley's analysis of the situation suggests that the parties in construction had grouped themselves along class lines, with the architect being at the top of the construction social hierarchy, followed by surveyors, then engineers, with the builder classified as being 'in trade' and therefore deprived of real influence in the industry. During the inter-war period there was some degree of modernisation by the industry, in the use of plant and new techniques for constructing buildings, but this took place against a background of steady consolidation of the divisions already existing, with the professions increasing their control over what they saw as their own areas of specialisation.

The general picture therefore changed but little in the first seventy-five years of this century, and the movements which have taken place over the last decade to change the organisational framework for building provision need to be seen in this light. While trends may be detectable, for example the increases in flexibility brought about by the relaxation of the RICS contractor's rule, and the changes in the architects' code of conduct to allow architects to become directors of development and contracting companies, these changes can only be subject to a valid historical analysis after a much longer period of operation.

The architect

In considering the role of the architect, a useful starting point is the view which the profession holds of itself. On the opening page of the *Handbook of Architectural Practice and Management*, the responsibilities of the architect are noted as being to 'society, his client, the profession, his own organisation, his colleagues in the design team, the contracting organisation and construction team'. This hierarchy of responsibility appears to be intended, since the paragraph on responsibility to society goes on to say:

> While maintaining his client's best interests, the architect must recognise the need to apply supra-client values to his decisions and advice, in order to serve the present and long term interests of society as a whole. For example, to develop the planning of a site or building in a way which will not prejudice the possibility of improved planning of the surrounding area in the future; or to design the building so that it will not be in conflict with others in the immediate environment.

Here we may discern one of the major areas of conflict faced by the architect in providing design services. In view of the obvious impact which buildings have on the environment, the insistence on responsibility to society at large is a laudable aim, but it is hard to see how this may be discharged in the light of the other responsibilities. In particular, the responsibilities in law which the architect (and other professionals) carries in relation to the client makes it difficult to understand how the primary responsibility can be any other than to the client. In theory, the architect must resolve any conflict by resigning a commission, rather than acceding to the wishes of an 'anti-social' client. This view of supra-client responsibility does however go some way towards explaining the increasing tendency for the architectural profession to consider itself to be legitimately involved in the field of social engineering. Under the Architects (Registration) Act 1931, and the Architects Registration Acts 1939 and 1969, only persons registered with the Architects Registration Council of the United Kingdom (ARCUK) may call themselves architects without committing a criminal offence, and admission to the register is limited to those who have passed an ARCUK recognised examination. Once admitted to the register, the architect must observe the Code of Professional Conduct; this code is similar to that laid down by the RIBA, but not identical. The RIBA code lays down three principles:

1. A member shall faithfully carry out the duties which he undertakes. He shall also have a proper regard for the interests both of those who commission and of those who may be expected to use or enjoy the product of his work.

This principle gives force to the wider responsibility noted earlier, but no real guidance on resolving the question of how an architect may avoid conflict of interest, other than by refusing or resigning a commission.

2. A member shall avoid actions and situations inconsistent with his professional obligations or likely to raise doubts about his integrity.

The aim of this rule must be applauded, particularly in the light of the changes in the rules in 1980 which allowed architects to accept directorships in development and contracting organisations. As well as the obvious warning about accepting bribes, the principle warns members against the conflict of interest which could occur if a client should inadvertently be led to believe that the architect was supplying independent consulting services, while operating through an organisation which was involved in contracting or other business. Where the conflict exists, the architect must only continue a commission with the full and informed consent of his client.

3. A member shall rely only on ability and achievement as the basis for his advancement.

The rules which elaborate on this principle make it clear that the architect must not gain commissions through bribery, must not quote fees without invitation, and must not engage in a 'dutch auction' over fees. A limited form of advertising is allowed, although strictly controlled, and the only architectural competitions which may be entered are those run under RIBA regulations.

While both ARCUK and the RIBA enforce their codes of conduct, it is informative to consider the types of misconduct which have been considered 'disgraceful' in a professional respect: 'soliciting business', 'accepting hospitality to such an extent that it was likely to affect judgement', 'involvement in a firm of Estate Agents and being a substantial shareholder in a building company' (pre-1980), 'giving substantial monies with a view to the introduction of work'.

Many clients and members of the public would look on this list of examples of disgraceful conduct with some alarm; not because the incidents are *acceptable* conduct, but because of the notable omission of incompetence as an exemplary basis for disciplinary action; little action appears to be taken on the grounds of incompetence even when this has been demonstrated through successful litigation.

Forms of practice

Traditionally, the desire to provide a professional service, unsullied by association with the profit motive, has led architects to practise through organisations based on sole proprietorships or partnerships. The codes of conduct have militated against the setting up of practices with limited liability, although this *is* allowed under the Architects (Registration) Act 1931, providing that any architecture carried out by the company is under the control of a registered architect. However, until the end of 1980 the RIBA code of conduct prohibited members from practising with limited liability. The controversy over whether architects should be allowed the protection of limited liability is similar to the debate conducted in other professional institutions in construction, and tends to polarise around two arguments; the first is that a true profession, where service to the client is paramount, cannot ethically operate where the professional is protected from the results of his actions through limited liability. The second is a reaction against the increasing amount of litigation being undertaken against professionals in the industry, the resulting difficulty in obtaining professional indemnity insurance and the escalating costs of such insurance. The arguments are complex, and the results so far have been inconclusive; the RIBA code of conduct since 1981 no longer prohibits architects from practising with limited liability, but fails to provide for mandatory professional indemnity insurance. The only protection offered for clients is through the ARCUK document, 'The Standard of Conduct for Architects' (1981), which provides for the possibility of disciplinary action against limited liability practices who do not make it clear 'beyond reasonable doubt' that they have limited liability. The controversial nature of the arguments and their commercial and ethical importance means that the situation is unlikely to be fully resolved for some time.

Appointment and services

The recommended (RIBA) form of appointment, and the conditions of such an engagement, are described in the booklet *Architect's Appointment*, published in June 1982. (A companion volume also exists for small works.) The scope of the services to be provided may vary according to the project, but the booklet does list which services are required on a particular job, and suggests a level of remuneration for those services. The fee scales are recommended, not mandatory, and an architect is free to submit fee quotations in competition with others, as long as he does not reduce his quotation to take account of other bids. The argument for the use of the recommended scales is that they are considered by the RIBA to be the minimum necessary to give sufficient income to allow the architect to provide a competent service. (Interestingly, this argument was eventually accepted by the Property Services Agency in 1984, two years after being instructed by the government

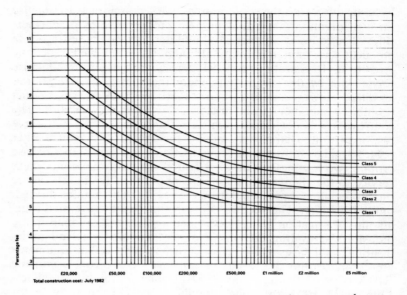

Figure 11. Recommended percentage fee scales: new works.

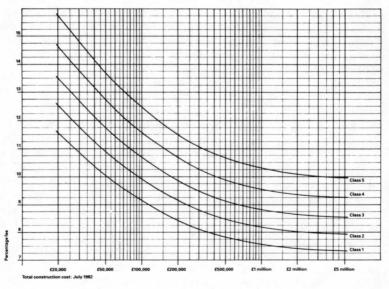

Figure 12. Recommended percentage fee scales: works to existing buildings.

to make all architects, engineers and surveyors compete for public contracts worth over £2 million.) The recommended fee scales are a percentage of the total costs of the construction work. These scales are reproduced in figures 11, 12 and 13.

The reduction in architects' workloads during the current recession has meant increased competition for work, and it has been suggested that in practice the recommended fee levels have been reduced by around 20%. In addition to the fee, architects may also claim out-of-pocket expenses for such items as printing, travel, hotel expenses, postage, telephone charges, and the cost of employing other consultants, but there is no reason why a client should not negotiate a lump sum fee which is inclusive of these sundry items.

The design services in *Architect's Appointment* are divided into 'Preliminary Services' and 'Basic Services', as noted in the Plan of Work; although this tends to assume that the traditional procurement model is being used, it is not difficult to adapt the design routine described in the plan of work to other procurement methods. The stages are:

Preliminary Services:
Work Stage A: Inception
Work Stage B: Feasibility

Basic Services:
Work Stage C: Outline proposals
Work Stage D: Scheme design
Work Stage E: Detail design
Work Stage F: Production information
Work Stage G: Bills of quantities
Work Stage H: Tender action
Work Stage J: Project planning
Work Stage K: Operations on site
Work Stage L: Completion

Type	Class 1	Class 2	Class 3	Class 4	Class 5
Industrial	Storage sheds	Speculative factories and warehouses Assembly and machine workshops Transport garages	Purpose-built factories and warehouses Garages/showrooms		
Agricultural	Barns and sheds Stables	Animal breeding units			
Commercial	Speculative Single-storey car parks	Shops Speculative offices Multi-storey car parks	Supermarkets Banks Purpose-built offices	Department stores Shopping centres Food processing units Breweries Telecom and computer accommodation	High risk research and production buildings Recording studios
Community		Communal halls	Community centres Branch libraries Ambulance and fire stations Bus stations Police stations Prisons Postal and broadcasting	Civic centres Churches and crematoria Concert halls Specialist libraries Museums Art galleries Magistrates'/county/sheriff courts	Theatres Opera houses Crown/high courts

	Dormitory hostels	Estate housing / Sheltered housing	Parsonages/manses / Hotels	Houses for individual clients
Residential	Dormitory hostels	Estate housing Sheltered housing	Parsonages/manses Hotels	Houses for individual clients
Education		Primary/nursery/first schools	Other schools including middle and secondary University complexes	University laboratories
Recreation		Sports centres Squash courts Swimming pools		
Medical social services		Clinics Homes for the elderly	Health centres Accommodation for the disabled General hospital complexes Surgeries	Teaching hospitals Hospital laboratories Dental surgeries

Figure 13. Classification of buildings, for guidance.

Part 1
Architect's services

This part describes Preliminary and Basic Services which an architect will normally provide.

PRELIMINARY SERVICES

Work stage A: Inception

Brief	1.1	Discuss the client's requirements including timescale and any financial limits; assess these and give general advice on how to proceed; agree the architect's services.
Information to be provided by the client	1.2	Obtain from the client information on ownership and any lessors and lessees of the site, any existing buildings on the site, boundary fences and other enclosures, and any known easements, encroachments, underground services, rights of way, rights of support and other relevant matters.
Site appraisal	1.3	Visit the site and carry out an initial appraisal.
Advice on other consultants' services	1.4	Advise on the need for other consultants' services and on the scope of these services.
Design work by specialist firms	1.5	Advise on the need for specialist contractors, sub-contractors and suppliers to design and execute part of the works to comply with the architect's requirements.
Site staff	1.6	Advise on the need for site staff.
Timetable and fee basis	1.7	Prepare where required an outline timetable and fee basis for further services for the client's approval.

Work stage B: Feasibility

Feasibility studies	1.8	Carry out such studies as may be necessary to determine the feasibility of the client's requirements; review with the client alternative design and construction approaches and cost implications; advise on the need to obtain planning permissions, approvals under building acts or regulations, and other similar statutory requirements.

BASIC SERVICES

Work stage C: Outline proposals

Outline proposals	1.9	With other consultants where appointed, analyse the client's requirements; prepare outline proposals and an approximation of the construction cost for the client's preliminary approval.

Work stage D: Scheme design

Scheme design

1.10 With other consultants where appointed, develop a scheme design from the outline proposals taking into account amendments requested by the client; prepare a cost estimate; where applicable give an indication of possible start and completion dates for the building contract. The scheme design will illustrate the size and character of the project in sufficient detail to enable the client to agree the spatial arrangements, materials and appearance.

Changes in scheme design

1.11 With other consultants where appointed, advise the client of the implications of any subsequent changes on the cost of the project and on the overall programme.

Planning application

1.12 Make where required application for planning permission. The permission itself is beyond the architect's control and no guarantee that it will be granted can be given.

Work stage E: Detail design

Detail design

1.13 With other consultants where appointed, develop the scheme design; obtain the client's approval of the type of construction, quality of materials and standard of workmanship; co-ordinate any design work done by consultants, specialist contractors, sub-contractors and suppliers; obtain quotations and other information in connection with specialist work.

Cost checks and changes in detail design

1.14 With other consultants where appointed, carry out cost checks as necessary; advise the client of the consequences of any subsequent changes on the cost and programme.

Statutory approvals

1.15 Make and negotiate where required applications for approvals under building acts, regulations or other statutory requirements.

Work stages F and G: Production information and bills of quantities

Production information

1.16 With other consultants where appointed, prepare production information including drawings, schedules and specification of materials and workmanship; provide information for bills of quantities, if any, to be prepared: all information complete in sufficient detail to enable a contractor to prepare a tender.

Work stage H: Tender action

Other contracts

1.17 Arrange, where relevant, for other contracts to be let prior to the contractor commencing work.

Tender lists

1.18 Advise on and obtain the client's approval to a list of tenderers.

Tender action and appraisal

1.19 Invite tenders from approved contractors; appraise and advise on tenders submitted. Alternatively, arrange for a price to be negotiated with a contractor.

Work stage J: Project planning

Project planning   1.20   Advise the client on the appointment of the contractor and on the responsibilities of the client, contractor and architect under the terms of the building contract; where required prepare the building contract and arrange for it to be signed by the client and the contractor; provide production information as required by the building contract.

Work stage K: Operations on site

Contract administration   1.21   Administer the terms of the building contract during operations on site.

Inspections   1.22   Visit the site as appropriate to inspect generally the progress and quality of the work.

Financial appraisal   1.23   With other consultants where appointed, make where required periodic financial reports to the client including the effect of any variations on the construction cost.

Work stage L: Completion

Completion   1.24   Administer the terms of the building contract relating to the completion of the works.

Guidance on maintenance   1.25   Give general guidance on maintenance.

Record drawings   1.26   Provide the client with a set of drawings showing the building and the main lines of drainage; arrange for drawings of the services installations to be provided.

It is recommended that the preliminary services be charged on a time basis, (hourly charges for principals by agreement, staff time charges not less than 15p per £100 of gross annual income), but it would be unusual for clients to pay a charge for these stages at all, unless the project was very large or peculiar. Part Two of *Architect's Appointment* covers services which are claimed to be outside the scope of the basic services, and should be paid for in addition to the basic fee, i.e. surveys and investigations, development services, (special) design services, cost estimating and financial advisory services, negotiations, administration and management of building projects (this last includes providing staff for *frequent* inspection of the works – normal services do not include a high level of site supervision), and work normally executed by other consultants – quantity surveying, structural, mechanical and electrical engineering, landscape and garden design, civil engineering, town planning, furniture design, graphic design, industrial design, and interior design. It is hard to imagine a project on which the architect is not expected to supply input on a number of these 'extra' areas, but it would be equally hard to find clients willing to pay an additional fee for them, unless the input in them was massive.

As with any other form of commercial contract, the exact services to be provided should be set down in an unequivocal form in writing, together with the level and basis of remuneration, and any other features which the contracting parties have agreed upon. *Architect's Appointment* contains a specimen memorandum of agreement, plus a schedule of services and fees which may be used to form the basis of an appointment; alternatively, these conditions may be incorporated by reference to them in a simple exchange of letters; there is a danger however that some important details may not be stated explicitly if this is done, and the pro forma memorandum does have the advantage of providing a useful aide-memoire when making an appointment. There is no reason why clients should not themselves set down in writing the services they expect, and the conditions of service, provided always that they are competent to do this, and have agreed the conditions with the architect; there is no legal or professional reason for strict adherence to the standard memorandum. Indeed, the RIBA form has long been criticised as being biased towards the architect, and a knowledgeable client may well obtain a better deal by writing his own clear and unequivocal memorandum. (The form to be produced by the BPF may give the lead to further developments in this area.)

Engineers

Unlike 'architect' the title 'engineer' in the UK is not protected by law, and anyone may call himself an engineer; indeed the title is used commonly to describe occupations ranging from semi-skilled workshop functions to research and development. Although the title of engineer may be abused, the right of entry to the professional engineering institutions is strictly controlled, and the tendency has been for the educational requirements for entry to one of the institutions to be steadily increased. The primary regulating authority for the *practice* of engineering in the UK is the Association of Consulting Engineers (ACE). The ACE exists to promote the activities of its members who practise as consulting engineers and was formed in 1913. It is a voluntary association, primarily concerned with professional practice matters, with membership restricted to senior members (usually fellows) of one of the following engineering institutions:

Institution of Civil Engineers
Institution of Mechanical Engineers
Institution of Electrical Engineers
Institution of Structural Engineers
Institution of Chemical Engineers

Institution of Mining and Metallurgy
Chartered Institute of Building Services Engineers

Members are normally sole proprietors or partners; in common with other professional organisations, the ACE has strongly resisted pressure for members to be able to practise with limited liability. The ACE 'Professional Rules and Practice' of June 1983 state that members may practise in the UK as sole practitioners, or as a partner, director or consultant in a Firm of Consulting Engineers, or *as any such but with limitation of liability by contract.* Where the engineer practises as partner or director, and the firm has a constitution providing for limited liability, then 75% of the voting power must be in the hands of engineers, the limitation must be apparent from all the firm's business stationery, and professional indemnity insurance must be maintained. For work outside the UK, the engineer has freedom to adopt limited liability providing the law of the country where the work takes place allows this. The ACE rules also provide that the engineer must comply with the rules of the professional institution to which he belongs; these may be more restrictive than the ACE regulations: for example, the Institution of Civil Engineers refuses to allow the title of 'Chartered Civil Engineers' to be used by a company.

The ACE has drawn up a set of standard conditions of engagement as the basis for a contract between client and engineer. These conditions are complex in comparison to the architects' conditions, and should be studied with care by any client intending to use them. There are four main forms of agreement, which relate to different types of engineering work, as follows:

Agreement 1; for reports and advisory work
Agreement 2; for civil, mechanical and electrical work, and for structural engineering work where an architect has not been appointed by the client
Agreement 3; for structural engineering work, where an architect is appointed by the client
Agreement 3 (1984); for structural engineering work, where an architect is appointed by the client (harmonised with the *Architect's Appointment*)
Agreement 4A(i) *Full Duties*; for engineering services in relation to subcontract works
Agreement 4A(ii) *Abridged Duties*; for engineering services in relation to subcontract works
Agreement 4A(iii) *Performance Duties*; for engineering services in relation to subcontract works
Agreement 4B; for engineering services in relation to direct contract works
(Note – in the last four, 'engineering services' refers to building services engineering).

In addition there is a pilot form (July 1985) for use where a separate client's representative is appointed under the BPF system, and also a form of engagement for use on PSA and Department of Transport contracts.

The agreements which will be most commonly encountered in building construction work are 3 and 4 above, where the engineer is working in a subordinate role to the architect (but Agreement 2 may be encountered on works where there is little architectural input, e.g. on the provision of roads and sewers as preparatory contracts). The fee scales recommended are for work of average complexity, and it is suggested that where the work is unusually complex, or where an abnormally large number of subcontracts is involved, or where the progress is retarded, e.g. through a number of phases, there should be a corresponding increase in remuneration. Conversely, an abatement is suggested where the work is simple or repetitive, or where the engineer has already done some of the work under Agreement 1. Given the level of competition in the market, and the increased attention paid by clients to the cost of professional services, it is unlikely that fees over the recommended scale would be paid, and more often an abatement to the scale would be agreed for a 'normal' service. The current agreements and fee scales were printed in 1983, and the government has recommended that the agreements be used for public sector projects; however, there has been no agreement as yet on the use of the fee scales in the current documents, and the public client is still being recommended to use the current agreement, but incorporating the 1979 scale of fees!

Agreement 3 (1984)
This was drawn up in 1984 to try to overcome the problems stemming from the non-alignment of structural engineers' design work with the design services provided under the architect's appointment. In the 1984 edition it is assumed that the design programme will be built around the RIBA plan of work. The normal services are therefore classified thus (in abbreviated form):
Outline proposal stage (RIBA Stage C) – visiting the site, studying data and information, considering reports prepared by others, advising on the need for geotechnical investigations, topographical surveys, etc., arranging same, consultation with local authorities, providing preliminary structural information to enable the architect to produce outline proposals and assisting the QS to produce the outline cost plan.
Scheme design stage (broadly within Plan of Work Stage D) – liaison with other members of the design team on the programme for the design work, developing the design from outline proposal stage, preparing further sketches, drawings, specifications to enable finalisation of the cost plan, consulting local authorities.

Detail design stage (broadly within Plan of Work Stages E plus part of F & G) – developing detailed design in collaboration with others, preparing calculations, drawings, estimates of reinforcement, final specifications to allow preparation of the bills of quantities and other tender information, advising the architect on the technical suitability of main and subcontractors, advising on any special tender conditions needed.

Production information stage (broadly within Plan of Work Stage F) – assisting architect and QS in assessing tenders, preparing final calculations and details, coordinating information from specialist suppliers and subcontractors, providing general arrangement drawings to allow their coordination by the architect with other information, preparing detail drawings, bending schedules, and any other production information required (NOT including temporary works drawings e.g., formwork, or shop fabrication drawings), examining fabrication drawings.

Construction stage (broadly following Plan of Work Stages J to L) – assisting in the preparation of contract documents, advising on the need for special inspections, advising on the appointment of site staff (paid for in addition to the fee), examining contractor's proposals where necessary, attending site meetings, and making periodic visits to assist the architect in monitoring work on site (NOTE: the frequency of site visits allowed for in the scale of fees is fortnightly unless agreed otherwise), advising architect on the issue of certificates, carrying out tests on site if required, providing client with a set of working drawings, assisting in resolving disputes.

Also appended is a list of additional duties which the engineer may be asked to perform, and for which an extra fee may be negotiated.

Fees for the normal service may be:

1.   Calculated on the cost of the project: this has the advantage of being aligned with the calculation of the fees for other consultants, and is easy to calculate as the cost of the project is known at any one time.

2.   Calculated on the cost of the works: (i.e. calculated on the cost of the works designed by the engineer). This was the method recommended until 1984, is familiar to practitioners, and is directly related to the engineer's work. The disadvantage is that the cost of the 'engineered' components has to be calculated for this purpose only.

3. A lump sum: this is appropriate where the scope of the work (and the length of the commission) is definable; the sum may be derived initially from the percentage scales. It has the advantage of ease of use, but requires either the engineer or the client to accept the risk of an inaccurate sum.

4. On a time basis: when the job is very small or difficult to determine, time charges at a predetermined level may be used.

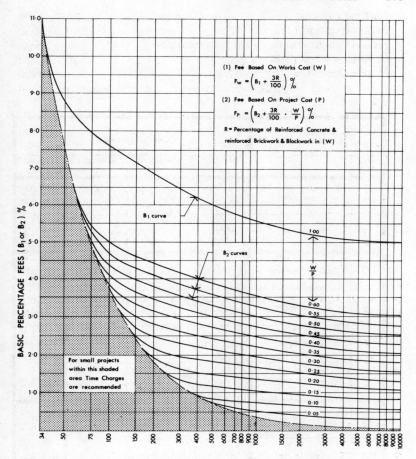

The following is within the figure:

(1) Fee Based On Works Cost (W)

$$F_w = \left(B_1 + \frac{3R}{100}\right) \%$$

(2) Fee Based On Project Cost (P)

$$F_P = \left(B_2 + \frac{3R}{100} \cdot \frac{W}{P}\right) \%$$

R = Percentage of Reinforced Concrete & reinforced Brickwork & Blockwork in (W)

B_1 curve

B_2 curves

For small projects within this shaded area Time Charges are recommended

$\frac{W}{P}$

1·00
0·60
0·55
0·50
0·45
0·40
0·35
0·30
0·25
0·20
0·15
0·10
0·05

BASIC PERCENTAGE FEES (B_1 or B_2) %

PROJECT COST OR WORKS COST IN £ DIVIDED BY 1000

(Based On August, 1984 Prices)

The Output Price Index in August 1984 was 212. The fee scale is determined from the graph against the corrected cost estimate, which is the current cost estimate at the time the fee is to be decided, multiplied by 212 and divided by the Output Price Index at that time.

N–9

Figure 14.   Recommended percentage (scale) fee for normal services on work of average complexity from ACE Agreement 3, 1984).

Where percentage fees are used the percentages are calculated from the graphs, as reproduced in figure 14.

The cumulative fee payments *recommended* at each stage of the service are –

Outline proposals	15%
Scheme design	36%
Detail design and tender documentation	60%
Production information	85%
Works complete	100%

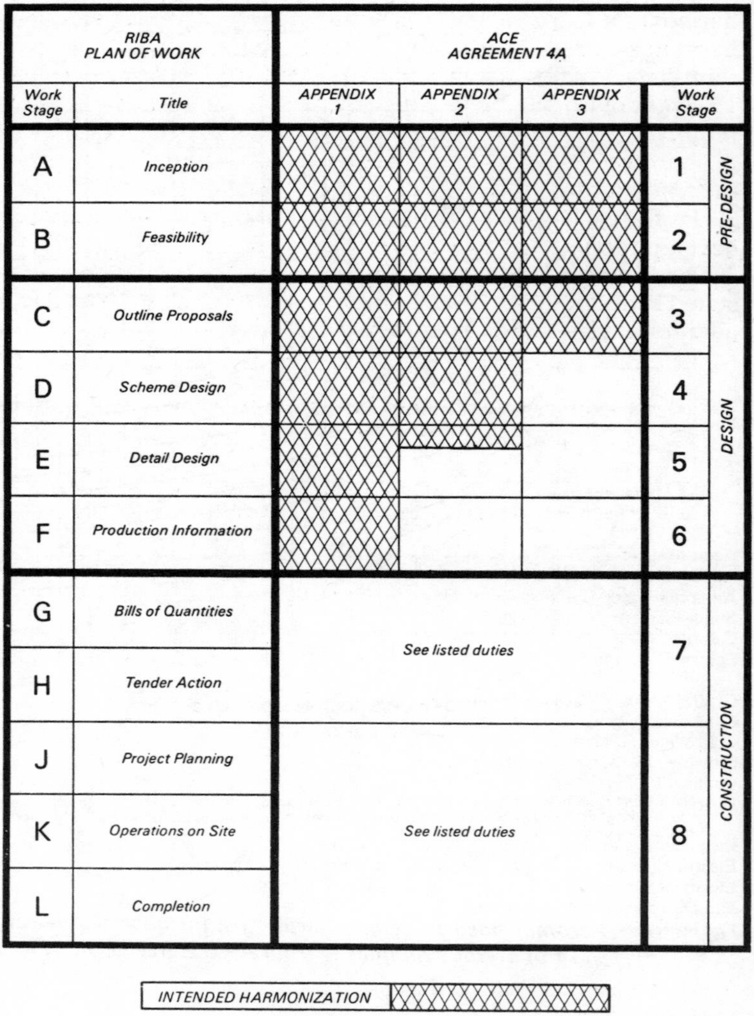

RIBA PLAN OF WORK		ACE AGREEMENT 4A				
Work Stage	Title	APPENDIX 1	APPENDIX 2	APPENDIX 3	Work Stage	
A	Inception				1	PRE-DESIGN
B	Feasibility				2	
C	Outline Proposals				3	DESIGN
D	Scheme Design				4	
E	Detail Design				5	
F	Production Information				6	
G	Bills of Quantities	See listed duties			7	CONSTRUCTION
H	Tender Action					
J	Project Planning	See listed duties			8	
K	Operations on Site					
L	Completion					

INTENDED HARMONIZATION

Figure 15.   Sequence of work stages (RIBA Plan of Work and ACE Agreement 4A)

Agreement 4A (i, ii and iii)

The agreements which refer to the provision of building services engineering are separated according to the extent of the engineer's involvement. The basic conditions of service are similar in construction to those for structural engineering, but the services provided and the fee scales are different, and too detailed for the purposes of this book. As in Agreement 3(1984) the stages are harmonised to some extent with the plan of work, and the broad harmonisation is shown for the three agreements in figure 15, reproduced from agreements 4A i, ii and iii. The three forms are:

1. *Full duties*; where a *full* design and supervision service is required.
2. *Abridged duties*; where a subcontractor is appointed to develop the *tender* drawings during plan of work stages E and F.
3. *Performance duties*; where a subcontractor is appointed to develop the *sketch* drawings during plan of work stages D to F.

The Elements which the engineer is expected to design are to be stated in an appendix, with those not required deleted, and those in addition inserted. The appendix is reproduced in figure 16 below.

**ENGINEERING SERVICES AND ASSOCIATED EQUIPMENT
(INSTALLED COMPLETE)**

Items not included in the Consulting Engineer's appointment to be deleted.
Special items covered by the appointment to be inserted.

Acoustical Design and Treatment
Air Compressors and Compressed Air Services
Air-conditioning and Mechanical Ventilation Services
Boiler Plants and Auxiliaries
Calorifier Plants
Central Dictation Services

Central Vacuum-Cleaning Installations
Clock Installations
Cold Water Services
Conveyor Installations and Equipment
Cooling-Water Services
Distribution Mains for any Services

Electrical Distribution Services
Electric Lighting and Power Installations, including Lighting Fittings
Electrical Sub-Stations
Fire Detection and Alarm Services
Fire Protection Services
Food Preparation, Cooking, Conveying and Serving Equipment

Fuel Gas Incoming Supply and Distribution
General Plant Installations
Heating Installations
Hot Water Services
Incoming Electrical Supplies
Laundry Equipment and Services

Lightning Protection Services
Lifts, Hoists and Escalators
Medical Gas Services
Medical Vacuum Services
Pneumatic-Tube Conveying Services
Public Address, Personnel-location and Call Services

Public Health and Plumbing Services
Radio and Television Installations
Refrigeration Installation and Cold Stores
Refuse Collection and/or Disposal Systems including Incinerators
Steam Services and Condensate-Return Services
Sterilising and Bedpan Washing or Disposal Equipment

Street Lighting
Telephone Equipment and Distribution Services
Thermal Insulation
Vibration Control
Water Treatment and Filtration
Window Cleaning Trolleys etc

Other Specialised Supply Systems and/or Plant:

....
....
....
....
....

Figure 16.   Appendix to Memorandum of Agreement

In all forms of ACE agreement, it is recommended that a
memorandum be prepared which sets out unequivocally the duties
to be performed, the fee scales which apply, the timing of interim
payments, time charges, etc. Given the complexity of the agreements themselves, it would be extremely risky for the client or the
engineer to attempt to incorporate the ACE conditions in a contract
merely by reference to them in letter form. It is preferable that
either a simple exchange of letters, which include details of the
service required, a straightforward statement of fee and timing, OR
a fully completed memorandum of agreement be completed; a
hybrid is to be avoided at all costs.

The quantity surveyor

Although quantity surveyors are to be found in private practice and
in contracting and client organisations, it is the first of these which
will be considered here. As with engineers, there is no statutory
regulation on the use of the designation 'quantity surveyor'. Most
quantity surveyors are members of the Royal Institution of
Chartered Surveyors, the quantity surveyors' division of which
comprises around 25% of the membership of the Institution, with
the remainder practising in other divisions, e.g. land, agriculture,
mineral, building surveying, general practice, etc.

Practice by chartered surveyors is governed by the Rules of Conduct (1983 edition, revised 1985) contained in by-laws 24–26, together with the regulations made under these by-laws. Although regulation 10(1) provides for the possibility of surveyors carrying on their business through the medium of a limited company, there are severe restrictions to this. The first is through by-law 24(4)(b) which states 'no Member shall carry on practice as a surveyor under the protection of limited liability', which probably has the effect of preventing the member limiting his liability by contract; and second through regulation 10(1) which requires the approval of the divisional council for a member to carry on business with limited liability; so far the quantity surveying division has resisted granting approval except where the work is carried on outside the UK, Ireland, the Channel Islands, or Hong Kong. Where the foregoing restrictions are satisfied, there are minimum limits on share capital of the company, and it must carry professional indemnity insurance.

The traditional service provided by the quantity surveyor has been the preparation of bills of quantities and variation accounts. This appears to have originated in the nineteenth century, with builders employing surveyors to assist them in submitting tenders and settling accounts, the cost of this service being paid by the client in the builders' overheads; clients saw the advantages of employing the surveyor directly, and through the use of bills of quantities could reduce the oncost paid to builders during multiple tendering. Since the Second World War, the massive increase in public sector construction has promoted the development of cost planning techniques, and has increased the influence of the quantity surveyor within the design team. Currently, the general quantity surveying service comprises all or some of the following:

1. Provision of cost advice during feasibility, outline and scheme design stages (as in the Plan of Work), to arrive at a cost plan which accords with an agreed design.
2. Cost checking during the development of the detailed design.
3. Advice on tendering/contractual method.
4. Production of bills of quantities from the fully developed design (in theory at least – see earlier note with regard to the tendency for the billing to be done in the absence of a fully developed design).
5. Reporting on tenders, and negotiating if necessary.
6. Preparing interim valuations.
7. Cost advice on variations proposed.
8. Agreeing the final account.

Although this traditional profile still accounts for a substantial proportion of quantity surveyors' work, the profession has taken note of the attacks made on the industry in general for inefficient, slow and expensive buildings, and has recognised in particular the vulnerability of practices built upon providing bills of quantities and the remeasurement of work. The premises upon which the BPF system has been formulated give a good example of the critical environment. The result has been a serious and apparently successful attempt to recast and relaunch the services which can be offered by quantity surveying practices, to the extent that many large firms now claim that less than half their workload is dependent on preparing bills of quantities. Using their basic expertise in the costs and economics of construction, a wider service, involving *inter alia* development surveying and project management, together with a more 'tailored' design and construction input, has been successfully marketed.

Where a surveyor is to be appointed for 'standard' quantity surveying services, the recommended form of engagement is that published by the RICS in *Appointment of a Quantity Surveyor* (Oct. 1983).

In a supplementary booklet, *Professional Charges for Quantity Surveying Services* (June 1983) nine different services and fee scales are itemised, as follows:

Scale 36. Inclusive scale of charges for quantity surveying services for building works.

Scale 37. Itemised scale of professional charges for quantity surveying services for building works.

Scale 38. Itemised scale of professional charges for quantity surveying services for civil engineering works.

Scale 39. Scale of professional charges for quantity surveying services for term contracts.

Scale 40. Scale of professional charges for quantity surveying services in connection with housing schemes for local authorities.

Scale 44. Scale of professional charges for quantity surveying services in connection with improvements to existing housing and environmental improvement works.

Scale 45. Scale of professional charges for quantity surveying services in connection with housing schemes financed by the Housing Corporation.

Scale 46. Scale of professional charges for quantity surveying services in connection with loss assessment of damage to buildings from fire.

Scale 47. Scale of professional charges for the assessment of replacement cost of buildings for insurance, current cost accounting and other purposes.

Of these, the most commonly encountered are Scales 36 and 37, and these are briefly described below; the scales are recommended, not mandatory, and clients have the right to seek competitive quotations for fees; for public sector contracts, the Minister of State for Consumer Affairs has emphasised that quality of service and calibre of performance are to be considered as well as actual fee levels.

(a) CATEGORY A: Banks; churches and similar places of religious worship; clubs; council offices; court-houses; crematoria; houses; libraries; old people's homes not exceeding two storeys; petrol service stations; police stations; public houses and inns; sports pavilions; teaching laboratories and industrial laboratories of a like nature; theatres; town halls; universities, polytechnics and colleges of further education (other than halls of residence and hostels); and the like.

Value of Work	Category A Fee	
£	£	£
Up to 75,000	190+6.0% (minimum fee £1,200)	
75,000– 150,000	4,690+5.0% on balance over	75,000
150,000– 300,000	8,440+4.3% on balance over	150,000
300,000– 750,000	14,890+3.4% on balance over	300,000
750,000–1,500,000	30,190+3.0% on balance over	750,000
1,500,000–3,000,000	52,690+2.8% on balance over	1,500,000
Over 3,000,000	94,690+2.4% on balance over	3,000,000

(b) CATEGORY B: Ambulance and fire stations; canteens; church halls; cinemas; community centres; departmental stores; enclosed sports stadia and swimming baths; halls of residence; hospitals; hostels; industrial laboratories other than those included in Category A; motels; offices other than those included in Categories A and C; old people's homes exceeding two storeys; railway stations; recreation centres; residential hotels; restaurants; schools; self-contained flats and maisonettes not exceeding two storeys (including old people's accommodation of this nature); shops; telephone exchanges; and the like, being works of a simpler character than those in Category A or works with some element of repetition.

Value of Work	Category B Fee	
£	£	£
Up to 75,000	180+5.8% (minimum fee £1,160)	
75,000– 150,000	4,530+4.7% on balance over	75,000
150,000– 300,000	8,055+3.9% on balance over	150,000
300,000– 750,000	13,905+2.8% on balance over	300,000
750,000–1,500,000	26,505+2.6% on balance over	750,000
1,500,000–3,000,000	46,005+2.4% on balance over	1,500,000
Over 3,000,000	82,005+2.0% on balance over	3,000,000

(c) CATEGORY C: Factories; self-contained flats and maisonettes exceeding two storeys (including old people's accommodation of this nature); garages; multi-storey car parks; offices with open floor space to be finished to tenants' requirements (tenants' requirements to be Category A); open-air sports stadia and swimming baths; warehouses; and the like, being works containing little internal detail or works with a large amount of repetition.

Note: When a building contract comprises a number of dissimilar buildings, with a resultant decrease in the amount of repetition, then the fees set out below may be adjusted by agreement between the employer and the quantity surveyor.

Value of Work	Category C Fee	
£	£	£
Up to 75,000	150+4.9% (minimum fee £980)	
75,000– 150,000	3,825+4.1% on balance over	75,000
150,000– 300,000	6,900+3.3% on balance over	150,000
300,000– 750,000	11,850+2.5% on balance over	300,000
750,000–1,500,000	23,100+2.2% on balance over	750,000
1,500,000–3,000,000	39,600+2.0% on balance over	1,500,000
Over 3,000,000	69,600+1.6% on balance over	3,000,000

Figure 17.   Scale 36

This scale of service is intended to be all-embracing, and covers the whole range of input from inception to completion (though not for civil engineering or public sector housing work), including budgeting, cost planning, advice on tendering, preparing tender documents, negotiations, interim valuations, remeasurement and variations, agreeing final account, (including also the cost of providing a 'reasonable' number of copies of the bill of quantities, and 'normal' travelling expenses). The inclusive fees for these services are noted in figure 17 above, and are related to the type of building, in Category A, B or C; where more than one category is involved, an apportionment is made. Fees are calculated on the total cost of the works.

The fee scales do not include the following, for which the RICS recommends an additional charge.

1. Quantity surveying services on air conditioning, heating, ventilating and electrical services; where a full service extends to these elements of a scheme, an additional fee is charged as in figure 18.

Value of Work	Additional Fee	
£	£	£
Up to 60,000	5.0%	
60,000– 120,000	3,000+4.7% on balance over	60,000
120,000– 240,000	5,820+4.0% on balance over	120,000
240,000– 375,000	10,620+3.6% on balance over	240,000
375,000– 500,000	15,480+3.0% on balance over	375,000
500,000–2,000,000	19,230+2.7% on balance over	500,000
Over 2,000,000	59,730+2.4% on balance over 2,000,000	

Figure 18.   Fees additional to Scale 36

2. Works of alteration: for these an addition of 1% to the scale percentage is recommended.

3. Redecoration and minor repairs: an addition of 1.5% to the scale percentage is recommended.

4. Excessive variations or abortive work: fee to be adjusted by agreement.

5. Services arising from termination of building contracts, liquidation, fire damage, arbitration, litigation and investigation of contractor's claims, taxation matters; it is recommended that these be charged on a time basis, but they must be the subject of specific instruction by the employer. It is also recommended that time charges be based on the gross annual *cost* of the employee(s) divided by 1650 (reckoned to be the annual hours worked by an individual); this hourly rate plus 145% (to cover profit and overheads) is charged for every hour worked.

Fees are recommended to be paid thus: half of the fee (based on the tender) at acceptance of tender (or if no tender is accepted, on the lowest *bona fide* tender), the balance by instalments to be agreed, ending one month after certification of final account.

Scale 37

This is an itemised series of scales covering separately the services which may be provided, and clients may appoint for one or more stages as appropriate; the scale covers some 28 pages and is too detailed for reproduction here, but the components are as follows:

1. Feasibility studies, approximate estimates, charged on a time basis.

2. Cost planning, charged on a percentage of the tender value, as an addition to the fee for providing bills of quantities.

3. Preparing bills of quantities, including preamble clauses but not including the preparation of specifications; on a percentage of tender value, the percentage depending on building type (similar to Scale 36).

4. Additional fee percentage for air conditioning, heating, and ventilating and electrical services.

5. Addition of 1% to the fee where works of alterations are involved.

6. Addition of 1.5% to the fee for works of redecoration or minor works.

7. Additional charges for preparing bills of reductions (but where the client has paid for cost planning and the tenders are higher than anticipated, through no fault of the client, the reductions are to be prepared at the surveyor's own cost).

8. Fees for negotiation of tenders.

9. Overall post-contract services, on a percentage basis, with additional amounts for air conditioning, etc.

OR

10 Itemised charges for post contract operations
   (a) Interim valuations
   (b) Variation accounts
   (c) Cost monitoring

11. As above, but for contracts based on bills of approximate quantities.

12. As above, but for contracts based on schedules of prices.

13. Prime cost contracts
   (a) Cost planning
   (b) Estimates of cost, including negotiating, adjusting and agreeing same
   (c) Checking prime costs, reporting for interim certificates, preparing final accounts
   (d) Cost reports and monitoring services

Professional liability

No discussion of the services offered by the professions in the construction industry would be complete without reference to the liability carried by them in relation to professional negligence. The professionals owe a duty to their clients in two main directions. First, there is the duty to perform the obligations laid down in the contract to the employer: these will be to a standard set down in the contract, or to one arrived at by implication. Second, and possibly more significant, is the duty in common law: the most frequent manifestation of breach of this duty is a suit for negligence.

A detailed treatment of the subject is beyond the scope of this book, (for further reading, see D. L. Cornes, *Design Liability in the*

Construction Industry) but the significant features may be summarised thus.

1. There has been an increasing tendency for designers to be held liable for failures in their buildings, to the extent that almost any failure may be held to be the result of a negligent act, allowing unliquidated damages to be recovered by the building owner.

2. The law on limitations has become extremely confused, to the extent that it is now difficult to state with certainty when the limitation period starts or ends in relation to a particular allegation of failure and negligence. The result is that designers may face open-ended liability in time, with the possibility of claims being pursued even when a designer has retired (or in some cases, after the designer has died).

3. Stemming from 1 and 2 above is the fact that it is becoming increasingly difficult for designers to obtain adequate and affordable insurance for the ordinary risks involved in building design. There are few designers who could contemplate a claim following a failure of any but the most modest size without the risk of bankruptcy. It is therefore normal practice for designers to insure against such risks; indeed, many clients, particularly in the public sector, will not consider hiring a designer who does not carry an adequate level of professional liability insurance. The high level of claims currently being made, and the open-ended nature of the liability in time, means that for the insurers the risks are high. Many designers have found themselves faced with increases in premiums of several hundred per cent each year, with those facing claims being penalised highest, often to the extent where it is impossible to obtain cover at any price.

The law on limitations is currently under review, with the intention of clarifying the extent of liability; once this exercise is completed, some sanity may return to reflect the resulting greater degree of certainty in the insurance market. However, any reduction in designers' liability will obviously have repercussions for the industry's clients. For the client, a limit on the liability in time for defects in his building is hardly attractive, and given the endemic nature of building defects at present, it is likely that clients will wish to see some form of alternative guarantee emerge. One possible solution, following the normal practice in France, would be for the designer or the builder, or both, to offer long-term (say ten year) guarantees on their buildings. Such insurance has recently become available for building owners in the UK, but it is relatively expensive (until a defect is discovered!) and involves the insurance company in a detailed scrutiny of the design as it is developed and constructed.

3.6   PRECONSTRUCTION PLANNING AND CONTROL

While much has been written on the need for planning and control of construction, relatively little advice or information exists on the control of design operations. In this respect construction differs substantially from other production industries, where the design of major capital goods, e.g. motor cars or other consumer durables, receives as much attention as the production phases. Much of the difference in attitude may be ascribed to the fundamental nature of the traditional procurement system, in which the contractor is under contract to perform an explicit service by a stated time, against the threat of a liquidated and ascertained damages clause. In contrast, the design team, if appointed under the standard conditions of engagement, suffers no such constraint unless the client chooses to make adherence to a predetermined programme an *additional* feature of the appointment.

The use of alternative methods of procurement means that the advantages of the alternative methods may be negated unless some kind of control of the design process is incorporated. This argument would hold, irrespective of whether the control was exercised by the design leader, the contractor or the client. It is useful to state here that the only reason for planning and control of preconstruction activities is to improve upon the performance of the project team in terms of the important parameters – usually variants on time, cost and quality. Against the desire for improvement can be raised the argument that bringing a high degree of regimentation into design is likely to lead to an inhibition of the creative process, and to a reduction in the time available for proper development of a detailed design, which in turn can lead to disruptive variations during construction, and a reduction in quality. If taken to extremes, this may indeed be true, but it is instructive to note that the research report 'Faster Building for Industry' (Building EDC) showed that there was no penalty to cost or quality in achieving good timing (the report also placed emphasis on the effectiveness of the customer in aiding and obtaining good timing).

The techniques which can be used for precontract planning and control are essentially the same as those used for any other planning operation, and may include bar-charting, arrow and precedence networks, resource scheduling, cost budgeting, etc. The nature of the operations in the preconstruction stages are quite different from those post-contract, but the number of activities is usually smaller, although the complexity of the interdependencies can be very high.

As a starting point for considering the nature of the design operation, the RIBA Plan of Work (the outline of which was given earlier) provides an excellent 'check list', as well as illustrating the dependencies which are likely to exist irrespective of the procurement system used. Although designed with the traditional system in mind, the plan may be interpreted and modified for use with most kinds of procurement method in order to provide identifiable project targets or milestones.

Control of time

Completion in the shortest realistic time which may be achieved without penalties may be critical to a project, but there are circumstances where the time parameter is not related to duration, but to particular dates or stages. Earlier discussion of the client input prior to and during briefing referred to the need for the client to assess accurately his internal mechanisms for feasibility assessment, his communications and authority relationships, and any other priorities attached to the project. In terms of time control, these priorities will probably resolve into:

1. A need for overall completion by a fixed date. This may be laid down by the client, for one of a variety of reasons, common examples being:
   (a) to meet a critical date for trading; e.g. supermarkets will wish to capitalise on pre-Christmas shopping, and this may mean a strict deadline for completion around September, in order to allow time for staff training, commissioning, and stocking;
   (b) to meet predetermined letting dates, where the client is committed to allowing beneficial occupation;
   (c) for decanting of other premises, e.g. in a rolling programme of housing rehabilitation, or where a production facility has to be moved while minimising loss of production.
2. A need for phased completion on fixed dates, for reasons similar to the above.
3. A need for a site start by a fixed date; e.g. to meet rules for the expenditure of monies in a particular budget year (more prevalent in the public than the private sector), or to meet the contingencies of legislation – there have been examples of government subsidies being available for particular development types, providing the work was seen to be committed (through a site start) by a particular date.
4. A need for tenders to be received and approved by or on a particular date, e.g. in the public sector in order to commit money in the current financial year, or to allow their approval by a board or committee which meets infrequently – if the tender is not presented at that time, there may be severe delays in gaining approval, by which time the tender acceptance period may have expired.
5. A need for design stages to be approved by a board or committee, for the reasons given in 4. above, with these stages and approval dates being established from the longer-term priorities of 1. to 4. above.

If the time constraints of importance to the client can be established at the outset, it should be possible quickly to determine whether they are at all realistic, or whether there is little probability of meeting them. Most clients with no building experience will need assistance in arriving at this judgement, and it is probably preferable if the initial assessment can be made prior to the selection of either the design team or the procurement method, as the selection of the system and the design/construction team should be based in part on their ability to meet the time schedule.

It is relatively easy to proceed if the time requirements are either easy to meet or completely impossible; in the former, detailed planning may commence, and in the latter the client is forced to reappraise his initial objectives. A more difficult situation arises when the time constraint is very difficult, but not quite impossible to meet. The client's choices in this situation condense into:

(a) Alter client's objectives.
(b) Provide the resources (including extra payments or other incentives) for an accelerated programme.
(c) Define the elements of the project most at risk if the programme is not met, and establish a fall-back position in the case of failure to meet time objectives.
(d) Define the elements of the project which will be at risk in the accelerated programme – in most cases these will be costs and quality factors – and decide how much risk may be acceptable on these, before the point is reached where such risk outweighs the advantages of meeting the time priorities.

Where it is possible to isolate the variables with accuracy, and allocate levels of probability to them, it may be useful to apply operational research methods to optimise the outcome; while these methods may be attractive in giving a measure of objectivity to the decision making, the difficulties involved in defining and quantifying the variables should not be underestimated. In practice, the creation of a management *environment* in which it is possible to derive and quantify the variables may produce more constructive results than actually using operational research methods.

One of the major difficulties in planning for design operations lies in defining in advance the boundary of each activity or stage. In most cases it will be necessary for the activities to be defined by the members of the design team. The format suggested in the BPF system where, as a condition of appointment, the design leader is required to produce a design programme containing details of the expected drawing production, could usefully be followed on most projects. The *environment* generated by such a discipline should lead to a situation in which the performance of individual team members could be identified with some certainty. This would also avoid the problem faced by many clients in deciding whether a statement by a designer that a stage had been reached is true;

without an objective guide, such as a predictable quantity of design information, any assessment of whether each design team member had reached a certain stage is at best subjective.

Control of cost

For most clients, it will be important to obtain the building at the lowest possible cost *consistent with an appropriate quality and timing*. Equally, most clients will want to know at the earliest possible date how much the project is likely to cost. As suggested in the discussion on procurement systems, the lowest cost and an early determination are often mutually incompatible if design quality is to be high.

The differences between the cost of the building and the overall cost of the project were demonstrated in the section on financial appraisal. It is necessary for the design team to appreciate at an early stage what the overall costs of the project (as opposed to the building) are likely to be as there will inevitably be some degree of interdependence between the factors making up the total cost. A common build-up might be:

Cost of building

Site investigations, site and building surveys, aerial photography, trial holes/bores, soil investigation, contamination testing.

Demolition; shoring of dangerous structures, protection of footpaths and neighbouring property, observing easements, demolition, protection against health hazards, e.g. asbestos, radio-active contamination.

Abnormal site works; e.g. treating contaminated soil on ex-industrial sites, excessive foundations, noise screens near railways, replacement of river walls.

Into this category might come the costs of construction and fees in connection with the negotiation of party wall awards.

External services; costs in providing services if none exist, e.g. bringing mains drainage, water, gas, electricity, telephones to the site.

Civil engineering works; providing roads, sewers, underpasses, bridges, etc., some of which may be required as part of a planning agreement.

The building contract.

Fitting out; the provision of equipment may dwarf the cost of the building, e.g. in teaching hospitals, electronics manufacturing plants, financial services buildings.

Landscaping, sculptures, fountains, etc.

Cost of design, management and supervision

This category will include the cost of managing the project, which may arise if a professional project manager is employed (although it could be argued that in this situation the total fee bill should not increase – see next chapter), or in the hidden cost to the client if members of his own staff are permanently seconded to the project. The fees for members of the design team should be realistically costed, either on the basis of negotiation or tenders, or as recommended by the professional institutions; to these must be added additional expense allowances (if agreed). Note that there may be an obligation to pay design fees also on the costs of fitting out, sculptures, etc, if arranged as part of the building work. There may be additional costs in the preparation of exhibitions, models and samples if a high level of presentation is needed, e.g. if a public enquiry is mounted. The fees for planning and building regulation approvals should be accounted for, and if the scheme is likely to be controversial, it might be prudent to make allowance for the legal and design team costs in pursuing a planning appeal.

The costs of supervising the works on site and the method of doing this should be considered with care. In the 'normal' conditions of engagement for architects, 25% of the fee is paid to cover supervision on site, but this does not provide for *exhaustive* inspection. On a protracted project, the costs of maintaining a reasonable site presence for the architect, resident engineer (if required), and clerk of works, together with their site accommodation, travelling, secretarial support, on-site computing etc., can be considerable. The demands of supervision should therefore be considered as a strategic issue early in the project planning.

Fluctuations: the balance to be struck in financial appraisals between the use of current data and projections was discussed earlier, and this need will be resolved in the light of the nature of the project, the needs of the client's financial environment, the length of the project, the incidence of decision points in the design process, and the risks which the client is prepared to accept. Any fluctuations in the building cost will have a corresponding effect on the level of professional fees where these are based on a percentage of building costs. Normally, the fees will be calculated on the total cost, not on the tender sum, even though it may seem inequitable that a client should pay a fee based on the tender plus fluctuations, when the design may have been done and paid for years earlier.

Other project costs

These would include costs of land, acquisition costs (agents and legal fees), costs of finance, allowances for risk and profit, advertising, letting and sales fees, legal fees on disposal, rent-free periods, plus possibly a contingency sum based on the building cost or on building cost plus other items as yet uncommitted.

The sum of the building costs, management, design and super-vision, and other project costs will give the total cost of the project. While the design team may be primarily concerned about the cost of actually providing the *building*, this cannot be divorced from consideration of the overall cost – first, because the design will have repercussions for other aspects of the appraisal, and second, because the client may have only a fixed sum to spend overall, and any variation from the sum allocated to design and construction will have to be found from savings elsewhere.

Timing of costs

The importance of considering the incidence of costs was demon-strated in the discussion of cash flow methods of appraisal, and in projecting the overall costs of a project, the client and the design team must consider the effect on the incidence of payments of the design solution used. Where it is necessary to fund part of the scheme through early income from a partial completion, the design must allow for this to be made physically and logistically possible by the method of construction, e.g. conflicts of access between the early tenants or buyers and the contractor must be avoided. This will often entail careful consideration of the construction method during evolution of the design solution.

Cost planning and control of design

Traditionally the cost planning of the design has been the role of the quantity surveyor, and considerable expertise has been established in this area since World War Two. Although the extent of the cost planning service is not explicitly stated in the standard conditions of engagement for quantity surveyors, it would be difficult to conduct the service without at least some element of cost planning being undertaken. However, where the itemised scale of charges (Scale 37) is used, cost planning must be specifically contracted for, and a prudent client will ensure that the extent of the quantity surveyor's (and designer's) responsibility is clearly recorded.

Any system of cost planning and control must serve first to aid the setting of the cost target, second to ensure that the cost target is met at either tender or final account stage or both (depending on whether the client accepts the risks of fluctuation or wishes to delegate this), third to provide guidance during the design develop-ment, to allow early corrective action on elements of the design which exceed their budget and, finally, to give the client good value for money.

In order to make objective judgements on the overall costs of building, and on the distribution of costs to design elements, it is useful to compare current proposals with other similar buildings.

The technique of elemental cost analysis allows costs to be allocated to functional elements of buildings, e.g. walls, floors, roofs, services, and these may be expressed in common units of cost per square metre. The common basis for expression allows recorded data on previous buildings to be compared with the proposals, and after isolating those variables which are not directly comparable, it is possible to draw conclusions about the costs of the proposals.

The historical data base may be internal to the surveying practice, or may be publicly accessible, such as the Building Cost Information Service (now available in hard copy or on-line).

The routine commonly adopted for cost control in relation to the plan of work is outlined in figure 19.

Inception	Feasibility	Outline Proposals	Scheme Design	Detail Design	Production Information
	Initial cost range limits indicated	Review cost range and/or cost limit	Prepare cost plan	Cost checking	

Figure 19.   Cost control related to RIBA plan of work.

In this process the cost range is established, then distributed to give a budget for each element; finally each element is checked against target as its design is developed.

During the outline proposals stage the cost plan may be determined as an overall sum, which may be divided by the area of the building in the favoured design solution to produce an overall cost per unit area; when the design solution is firmed-up at the scheme design stage, this overall cost/unit area may then be apportioned amongst the elements to give the cost plan. The cost plan must not be seen as an absolute cost straitjacket, but as a means of control; where the design for an element is calculated to fall outside the element limit, this must be compensated for by savings on other elements, so that the overall limit is not exceeded. The cost distribution may be done on the basis of updated historical data from other buildings, or by pricing approximate quantities taken from the scheme design, or by a combination of both methods. Where the data is historical, care must be taken to ensure that the comparisons are valid, particularly in respect of quality; here there is a need to ensure that all members of the design team (and client) have a common understanding of the quality being proposed, and probably the simplest method is through joint visits to comparable buildings. Provision must also be made at the cost planning stage for two factors which could present a risk to the plan. The first is the possibility of price increases between the date of the cost plan and the date of tender; for small jobs this is unlikely to cause problems except on those elements where price movement is foreseeable, but on a protracted design the contingency for price increases must be as accurate as possible. Secondly, there is a risk that the design team may not be able to comply with the cost plan, due to underestimates of complexity, unforeseen planning or legal difficulties, or problems outside the expertise of the designers.

The procedure for checking against a cost plan is relatively simple; as the detailed design for each element is finished, the information is passed to the quantity surveyor who will calculate the probable cost (obviously the element design must be complete for this to work, as little of value could be measured or compared from an incomplete element) and compared with the planned cost; if the element is outside an acceptable deviation from the plan, the designer must redesign, or be prepared to reduce the cost of other elements in compensation. In order for the process to be successful, communications between designers and surveyor should be rigorously maintained, and it should be made relatively easy for the client to receive copies of the communications, or for summaries to be provided at regular intervals.

Quality

Whereas time and cost may be measurable and therefore controllable in an objective sense, the concept of quality is more nebulous. Even in the unlikely event of the client having unlimited resources, the establishment of a benchmark for quality is difficult, and it is probably even more difficult to measure and control it during design.

The first difficulty arises through the lack of a common vocabulary between client and designer which will allow the client to describe the quality requirements of the scheme. Is 'high' design quality to relate to 'uniqueness', or predetermined notions of 'style', or to absolutes (if they exist) in relation to the 'architectural quality' of the building, or to the use of the 'best' (and presumably the most expensive) materials, or to the provision of materials and equipment which will minimise maintenance costs? As some of these variables may be mutually incompatible, a clear understanding of the criteria applying to quality must be obtained at the briefing stage, and unequivocally agreed in the approval of the scheme design. The question of a lack of common vocabulary may be resolved by the designer and client touring buildings together and coming to a common understanding and assessment of quality values by reference to samples of work in those buildings.

Once the scheme design and cost plan are agreed, the cost plan may be able to supply part of the control mechanism needed to ensure that the development of the design matches the desired quality, provided that the plan faithfully represents the quality deemed appropriate.

A further danger area may lie in the design intent, which ostensibly represents the desired quality standards: can the project in fact be built as intended? Architects, engineers and surveyors may justifiably feel frustrated when a carefully thought out design is destroyed through poor management, carelessness, and poor workmanship on site. But an equal contributor to such frustration (also felt by responsible site managers and foremen) is a lack of appreciation of what can be physically achieved on site. Over-detailing can lead to excessive demands on workmanship, which may not be totally unreasonable provided the contract documents clearly express the difficulty to be expected: unfortunately the traditional bill of quantities is a poor vehicle for transferring this kind of information, and the communication problem is exacerbated when some of the most important details may not be designed until well after the bill is prepared. Similarly, high quality (and often fragile) materials or components may be detailed so that they can only be fixed early in the construction programme. While the bill or specification may contain standard clauses on protection, it is naive to suppose that protection can ever be absolute. The 'buildability' of the design is a quantity which can only be improved through education, training and experience, and at present such knowledge is mainly confined to contracting organisations, or such design practices as have had close liaison with them, and have identified the issue as one to be taken seriously.

In summary, the success or otherwise of planning and control in the design process originates in the briefing provided by the client, and in the determination of the client or his representative to ensure that the process is controlled. The quality of the brief, and its early finalisation, will provide the benchmarks needed for establishing time, cost and quality parameters. But equally important, the part of the brief which deals with the requirements of the client's procedural systems will define the extent to which the client commits both himself and his consultants to a programme of regulation.

4 Project Management

4.1 INTRODUCTION

There is probably a greater potential for confusion in the study of project management than of any other contemporary issue facing the construction industry. Not only are there problems of terminology, but also of emphasis and bias caused by the large number of people and organisations attempting to enter the field, and claiming proprietary rights in the subject.

The main problem in terminology is the use of the term 'project manager' to describe the person responsible for the construction phase, usually based on site. In one sense this usage is quite legitimate; in considering how project management is different from operations management, it is clear that the latter is concerned with preserving an existing and continuing system, while the former is involved with the management of *change*. It follows therefore that a 'project' will have a beginning and an end, even where these points are difficult to define. Anyone with the responsibility of managing an operation which produces change and has fixed start and finish points could therefore be termed a project manager. But this does not help in identifying the service under discussion here, in which the term 'project management' relates to a much wider responsibility than that for the construction phase.

There have been many attempts in recent years to define project management in its current, wider professional sense. While many of them are valid in particular contexts, the definition which will be referred to here is that used in the Chartered Institute of Building publication *Project Management in Building*:

> *The overall planning, control and coordination of a project from inception to completion aimed at meeting a client's requirements and ensuring completion on time, within cost and to required quality standards.*

Even if the construction companies were to cease using the term project manager to describe *site* management, the problems of identifying the service would not entirely disappear, as there is no guarantee that merely because there is a person with the title of project manager, the project will benefit from overall management.

Conversely, it is quite possible for project management to exist in a development without anyone carrying the title of project manager – the important factor being whether there is an identifiable *process* providing a *focus* for the coordination and control of the project, whether this exists through the authority of one person, or through an organisation.

The process of project management essentially exists to meet all of a client's requirements on a project, and in an ideal world, these responsibilities would be discharged by the client himself. In practice, this situation does not arise very often, either because the client is inexperienced, or because his resources are already committed. As the project management service in the sense of the CIOB definition is being provided by a 'surrogate client', it is logical that the service should be unbiased and therefore unattached to any of the other commercial interests which exist in the provision of the design and construction.

Before examining the process in detail, it is useful to reflect on the pressures which have caused the service to appear, and on the manner in which these pressures have shaped and defined the service as it is developing at present.

4.2　EMERGENCE OF PROJECT MANAGEMENT

In Chapter 3 the historical development of the design team specialisms were traced, together with the generation of the traditional and alternative forms of procurement. In the case of the alternative forms of procurement, these could be seen as a reaction to the dissatisfaction expressed by clients over the service obtained from the industry as a whole. In many ways the development of project management may be seen as a further extension of this tendency. The traditional system has been criticised mainly for the fragmentation it brings to the process of building procurement, made worse by the fact that there is no inbuilt compensatory mechanism to supply the integration which is needed by a complex, interdependent series of contractual and communication relationships. The integration which is supplied by the architect in the traditional process must be less than optimal, even with the best of intentions on the part of the architect, owing simply to the conflict of interests which exists between the duties of the architect to his client, as a designer and as a manager. As a designer, the architect must respect the process of design itself and its outcome as an end in itself; as a manager, the architect must coordinate his own work with that of others, and must in administering the construction contract hold the scales fairly between client and contractor. Even if the education and training of the architect did provide a reasonable foundation for the range of skills necessary for such an Olympian task, it is scarcely credible that in the event of a conflict of interests his advice to the client would in fact be unbiased – for example where, due to poor coordination of structural engineering and architect's drawings work has to be removed on site, and the contractor claims an extension of time and extra reimbursement. Is the architect really to be expected to volunteer to pay for the defective work and the delay? No doubt there are those who would, and many who believe that this is what should happen; perhaps in the days when high levels of professional integrity were maintained and expected this would indeed have been the case, but the pressure on professional practices to operate as commercial entities militates against this being the norm. Nor is the criticism confined to the architect, although the profession has tended, perhaps not always fairly, to bear the brunt of the criticism.

The conditions of engagement for other consultants provide similar, though perhaps less far-reaching conflicts. The general contractor has not remained unscathed, as the standard forms of contract have become viewed as a 'contractor's charter', and many contractors have taken every opportunity offered by that document; the contractor would point out quite correctly that the contract is signed freely by both parties, and any 'claim' is only a reasonable exercise of the contractual right to the recovery of monies owed through actions by the client or his agents. In addition to the acquisition of a reputation for claims-consciousness, the contractor is also criticised for being able to avoid responsibility for the performance of the building, unless he has blatantly disregarded his obligations on workmanship and materials. Nor is the fragmentation confined only to the design phase; the increased tendency towards subcontracting rather than the use of direct labour has increased the need for integrative management, and this need is compounded by the use of both domestic and nominated subcontractors, with different commercial parameters applying in each case. The problem is possibly less severe in its implications for the client, as in the case of domestic subcontractors at least, the responsibility for their performance still lies with the general contractor. Each component of the industry may well feel able to contemplate its own obligations and performance and conclude that the service it has provided is not at fault.

But this is of little consolation to the client, who is obliged to contract with a number of separate organisations, each with a different service to offer and subject to conditions of service only understood by those privy to their mysteries, with the interrelationships and responsibilities of each party only really being understood by those solicitors and barristers whose income is derived from a constant presence in the High Court dealing with building matters. The issue of fragmentation is not one which has survived through lack of identification or recommendation; a series of reports since the Second World War has drawn attention to the problems, and has suggested solutions:

(a) The Phillips report in 1950 commented upon the lack of joint education for people involved in design and construction, and on the problems of late issue of information, and the ease with which variations could be introduced.

(b) The Emmerson report in 1962 identified problems within the design professions, and in the placing of contracts, and stated 'in no other important industry is the responsibility for design so far removed from the responsibility for production'.

(c) The Banwell report in 1964 reinforced criticisms of inefficient practices in the design professions, and the industry's failure to provide a coherent and integrated service.

(d) The 'Action of Banwell' report in 1967 found that little progress had been made in response to the criticisms raised in the 1964 report.

(e) The report *Communications in the Building Industry* produced by the Tavistock Institute of Human Relations and the NJCC in 1965 found the same types of failure due to poor communications and fragmentation, but attributed these to the fact that 'the basic relationship which exists amongst resource controllers has the character of *inter-dependent autonomy*. There is a lack of match between the *technical interdependence* of the resources and the *organisational independence* of those who control them' (resource controllers in this context were those organisations – design practices, contractors, etc. – which contained and controlled the resources needed for a project) and went on to say 'any attempt to reorder the division of responsibilities among resource controllers that might arise from a purely technical study would very soon run up against deep seated difficulties of conflicting values and vested, professional technical and commercial interests. These often represent the commitments of a lifetime, and demand respect'.

(f) The Wood report in 1976 commented on the use of inappropriate tender methods, a lack of integrated project control, and restrictions arising from public accountability concepts and a reluctance to innovate which hampered obtaining value for money. It also recommended that (for public clients) a senior officer of the user department should be appointed as the client's representative for each project to coordinate requirements; and for larger developments, that a project manager should be appointed to assume overall responsibility (but not to interfere with the contractor's or consultant's responsibilities).

During the ten years prior to the Wood report, the industry saw the beginnings of a change in practices, at least in the willingness of some contractors to experiment with alternative procurement models, particularly in fee and management contracting. It would be encouraging if one could say that these alternatives were produced as the industry's response to public criticism, but a more realistic judgement would be that they were a commercial response by companies which saw a market for a different service, and subsequently took full advantage of the possibilities. Also, during the seventies, the professions were under attack from the Monopolies and Mergers Commission over their fee scales and professional codes. This attack in a more muted form has continued up to the present time in the form of pressure from the Property Services Agency, which has had a limited amount of success in fostering competition for design contracts; the PSA has also been active in attempting to pass a greater amount of risk on to the construction companies, by asking for prices to be fixed (i.e. through 'no fluctuations' clauses) on contracts up to two years in duration, and for contractors to supply estimates of likely charges for disruption at tender stage (i.e. asking contractors to estimate the likely extent of their claims). The result of this series of reports and recommendations has been an increased awareness within the industry and outside of the deficiencies in the traditional system, and a recognition of the need for some kind of overall management of projects.

Further impetus towards the generation of a project management function has come from dissatisfaction expressed by clients when contrasting their experience in the UK with their experience in operating overseas, particularly in the USA. Many UK developers have a substantial presence in North America, and the differences in practice between the UK and the USA have put the UK performance on speed, time and value for money in a poor light. The most obvious manifestation of this discontent has been the production of the BPF system, arising largely from the influence of USA practice on British developers. (For a fuller description of the British Property Federation system for building design and construction, see section 3.4.) In the BPF system, great emphasis is placed on the separation of the design function from the management function, with a 'client's representative' being appointed for the latter – a project manager by another name.

Since the 1970s there has been considerable jockeying for position in the race to establish 'proprietary rights' over the ability to offer project management services. The general contractors offering fee and management contracting claim to have been doing this in all but name for a number of years and have expanded their list of services to include design and design management; quantity surveyors have laid claim to the title through their experience in managing the financial aspects of development from inception to completion; development surveyors have established a considerable presence through their being involved at the site finding/feasibility/disposal stages, and thus in the commercial aspects of development onto which it may be relatively easy to graft the management of design and construction; architects have attempted to make a claim to be the natural candidates for the project management role, through being involved with a scheme from its inception, and having a thorough understanding of the client's needs; multi-discipline design practices claim to be able to offer the service as a matter of necessity, through the need to integrate several design disciplines within one practice.

The result is the emergence and establishment of a 'new' discipline in the construction industry, with practitioners drawn currently from diverse backgrounds. The discipline as currently (ill-) defined and practised is unlikely to be the pattern for the future. The embryo nature of the service, and the lack of a commonly agreed format, means that there is considerable scope for development and flexibility within the role.

4.3   MANAGEMENT FOR CONSTRUCTION PROJECTS

The extent to which an overall project management service is supplied on a project may be demonstrated by comparisons of the 'ideal' (i.e. where there is an identifiable single focus for management), with the management input to the project system under the common forms of building procurement. In figures 20 to 23, the degree to which a single source of overall management input is supplied is graphed against the three main project stages, simplified as inception, design and construction. It is assumed that there is an overlap between each of the stages.

In figure 20, the 'ideal' management system is shown, with a single source being responsible for overall management at each point in the gestation and realisation. The functional responsibility for carrying out each of the main stages could be carried by the project manager (individual or corporate, depending on project size and complexity), or might be allocated to a leading participant in each of the main functional groups; for example, the design coordination might be carried out by the project manager, or could be delegated to the principal designer or design leader. Similarly, the construction phase might be coordinated and managed by the project manager, perhaps on a single trades or construction management basis, or if the contract is to be let to a main contractor, there would be delegation to that contractor. In any event, the level of delegation of coordination or control would be planned and deliberate, and would comply with the overall requirements of the project system.

This may be compared with the overall management input through a single focus on three of the common procurement systems. Figure 21 shows the amount of overall management offered in the traditional system. This assumes that the architect provides the single focus on a 'full service', being appointed some

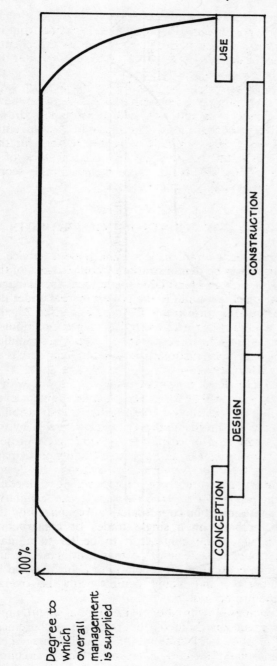

Figure 20. Degree to which an identifiable single focus for management exists: ideal.

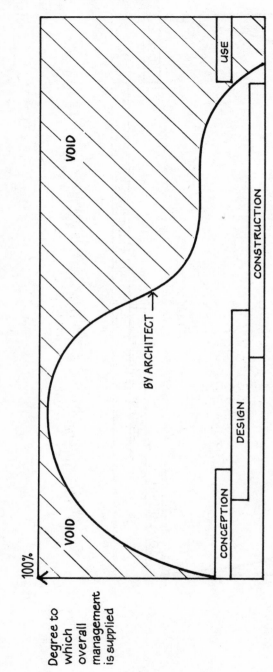

Figure 21.   Degree to which an identifiable single focus for management exists: traditional system.

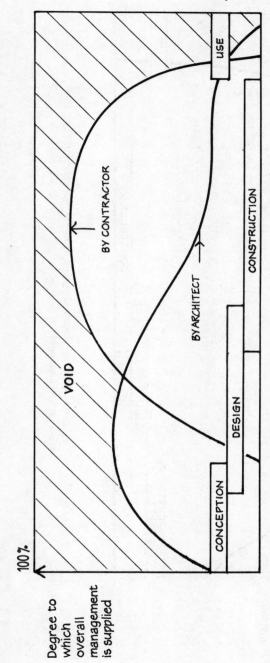

Figure 22.   Degree to which an identifiable single focus for management exists: management contracting.

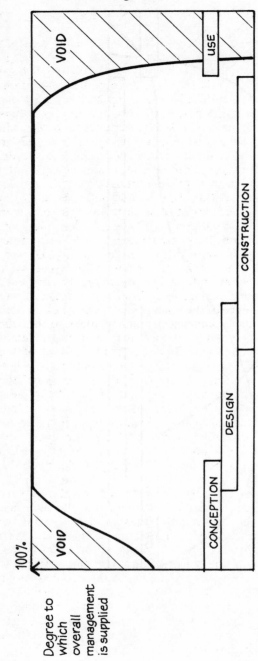

Figure 23.   Degree to which an identifiable single focus for management exists: design and build.

time after the client has made an initial decision that only building provision is likely to satisfy his needs.

The architect's influence on the project can be seen to build up rapidly after his introduction, and reaches a peak during the design stages. However, as the architect in his traditional role has no legal or contractual authority over the other members of the design team, it cannot be said that even in this phase he can provide a total focus for making or implementing decisions affecting the other members of the team. The overlap between design and construction (which in the traditional process should be minimal) means that the design coordination role continues into the construction phase; however, the overall management input at this time must drop considerably, as the architect has few powers to influence the course of the project once the building contract (i.e. JCT Standard Form) has been signed. A competing focus for control of the project emerges with the contractor in almost total control of the project time scale (subject always to penalities for non-compliance with the contract conditions) and arguably in control also of project quality and cost.

Figure 22 indicates the comparative position in respect of a project let on a management contracting basis, where the architect's ability to be the primary management focus reduces even more quickly due to the influence of the management contractor on both the design itself, and its sequencing. Complementary to this, the contractor's ability to provide overall management increases quickly after appointment, and continues until the end of the scheme. The intersection point and the gradients of the curves will depend to a great extent on the nature of the project, and the amount of design work complete at the time of the management contractor's appointment. The management contractor is not however able to offer a *complete* management service, first because he is unlikely to be appointed ahead of the design team, and secondly because he does not have contractual control of the design team unless the management contract is expanded to include this responsibility.

Figure 23 shows the extent to which a design and build contractor may provide a single focus. Here it is assumed that the client has made an initial appraisal of his requirements, prior to selecting the design and build contractor. After appointment, the contractor's ability to control the project is to all intents absolute, as he has control of the design and the construction phase, subject only to whatever scrutiny the client has retained over the detailed design development. The nature of the design and build operation is likely to impose considerable constraints on the client's ability to disrupt this stage, unless the contractor is blatantly unable to fulfil whatever performance specification is to be met. Similarly, there will be severe inhibitions on the discretion the client may exert during the construction phase unless the contractor fails to construct to the required standard; as the contractor will have been responsible in large measure for predetermining the standards to be met, this should not be a major source of contention.

In terms of the efficiency of the project system which may be derived from the existence of an overall management focus, the design and build system would appear to satisfy these demands almost completely; however, the efficiency here is an *operational* efficiency, and ignores to a great extent the 'efficiency' requirements which may be attributed to the quality of the design. Where there is the likelihood that aesthetic or functional qualities may be subordinated to operational optimisation in construction, the client must be prepared to accept this trade-off, or be prepared to introduce further lead time in the procurement process in order to gain design advice, and be prepared to make the quality of the design an intrinsic part of the design and build contractor's contract.

4.4   MANAGEMENT STRUCTURES FOR PROJECT MANAGEMENT

From the viewpoint of the client, the optimum arrangement must be one in which the project manager takes full responsibility for the management of the project. However, in this deceptively simple proposition lies one of the difficulties in defining what the project management service should be. Within the statement is an implied assumption that the project manager will not only be responsible for managing, but also for the outcome of the project in terms of cost, time and quality. This assumption brings with it two important considerations. First, is it desirable, in attempting to provide an overall management focus, to introduce the commercial bias which would arise from an organisation's being responsible for every aspect of the project outcome? It could be argued credibly that if the project manager is responsible in this way, his advice would be biased towards minimising his own risk, rather than maximising the outcome for the client. Set against this would be an equally persuasive argument that many clients would prefer to accept the protective attitude of the project manager, as this would build in a similar protection for the client, on the basis that many clients would be prepared to accept more 'mundane' buildings if there was a guarantee that those buildings would be delivered on time, at reasonable cost, and free of the defects which appear to be endemic today. Second, is the question of whether project management organisations are financially capable of accepting such a level of responsibility. Many such organisations are relatively small, and the total risk from failure on quality, cost and time would be high on even modest projects. Professional liability insurance for such risks, even where it could be obtained, would be prohibitively expensive in relation to the fee income generated from the project management service. It could be argued that the project manager could obtain a level of indemnity from the designers in the event of a design failure, could set-off the risk by applying a liquidated and ascertained damages clause to both contractors and designers, and could find a form of professional contract which could oblige the designers to design strictly within cost budgets, with a damages clause for non-compliance. While these safeguards are possible in theory, they would undoubtedly be difficult to implement unless adopted as industry 'standards', and would add to the total risk undertaken by the project manager and other team members, with a corresponding rise in charges to the client.

The difficulties in adopting a form of construction project management which combines a single overall management focus with single source responsibility serve to explain the current models for management structures in project management, which are mainly based on the provision of a professional management service without primary contractual responsibility for time, cost and quality.

The two most common vehicles are described in the CIOB publication *Project Management in Building* as 'non-executive' and 'executive' project management.

Figure 24 shows a structure where the management is *non-executive*, i.e. where the project manager acts in parallel with other participants, particularly in the design phase. Here, the project manager has no authority to *direct* the other members of the team, and tends to be more concerned with coordination and communication. This model could find application in an organisation which itself provides some or all of the participants in the design and construction process, for example in a public sector body such as a local authority or health authority – i.e. as part of the client organisation. In this case the final arbiter over the project would be the organisation itself, and it would be meaningless, except as a management accounting exercise, for the organisation to attempt to provide 'independent' management of part of its own activities. One other application for such a project management structure could be in *partial* project management, where an identifiable project could exist as a subsystem to the project as a whole, for instance in the case of a multi-discipline design practice undertaking the whole of the design for a project; here the project manager would be the manager for the *design* of the project, within the practice as a whole, but would not be responsible for the design itself.

Figure 25 indicates the authority available in *executive* project management, where the project manager has the authority to make and implement decisions concerning all aspects of the project. The discretion to be reserved to the client for key decisions, and the

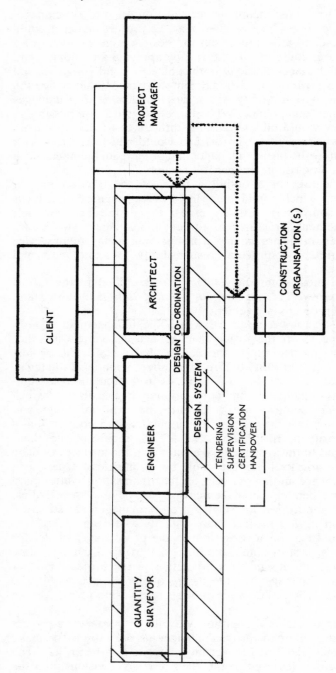

Figure 24.   Non-executive project management.

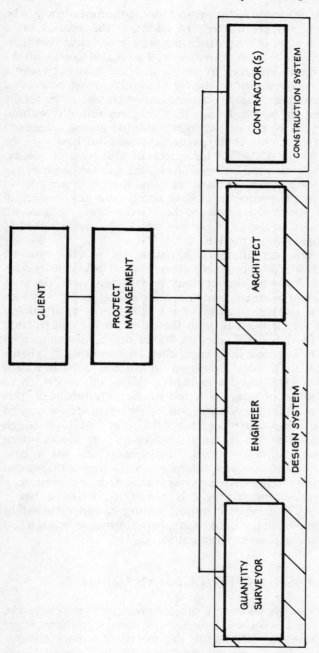

Figure 25. Executive project management.

amount to be delegated to the project manager, must obviously be clearly and accurately framed. In addition, the conditions of engagement for the other participants must make clear that their responsibility is to the project manager, who is able to act with the authority normally exercised by the client. There have been severe criticisms of such a structure, mainly from other construction and design organisations whose comment cannot be said to be totally unbiased, centring on the premise that this gives authority without responsibility, as the project manager is able to exercise judgement and authority over the other participants without having to be responsible (as noted earlier) for aspects of time, cost or quality. This could be countered by emphasising the fact that contractual responsibility for *managing* does exist, and that there are distinct advantages in the project managers not having any conflict of interest. This structure is similar to the 'construction management' system operated in the USA, and of late by a small number of American companies in the UK.

There are however differences in commercial practice between UK methods of project management and USA construction management. Although the relationships between client, designer and construction manager may be similar in both countries, with both designers and construction/project managers being appointed as agents of the client, it is often the case that the construction manager in the USA will accept a higher degree of commercial liability for the outcome in terms of cost, time and quality; clients are prepared to demand, and get, maximum cost and time guarantees from construction managers. Where this occurs, there exists the conflict of interests noted in the introduction to this chapter. Payment for the construction management service may be on the basis of lump sum or percentage fee, as in the UK (although when the client is given a guaranteed maximum sum, this will often be inclusive of the construction management fee). Many contractors in the USA are now offering construction management services not only to improve turnover, but to reduce their trading risks; construction management is considered to be a better commercial risk than general contracting, to a considerable extent due to the removal of the need to supply performance bonds when offering a construction management service.

4.5   PROCESSES IN PROJECT MANAGEMENT

As the reason for appointing a project manager is to relieve the client of the need to become intimately involved with the management of his project, it follows that the process of project management should be directly related to the needs of the particular client and his project. This would suggest that there can be no definitive specification for the project management role; not only will the project itself dictate the description and the level of sophistication of the service to be provided, but the degree to which the client wishes to retain an involvement will dictate the authority available to the project manager.

Within this need to retain sufficient flexibility in role definition, it is possible to generalise about the characteristics of the project management service, and to extend such a description to embrace project management as a concept, without specific application to the construction industry. We may take as a starting point some of the related activities which (with a number of variants of title and emphasis) are commonly seen as the process of management:

PLANNING
ORGANISING
MOTIVATING
COMMUNICATING
CONTROLLING

Although these are useful headings for defining some of the essential features of a management service, they cannot in the project management context be considered as self-contained entities; each overlaps with the others and is supported by others, and in some cases a strong cause and effect relationship exists.

Planning

Planning must also embrace the concept of forecasting, in order to establish a client's needs in the context of what is available and desirable in the future, given the constraints which may be predicted within the planning horizons of the project. The planning horizons to be employed must also be a function of the project needs, and may be subject to change or at least redefinition as a result of the planning process itself. Within this stage, the project manager must be concerned with establishing the project objectives, and refining these so that they may be expressed as operating objectives which can guide the other participants. These objectives may be framed in terms of cost, time, method and quality so that they are communicable to others, and able to be monitored.

Organising

This stage is concerned with establishing whatever form of organisational framework is necessary to implement the objectives derived at the planning stage. Probably the most important issue here is the identification of the resources required for the project, and in particular the identification and appointment of the leading participants. As part of the appointment process, the boundaries of the responsibility allocated to the participants will need to be defined, together with the lines and methods of communication necessary for monitoring and reporting.

Motivating

It is crucial to the operational success of the project that each participant, whether an individual or organisation, is committed to achieving the performance level set at the planning and organising stages. There must be a will to succeed, to overcome difficulties and to cooperate with others; for this to be accomplished there should be a good match between the project objectives and the individual participants' objectives. In theory, if the planning and organising stages have been thoroughly explored, there should be little problem in achieving the high level of match required. In practice, changes in the operational briefs and in the project environment will mean that constant attention to motivational issues will be required throughout the project.

Communicating

This is probably the one aspect of managing projects which pervades all others, and without a well-conceived and effective basis for communication it is only by accident that the project can succeed. One of the primary tasks at the planning and organising stages will be the creation of the communications system, covering methods, timing and levels of communication to be employed at each stage of the project's lifetime. Communications between human beings have considerable potential for breakdown and misunderstanding, and the level of morale within the project system as a whole and between the interdependent parts will be closely related to the effectiveness of the communications system and the manner in which it is interpreted and implemented. With the advent of modern electronic communications, the problem of establishing and maintaining a communications system is compounded; while a paper and telephone system may appear crude and slow, it does have the benefit of largely standardised hardware which is well understood in every section of business and commerce. The potential offered by information technology in its widest sense as a management tool is enormous, and few projects, except for the most modest, can expect to remain untouched by its impact. However, in the planning of a communications system for a project, the use of such facilities brings with it further problems in defining a system which will be effective, understood by all of the participants, and untroubled by questions of machine and software compatibility.

Controlling

Control is concerned with the overall direction of the project, the identification of deviations from planned targets for time, cost and quality, and the actions necessary to correct or minimise the effect of such deviations. Control in these terms is virtually impossible unless the other processes above are effective. Without proper planning and organising there will be no targets against which performance deviations can be measured; without motivation there will be little incentive for the participants to consent to a regime in which control may take place, and without an effective communications system there will be no reliable means of ascertaining whether deviations are taking place, or whether corrective action is successful.

Against this generalised background of the processes which must take place in project management, it is possible to develop the spectrum of duties and responsibilities to be undertaken during the management of a construction project. The list which follows is reproduced from the Chartered Institute of Building publication *Project Management in Building*. The levels of authority, responsibility and breadth of service to be provided by the project manager will depend on the client and the type of project, and it should not be assumed that all project managers will supply all of the services noted, or that the list is exhaustive.

Initial stages with the client

Project Manager's brief	(a)	Set out the terms of engagement and basis of reimbursement of the Project Manager and establish the full extent of his authority and responsibility in unambiguous terms.
Client involvement	(b)	Define the degree of involvement required from the client and define clearly a 'modus operandi' between the client and Project Manager.
	(c)	Set out clearly the approvals required by the client, indicating time constraints on approvals.
Viability of project	(d)	Assess the financial and technical viability of the project from the initial information provided by the client.
Funding	(e)	Establish what funding arrangements exist for the project. If necessary assist the client in obtaining finance and making adequate financial arrangements for the project.
Communication and reporting	(f)	Set out lines of communication and extent and frequency of meetings to be held between client and Project Manager.

(g) Establish the reporting required by the client and report on a regular basis on such subjects as:

    (i) expenditure against budget and estimated cost to completion;

    (ii) actual progress compared with programme and define work still to be completed;

    (iii) regularly update schedules and budgets;

    (iv) design changes.

Grants

(h) Investigate the question of Industrial Development Certificates, other development certificates and development grants and examine the taxation position.

Feasibility stage

Develop brief

(a) Examine the client's basic proposals for the project and collect and examine all available existing data.
Develop in conjunction with the client a firm clear brief for the project in qualitative and quantitative terms. Such a brief should clearly set out all management and technical functions and establish their boundaries. Develop the brief as necessary, including such means as flow lines and flow process charts and establish the best requirements for the client regarding plant, layout, selection of plant, handling, loading, storage of raw material and finished products, building type, environment, and labour force provisions. Investigate as instructed by the client new machinery and processes applicable to the development.

Project feasibility

(b) As the brief is defined, establish that the client has a viable proposition and that development is both technically and financially feasible.

Programme

(c) Prepare a programme for the total project and establish a total time scale in conjunction with the client's requirements.

Design team

(d) Advise the client on the selection of the design team and its term of appointment and terms of reference. Select the team and recommend its appointment to the client.

Site

(e) Ensure that preliminary investigation of the site or sites is carried out and examine alternative designs and layouts. Establish the optimum requirements regarding the basic layout and site requirements.

(f) Advise on the site location and the suitability. If necessary assist the client in the selection and purchase of a site, including the prior checking of any legal or planning restrictions affecting the site. Ensure that site possession will be available when required.

Government approval

(g) Assist the client in obtaining basic approvals necessary from the government and local government.

Site investigation

(h) Arrange for such site investigation including topographical surveys, soil reports, bore holes and such other geotechnical tests as necessary for the satisfactory design and construction of the project.

Preliminary drawings	(i)	Ensure that preliminary architectural and engineering drawings and a preliminary material and equipment specification are prepared for the purpose of planning approvals and establishment of budgets.
Budget	(j)	See that a budget is prepared for the project with investment proposals including cash flow projections.
Outline planning approval	(k)	Define the basic building and structural requirements and establish outline planning approval within the required time scale. Investigate and resolve any adjacent owner situations, preservation order situations, rights of way or easements. Ensure that the statutory authorities can provide the basic services required.
Feasibility report	(l)	Prepare a feasibility report outlining all aspects of the project for the client's approval.

Pre-construction stage

Contractor selection	(a)	Establish with the client the general procedures for selection and appointment of contractors, including the form of tendering, form of contract, terms of payment, degree of sub-contracting required and labour relations policy.
Management structure	(b)	Set up a management structure for the project with clear procedures for communication to all participating parties and clear definition of interfaces between contributing members. Define the responsibilities of all parties and manage them to carry out their tasks efficiently.
Communication	(c)	Set up procedures for clearly defining responsibilities of the team in respect of administration, accounting, purchasing, approvals, reports and meetings and indicate documentation circulation. Hold such progress meetings as are necessary for satisfactory co-ordination of the works.
Programme	(d)	Produce a master programme for the design and construction phases and communicate to all parties.
Design proposals	(e)	Following approval of the feasibility study obtain from design consultants firm proposals regarding conceptual design, structural requirements, plant layout, services and equipment. Check at all times that the design produced complies with the overall cost budget. Ensure design consultants produce specifications for all aspects of the works and in preparation consider such items as cost efficiency in operation and maintenance. Ensure adequate provisions are made for the most effective form of heating, ventilation, air conditioning, recycling of heat and waste products, hoisting facilities, lifts, fire precautions, sprinklers, alarms, smoke detectors, security provisions, special storage requirements, means of escape, fire fighting requirements, smoke control, refuse disposal and window cleaning and note the effect of design decisions on such matters as future insurance requirements. Consider future maintenance and replacement of building fabric, finishes and services from the viewpoints of cost and practicality. Ensure that adequate access is provided to service installations for such maintenance and future replacement. Consider energy saving measures.

(f) Ensure that the client is aware of developing design and specifications and that his approvals are obtained at the agreed stages of design and specification developments. Ensure at all times that all elements of design are properly coordinated and integrated within the master programme requirements and that the design fully takes into account the Offices, Shops, and Railway Premises Act, the Health, Safety and Welfare at Work etc Act and other statutory requirements including Government circulars, Codes of Practice and relevant British Standards.

Monitor budget

(g) Following completion of the initial conceptual design and master programme, re-examine and revise the preliminary project budget to produce a definitive budget for cost control purposes.

Costing

(h) Establish costing systems to continuously monitor the budget in accordance with the feedback costs required by the client. Produce and update cash flow requirements.

Pre-ordering

(i) Check on material availability and initiate orders on the client's behalf for long delivery plant and equipment in accordance with programming requirements. Monitor manufacturers' progress in design, fabrication and delivery.

Accounting

(j) Establish accounting procedures and cost controls to cover the various stages of the project, ie Project Management, planning and design, purchasing, construction costs, inspection, commissioning and co-ordinate contributions from all participants. At all times monitor the project's viability on the client's behalf.

Planning permission Building Regulations

(k) Ensure that planning approval and building regulation approval is obtained in accordance with the programme requirements. Obtain building regulation waivers where necessary.

Contract documents

(l) Compile all contract documents for the construction phase in accordance with the agreed policy regarding tendering and selection of contractors. Ensure that all quality control and testing requirements are clearly defined. Establish the client's requirements on such matters as liquidated damages, insurance requirements, performance or other bonds.

Contractor pre-qualification

(m) If contractors are to pre-qualify, obtain pre-qualification information from selected contractors well in advance of tender dates.

Selection

(n) Produce a recommended list of contractors who will be invited to tender for the client's approval and send out tender documents to approved contractors.

Tender evaluation

(o) Evaluate tenders received and make recommendations to the client regarding the appointment of contractors. See that the contract documents are properly executed before work starts on site. Ensure the contractor has complied with insurance and bonding requirements.

Site inspection

(p) Ensure that adequate staff are available for the site inspection and quality control checking and for monitoring the progress of works during the construction phase.

Construction phase

Monitor progress	(a)	Advise the contractor of programme procedures and requirements. Arrange for all necessary feedback required and set out reporting procedures regarding progress. Ensure that potential delays are fully reported. Approve any sub-letting in accordance with the contract requirements. Monitor design information flow and client approvals and ensure that programme requirements are being achieved.
Hoarding and existing site conditions	(b)	Ensure the contractor erects hoardings and protection to other areas as specified and record with the contractor the condition of adjacent buildings and surroundings, including pavings and roads.
Meetings	(c)	Set up regular progress meetings with designers, contractors, sub-contractors and suppliers and attend and chair such meetings as necessary.
Inspect works	(d)	Co-ordinate, direct and inspect all construction work.
Certify payment	(e)	Arrange for the work to be measured, valued and certified regularly and that payments are made on behalf of the client to the contractor in accordance with contract requirements.
Safety	(f)	Ensure that site security and safety standards are maintained at all times.
Quality control and testing	(g)	Ensure that construction works are carried out in accordance with the specification and that quality control procedures, testing and other performance criteria are maintained, as set out in the contract document.
Anticipate	(h)	Identify with the contractor problems, anticipate problems and take such measures as are necessary to resolve these to the best advantage of the client.
Monitor budget and variation orders	(i)	Ensure that design information is produced in accordance with the master programme requirements and that variations are kept to a minimum. Establish procedures regarding the issuing of variations and their costing and feedback into the overall cost budget position and produce costs-to-completion information on a regular basis and ensure that the client is fully informed.
Training	(j)	If necessary, arrange for the recruitment and training of personnel to operate the completed installation on behalf of the client.
Certify	(k)	Issue on the client's behalf all certificates required under the conditions of contract.
Statutory undertakers	(l)	Where not the contractor's responsibility, place orders on behalf of the client and ensure that all statutory undertakers carry out their works in accordance with master programme requirements.

Completion

Pre-commission	(a)	Ensure that all necessary pre-commissioning checks are carried out as necessary for the plant, equipment and buildings.
Final account	(b)	Ensure that all final accounts are dealt with in accordance with the contract conditions and that any claims are settled.
Commission	(c)	Assist the client in carrying out commissioning and arrange for suppliers and contractors to put into operation such equipment and services necessary for the commissioning and any performance tests.
Manuals	(d)	See that all necessary operating manuals, drawings, planning and lease conditions and instructions are supplied to the client.
Defects liability period	(e)	Monitor the works during the defects liability period and inspect at the expiration of this time. Release retentions on completion of any remedial works and issue all necessary certificates in accordance with conditions of contract.
Feedback	(f)	Advise the client of the final plant and machinery costs for grant and tax purposes and assist in obtaining grants in accordance with the original brief.
	(g)	Supply final cost feedback information as required by the client.

4.6   FUTURE DEVELOPMENTS IN BUILDING PROJECT MANAGEMENT

The current 'state of the art' in building project management defines the project manager as a surrogate client, making him thereby into a separate professional, detached from the commercial aspects of being responsible for designing and producing the building, but with a responsibility for the integration of interdependent but commercially separate entities. But it must be questioned whether this is the ideal formula for the management of projects. If a system for conceiving, designing and constructing projects were to be designed from scratch, would the present formula be acceptable? Probably not. In that case, would it be more accurate to see the current system of project management as merely a transitional stage in a wider revision of the industry's structure as a whole, providing an interim method of coordination during a period of readjustment of professional and managerial roles?

For a number of years the industry has, without great enthusiasm, addressed the questions of fragmentation but it has as yet been unable to provide any formula for remedying the malaise at source. The considerable vested interests and the inertia of a massive industry with a number of powerful lobbies have been resistant as yet to all but the mildest revisions, and even those have come about as a reaction to commercial pressures, rather than as a result of rational discussion.

It is unlikely that in the run-in to the twenty-first century any section of the industry will remain untouched by change: there will be pressure on the architectural profession to examine whether its service need be based on artistic ability rather than technology and management, with implications for architectural education and forms of practice; the quantity surveyors will undoubtedly need to re-examine their service even more than has been done already; there is a feeling that the level of specialisation and depth of education in engineering has gone beyond the point at which increased returns can continue to be expected for the effort put in; while main contractors have already seen massive inroads into the traditional services provided by them under the JCT forms of contract, through the use of management contracting, and have to face the as yet minor threat posed by the introduction of USA-style construction management.

New factors as yet largely unrecognised by the UK industry may in the medium term produce rapid change. One is the arrival of the unified Common Market in 1992. As well as offering possibilities for more trading for contractors in Europe, this change will bring with it a greater unification of professional qualifications, and a greater impact by European designers in the UK market. The second is the presence of major Japanese developers and contractors in Britain. Already at least six major Japanese contractors have established offices, and have begun development projects. Two features may serve to give these companies the opportunity to change the UK industry's practices. The first is their massive financial muscle, which provides strength and stablility not usually possessed by contractors in this country. At least one Japanese company has stated its intention to buy a major British contractor. The second is a cultural factor; Japanese companies are willing and able to plan their operations over a much longer time scale than their British counterparts, and have the finance to do so. One manifestation of this is a willingness to invest in research and development, to develop new methods, techniques and equipment, on a scale which dwarfs the British efforts in this area.

Although it is not yet possible to predict the shape of the industry in the year 2000, and the management systems likely to be employed in the management of projects, it is probably safe to say that the rate of development of new forms of integration and groupings will continue to accelerate for the remainder of the century.

5 Problem Solving

There can be few if any developments where no problems have appeared, whether through the intervention of uncontrollable forces or through simple human error. In the latter case, there are few such problems which are unique, since the human species appears to have an infinite capacity for failing to learn by experience.

The diversity and complexity of the activities which are required to generate and realise any building project give ample opportunity for things to go wrong, and this diversity itself leads to difficulties in resolving the problems. Where the problem is related to simple mechanical breakdown, one may diagnose the fault, rectify it, and assume that no further action is necessary. Unfortunately, few problems are as simple as this, as most are composed of a messy web of human, technical and extraneous factors. (But to return to the simple mechanical breakdown – is even this as simple as it might appear? Is this the first such occurrence? What was the *expected* service life of the component? Is anything else causing the failure? Is anything else designed/built by the same company/sub-contractor/designer causing problems? Or was the simple mechanical repair just an easy short-term solution to a much larger problem?)

The study of problem solving is intrinsically difficult – first, because in describing any problem in order to allow experience to be gained there will be factors which are omitted or simplified, thus introducing a degree of artifice and loss of realism; and second, because many of the techniques designed to facilitate a logical approach to problem solving depend on highly structured techniques, which in turn depend on the existence of a sufficient data base to allow elements of mathematical modelling. In the management of building projects, it is relatively unusual for the complex mix of factors to be analysable using operational research techniques, if for no other reason than the fact that human beings rarely display such simple and predictable characteristics that they may be addressed in this way. Yet it is possible to draw on some of the techniques developed for problem solving and adapt them as the basis for an orderly approach to the analysis and solution of problems. Before examining techniques, it would be wise to introduce here a note of caution in referring to 'solutions'. There are probably few problems in development and construction which have an ideal solution; the best which may normally be hoped for is to pick the most favourable of a range of possible actions, and even then the 'solution' is only the most 'favourable' within a carefully defined set of circumstances.

5.1   THE KEPNER-TREGOE METHOD

One method of deducing the causes of problems is described by Charles Kepner and Benjamin Tregoe in their book *The Rational Manager* (McGraw-Hill). The authors suggest a seven-step approach as follows:

1. Define an adequate standard of performance to be expected, i.e. a 'should' case against which the 'actual' may be compared. The expected standards of performance will be well defined in many cases, but it is quite possible that the standard expected will not be recorded, except by implication; in this case it may be necessary to examine evidence outside the project system to try to identify the required standard.

2. The 'problem' is defined as a deviation from the standard expected. In monitoring the performance of any project, a manager will identify many deviations from planned performance, and one of the difficulties will be to prioritise these deviations, in order to give attention to those with the greatest implications for the project.

3. The deviation must be identified and described as accurately as possible; Kepner and Tregoe suggest that precision be ensured by describing the deviation in four dimensions; identity, location, time and extent. Complementing this analysis of what the problem *is* must be the removal of extraneous detail, i.e. the removal from consideration of what the problem is *not*. This last step is often extremely difficult in building projects, due to the interdependency of many of the operations and their participants, but it is still necessary to undertake this part of the routine in order to remove non-essential detail.

4. Identify those areas which have been affected by the cause of the problem; these will be distinguished by changes, which set them apart from those areas not affected by the cause of the problem.

5. The cause of the problem is always a change which has taken place through some distinctive feature, mechanism or condition to produce a new, unwanted effect; but only those changes connected with distinctive areas of the deviation are relevant and should be considered.

6. The possible causes of the deviation may be deduced from the relevant changes discovered in analysing the problem.
7. The most likely cause of the deviation is one that exactly explains *all* the facts in the specification of the problem.

Once the cause of the problem is identified, the best course of action may be determined through a further series of steps:

1. Establish the objectives of the decision.
2. Classify the objectives in order of importance.
3. Consider possible alternative actions.
4. Compare and evaluate alternative actions against the objectives.
5. Tentatively decide on the best alternative.
6. Test the 'best' alternative for possible adverse effects.
7. Provide mechanisms to ensure that adverse effects are minimised, and ensure that the final decision is implemented.

The range of actions available to managers may be condensed to the following:

1. Interim action – allows 'breathing space' while the cause of the problem is discovered.
2. Adaptive action – where some of the effects of the problem are tolerable, or where it is not possible to eradicate the cause, this may provide a means of living with the problem.
3. Corrective action – eradicates the known cause of the problem.
4. Preventive action – removes the possible cause of the problem, or reduces its probability.
5. Contingency action – provides standby arrangements to offset or minimise the effects of a serious potential problem.

One last caveat must be registered before embarking on any structured analysis of problems, particularly where the problems are multi-faceted: the success of a structured approach relies at least in part on the ability to find and use 'hard' information, and to be able to rely on that information. In real life, there is always a shortage of hard information, and it is easy to be diverted from making a decision in the correct time frame by the argument that the information needed is not complete. It is preferable to start from the assumption that the information will never be complete in the sense that it would have to be in, say, a criminal trial; the manager's problem then becomes one of knowing when the benefits of taking a decision on the basis of incomplete information clearly outweigh the disadvantages of delaying a necessary action. One further complication in using information is that in real life the 'truth' may be an intangible quantity. This may stem from the fact that people do sometimes tell lies in order to protect their position, and also from the fact that the 'truth' is often a function of an individual's own perceptions of facts and the perspectives which determine that perception. Managers must be alive to the need to cross-check information upon which decisions are to be based according to the importance of the outcome of the decision being considered.

5.2   PROBLEM SOLVING EXERCISES

The examples which follow are designed to be used as the basis for discussion in class on the issues which arise out of them. For this reason they are deliberately simplified so that a range of 'what if' questions may be generated to add extra dimensions to the problems. All of the examples are based on real projects, although names have been omitted and some of the details altered to disguise the identity of the developments.

EXAMPLE 1.   *Imposition of onerous planning conditions*

The developer is a major public sector landlord, operating in an inner city environment where the majority of the housing stock is Victorian and in poor condition. The developer uses public funds to convert the old houses into one- and two-bedroom self-contained flats. The local authority in whose area the developer owns several hundred such flats, and produces around a further 200 every year, has become alarmed at the total amount of conversion taking place. The grounds for concern are that some of the conversions produce very small units of accommodation, that there may at some time in the future be a shortage of larger units in the area, and that the environmental standards of the conversions, particularly in terms of sound transmission between the units, are poor. The authority has decided to adopt a formal policy on such conversions, whether done by the public or private sectors. The published policy lays down minimum areas for converted flats, and minimum room size and circulation standards, plus a requirement for the units to meet the building regulation standards for sound reduction between adjoining units. In the last two weeks the developer has had 12 applications for planning permission refused, on the grounds that they do not comply with the authority's published standards. In all cases the shortfall in total area is no more than $4m^2$. The developer estimates that to comply with the council's suggested method of reducing sound transmission would cost approximately £1500 per unit, and could not be guaranteed to succeed technically.

For consideration: What action should the developer take? Is the council's policy *intra vires* the planning legislation? What is the chance of an appeal succeeding, and is the cost justified? What is the implication of not appealing for the rest of the developer's programme of activity? On what technical grounds could the developer mount an appeal?

EXAMPLE 2.   *The impoverished client*

A major speculative development of warehousing and offices (approximately 20,000m^2) is on site, three quarters through a two year contract period. The developer is a private company, being a wholly owned subsidiary of a group which contains several well known companies operating in diverse fields. The construction has been let on a fee contract to a national company. The contractor's site staff have been troubled throughout the contract period by the issue of details which are difficult or impossible to build, and this has led to considerable delays and friction between contractor and architect. The architect is unsympathetic to the contractor's comments on the detailing, and the client has ignored requests for meetings to discuss this. For the last six months the client has been late in meeting certificates for payment, and on the last two certificates has paid with post-dated bills of exchange, which have been accepted by the contractor with great reluctance. A letter now arrives from the architect to the contractor, informing the contractor that the client has secured a tenant for the scheme, who wishes to take possession the day after the contractual completion date. The letter also rejects the contractor's earlier suggestion that a three-month extension of time is justified, and reminds the contractor of the substantial amount of liquidated and ascertained damages which would be payable if the development were not completed on time.

For consideration: What should the contractor's reaction be to the letter? How seriously must he consider the rejection of the extension claim? How sound (financially) is the client? How can the contractor find out what the client's financial position is? Should the contractor attempt to accelerate progress on site (presumably at his own cost)? Can the contractor afford *not* to try to meet the deadline?

EXAMPLE 3.   *Private house sales to the public sector*

A major inner city local authority with a consistently large socialist majority is considering buying a 300 house and flat estate as a package deal from a speculative housebuilder. The authority's reasons are first that it needs the housing (in a prosperous middle class suburb) for decanting the occupants of an inner city area due for rehabilitation and redevelopment, and second that the authority has had for some time a policy of trying to install socially owned housing in the suburb. The houses and flats under consideration are in one phase of a much larger scheme, which has been selling well for two years. The section being considered has just started on site, with foundations well under way. On a visit to the site to familiarise himself with the construction used, the council's senior architect notes that the construction details are 'minimalist', i.e. they would work theoretically and would comply with building regulations and NHBC standards, but only with a high degree of supervision. These reservations are reinforced when the builder supplies the drawings and specifications which are to form part of the contract document-ation. The builder is unwilling to make any but the most cosmetic changes to the specification, as for him there is only the most marginal commercial advantage in selling to the council rather than on the open market. When the architect's reservations are reported to the chairman of the council's housing committee (which has delegated powers to formalise the agreement) the chairman's only comment is that the dwellings meet current national standards, and it is the architect's department's job to supervise and make sure that the job is done properly. The contract is then signed without further modification.

For consideration: What are the essential differences between the specifications which are appropriate for the private and public sectors (if indeed there are any)? What difficulties are likely to ensue for the architect's department in acting as 'supervising officer' during the course of the contract? What problems may be antici-pated after occupation? What precautions can be taken during the construction period?

EXAMPLE 4.   *Defective building*

A large five-storey office building was built during 1975 with a reinforced concrete frame clad with brickwork. Since a few years after completion cracks have been appearing between the brick balcony cladding and the concrete slab projections which support the balcony, and on corners of the building in a number of locations. The cracks have slowly become more unsightly, and action has been prompted by a new maintenance manager who has asked the original architects and structural engineers to investigate. Their report suggests that the problem lies in a combination of dissimilar thermal movement, and early moisture expansion of the brickwork (a search of the site visit reports supports the second assumption, as there was a severe brick shortage on site at the time, and bricks were being unloaded straight from the brickworks onto the scaffold and used immediately). The report also suggests that the fault lay with the contractor (now in liquidation), but that no major remedial treatment is necessary other than repeated repointing of the cracked areas – this will be necessary in perpetuity.

For consideration: Is the technical diagnosis accurate, or could it be biased towards protecting the consultants? How entitled is the building owner to a building which is not only structurally sound, but free from a shabby and repaired image? Who should pay for the repairs, and how much repair should be undertaken? How could the problem have been avoided?

EXAMPLE 5.   *Cost escalation*

A wealthy businessman wished to have a large private house built for his own occupation. As the property was to reflect his status in life, he commissioned a small architectural practice who have a reputation for winning design awards. The client accepted one of the scheme design proposals, and set a budget limit. On this basis the detailed design was completed, and a contract signed for construction with a local builder, the contract sum being only slightly over the client's budget figure. Two months after work started, the client was disturbed by sight of a number of variation orders, and even more disturbed when monthly cost statements projected the final account at 50% over the contract sum. The client refused to pay the variations element in the certificates as he did not consider that he had generated or authorised any variations.

For consideration: What rights does the client have in refusing to pay? If he has to pay, can he pass the cost on to anyone else? What action should the builder take? What steps should the client take to stabilise or correct the situation? Could it have been avoided, and how?

EXAMPLE 6.   *Delayed feasibility study*

A private developer has taken a three month option on a piece of land on which he considers it would be possible to develop a small office building and some high quality private housing. He asks an architect and a quantity surveying practice who have worked for him on several projects to conduct feasibility studies on the scheme on a 'no-job-no-fee' basis. They agree and after initial investigations discover that there will be severe structural problems in the foundations due to old sewer works. It is not believed that the problems would destroy the feasibility of the scheme, but in order to verify this the architect asks an engineering practice with whom he has often worked to check the extent of the extra engineering works required. While this extra work is in progress, the option period expires without the developer being in a position to make a firm offer. Shortly afterwards the landowner informs the developer that he has sold elsewhere. One month later the developer receives an account from the engineer for £3000, for work on the aborted project.

For consideration: Is the engineer entitled to payment, and if so, why? If there is an entitlement, who is likely to have to pay? Would the developer be entitled to reject the payment on the basis that the engineer's failure to complete the calculations on time was the reason for the scheme's being aborted? If so, is there any basis for a counter claim?

EXAMPLE 7.   *Coordination of drawings*

The building of a supermarket has been let on a management contract basis to a national contractor, the design having been done by the supermarket chain's in-house design department. One of the major nominated subcontracts is for the design and installation of an escalator from the sales area to the roof car park. The architectural and engineering sketch designs were sent to the escalator company (based in West Germany) at an early stage, so that the company would be able to design and deliver in order to meet the contractor's programme requirements. The escalator was delivered one month late, and when installation was attempted it was discovered that it was 150mm wider than the opening in the slab. The manufacturer's conditions of sale, printed in German on the back of the order acknowledgement form, contains a clause that all builder's work will be completed in compliance with the manufacturer's shop drawings. The client's design team then discover that shop drawings were in fact supplied to them at the proper time, but that a new office junior had filed them on arrival, without circulating them first. The client now claims that the management contractor is responsible for coordinating all drawing progress, and that the extra work should be paid for by the contractor, who must also accelerate the project at his own cost to ensure that the supermarket is open in good time for Christmas trading.

For consideration: How valid is the client's stance? How many of the participants here could be at fault? How should the contractor react? Does the fact that the escalator company is outside the UK make any difference?

EXAMPLE 8.   *The over-extended contractor*

A private developer has let the contract for the conversion of a Victorian church into 12 high quality flats to a local contractor. The contractor has been in business for ten years, has expanded steadily, and has a reputation for good quality work. This is one of the largest contracts handled by the builder, whose tender at £250,000 was £50,000 lower than the next tenderer. For the first two months, progress is good, and the first two valuations are slightly higher than might be expected. In the third month, delays are reported, and the valuation drops considerably. In the fourth month, there are further delays, apparently through insufficient labour being on site. The architect receives complaints from subcontractors that they have not been paid, and on checking with other clients finds that the same situation is occurring on other sites being run by the contractor.

For consideration: What action should the architect or client take? What are the risks in the alternative courses of action? Could the problem have been avoided, or is it one of the 'acceptable' risks in speculative development?

EXAMPLE 9.   *Limits of contractor's responsibility (1)*

The owner of a large department store has decided to convert part of the ground floor into a banqueting suite. The store's maintenance surveyor has produced scheme drawings, and a performance specification, and has invited tenders on the basis that the contractor will be responsible for translating the outline scheme and specification into the completed product. The winning tenderer, who has already employed a building services engineering practice and an interior designer to assist in his tender preparation, commences work on site, and after a few weeks discovers that the condition and the nature of the structure is quite different to that previously believed to exist, most of the structure having been well disguised by the shopfittings. In order to make progress, the contractor prepares the necessary alterations to the detailed drawings, and gains the necessary statutory approvals. As the alterations do not affect the layout or the standard of the completed works, the client's surveyor is happy to give his blessing to them. In his next application for payment, the contractor includes the cost of the alterations so far completed, plus the additional design fees for the engineer and interior designer.

For consideration: What is likely to be the client's reaction, and why? How strong is the contractor's case? What should be done by both the client and the contractor to resolve the problem?

EXAMPLE 10.   *Limits of contractor's responsibility (2)*

A pension fund has bought a terrace of 12 listed Georgian houses and has permission to convert them to offices. The fund has engaged a prestige firm of architects to design and supervise the conversion, in the knowledge that the architects' admitted lack of experience in this field will be compensated for by their acknowledged design ability. The architect recognises the problems which may be faced, and thinks it would be sensible to get early advice from an experienced contractor, and invites tenders on a two-stage basis. The winning contractor then spends several months being heavily involved in the design stage, and negotiates a final price which is acceptable to the client. On commencing work, the site agent discovers that the dimensions on several drawings do not agree, and that there are a considerable number of dimensions missing. On the strength of the relationship with the architects, the site agent and contracts manager make their own interpretation of the information required, and construct accordingly. At the architect's next site visit, the contractor's staff discover that the architects are furious about the 'ad libbing' as some sensitive areas of design have been mishandled, and they demand that the contractor remove the work at his own expense.

For consideration: On the face of it, this sort of problem should not have occurred – the parties seem to have cooperated to ensure that this kind of problem was avoided. Where has the failure occurred? Who will have to pay for the abortive work? What should be done to stabilise the position and avoid a repetition?

Further Reading

Chapter Two – Project Appraisal, pp. 21–102

GRANT, M., *Urban Planning Law*, Sweet & Maxwell, 1982
DENYER-GREEN, B., *Development and Planning Law*, Estates Gazette, 1982
GARNER, J. F., *Practical Planning Law*, Croom Helm, 1981
HAMILTON, R. N. D., *A Guide to Development and Planning*, Oyez Publishing, 1981
RATCLIFFE, J., *Land Policy*, Hutchinson, 1976
RICHMOND, D., *Introduction to Valuation*, Macmillan, 1975
DAVIDSON, A. W., *Parry's Valuation and Conversion Tables*, Estates Gazette/College of Estate Management, 1978
CADMAN, D. & AUSTIN CROW, L., *Property Development* (2nd ed.), E. & F. N. Spon, 1983
DARLOW, C. (ed.), *Valuation and Development Appraisal*, Estates Gazette, 1982
STONE, P.A., *Building Design Evaluation*, E. & F. N. Spon, 1980

Chapter Three – Preconstruction Process, pp. 103–192

BUILDING, E. D. C., *Thinking About Building*, HMSO/NEDO, 1985
R.I.B.A., *Handbook of Architectural Practice & Management* (4th ed.), RIBA Publications, 1980
MELVILLE, I. A., & GORDON, I. A., *Professional Practice for Building Works*, Estates Gazette, 1983
BOWLEY, M., *The British Building Industry*, Cambridge University Press, 1966
CORNES, D. L., *Design Liability in the Construction Industry*, Collins, 1985
ADRIAN, J. A., *Building Construction Handbook*, Renton Publishing Co. Inc., 1983
AQUA GROUP, *Tenders and Contracts for Building*, Granada, 1982
N.E.D.O., *Before You Build*, HMSO, 1974
FRANKS, J., *Building Procurement Systems*, CIOB, 1984
N.J.C.C., *Code of Practice for Two Stage Selective Tendering*, RIBA Publications/RICS/BEC, 1983

MOORE, R. F., *Response to Change – The development of non-traditional forms of contracting*, CIOB, 1984

MCKINNEY, J., *Management Contracting*, CIOB, 1983

BRITISH PROPERTY FEDERATION, *Manual of the BPF System*, BPF, 1983

R.I.B.A., *Architect's Appointment*, RIBA Publications, 1983

R.I.B.A., *Code of Professional Conduct*, RIBA Publications, 1984

CANTER, D., *Psychology for Architects*, Applied Science Publishers, 1974

R.I.C.S., *Appointment of a Quantity Surveyor*, Surveyors Publications, 1983

R.I.C.S., *Rules of Conduct – Disciplinary Powers and Procedure*, Surveyors Publications, 1985

R.I.C.S., *Professional Charges for Quantity Surveying Services*, Surveyors Publications, 1983

ASSOCIATION OF CONSULTING ENGINEERS, *Conditions of Engagement –* Agreements 1, 2, 3, 3(1984), 4A(i), (ii), (iii), 4B, ACE, 1983

Chapter Four – Project Management, pp. 193–217

MORRISON, M. C., *Total Project Management*, British Institute of Management, 1984

MORRISON, M. C., *The Management of Contracts*, British Institute of Management, 1984

C.I.O.B., *Project Management in Building*, CIOB, 1982

WALKER, A., *Project Management in Construction*, Granada, 1984

'PHILLIPS REPORT', *Report of the Working Party on the Building Industry*, HMSO, 1950

'EMMERSON REPORT', *Survey of the Problems before the Construction Industry*, HMSO, 1962

'BANWELL REPORT', *The Placing and Management of Contracts for Building and Civil Engineering Works*, HMSO, 1964

'ACTION ON BANWELL', *A Survey of the Implementation of the Recommendation of the Committee under the Chairmanship of Sir Harold Banwell on the Placing and Management of Contracts for Building and Civil Engineering Works*, HMSO, 1967

HIGGINS, G., & JESSOP, N., *Communications in the Building Industry*, Tavistock Publications, 1965

Chapter Five – Problem Solving, pp. 218–227

KEPNER, C. H., & TREGOE, B. B., *The New Rational Manager*, Princeton Research Press, 1981

MARGERISON, C. J., *Managerial Problem Solving*, McGraw-Hill, 1974

LYLES, R. I., *Practical Managerial Problem Solving and Decision Making*, Van Nostrand Reinhold, 1982
NELLIST, A. IVAN, *Pippit Dotterel and Others*, Construction Press, 1978

Index